The Colonists' American Revolution

The Colonists' American Revolution

Preserving English Liberty, 1607–1783

Guy Chet

WILEY Blackwell

This edition first published 2020
© 2020 John Wiley & Sons, Inc.

Registered Office
John Wiley & Sons, Inc., 111 River Street, Hoboken, NJ 07030, USA

Editorial Office
111 River Street, Hoboken, NJ 07030, USA

For details of our global editorial offices, customer services, and more information about Wiley products visit us at www.wiley.com.

Wiley also publishes its books in a variety of electronic formats and by print-on-demand. Some content that appears in standard print versions of this book may not be available in other formats.

Library of Congress Cataloging-in-Publication Data
Names: Chet, Guy, author.
Title: The Colonists' American Revolution : Preserving English Liberty, 1607–1783 /
    Guy Chet, University of North Texas, Denton.
Description: First edition. | Hoboken : Wiley, 2019. | Includes bibliographical
    references and index.
Identifiers: LCCN 2019033177 (print) | LCCN 2019033178 (ebook) | ISBN 9781119591863
    (paperback) | ISBN 9781119591931 (adobe pdf) | ISBN 9781119591986 (epub)
Subjects: LCSH: United States–Politics and government–To 1775–Juvenile literature. |
    Great Britain–Politics and government–1760–1789–Juvenile literature. |
    Revolutionaries–United States–History–18th century–Juvenile literature. |
    Revolutionaries–Great Britain–History–18th century–Juvenile literature. |
    United States–History–Revolution, 1775–1783–Causes–Juvenile literature.
Classification: LCC E210 .C49 2019 (print) | LCC E210 (ebook) | DDC 973.3–dc23
LC record available at https://lccn.loc.gov/2019033177
LC ebook record available at https://lccn.loc.gov/2019033178

Cover Design: Wiley
Cover Image: © Marcus Baker/Alamy Stock Photo

Set in 10/12pt Warnock by SPi Global, Pondicherry, India
Printed and bound in Singapore by Markono Print Media Pte Ltd

10 9 8 7 6 5 4 3 2 1

Prudence, indeed, will dictate that Governments long established should not be changed for light and transient causes; and accordingly all experience hath shewn, that mankind are more disposed to suffer, while evils are sufferable, than to right themselves by abolishing the forms to which they are accustomed. But when a long train of abuses and usurpations [...] evinces a design to reduce them under absolute Despotism, it is their right, it is their duty, to throw off such Government, and to provide new Guards for their future security.
American Declaration of Independence, 1776.

Contents

Preface

As an immigrant to the United States, I know firsthand that American values are simultaneously familiar and exotic to foreigners. On the one hand, America seems recognizable to outsiders because they are often well acquainted with American culture and institutions, and even American history. They might even see American culture, beliefs, and values as similar to their own. On the other hand, immigrants and foreign observers are often perplexed by various American peculiarities – from the natives' attachment to cars, firearms, and work, to their religiosity, their fear of governmental power, and their veneration of a Constitution written over two hundred years ago. This sense of bewilderment or frustration revolves most persistently around issues relating to liberty versus security. Whereas most Americans assume that the tension between the two is visible and visceral to all, many newcomers truly do not understand why Americans see tension between the two. My intent is to clarify to those – foreign and domestic – who are mystified by the origins and nature of Americans' conception of liberty.

Americans who revere the United States Constitution, admire the Founders, and share their ideological belief system easily identify the differences between the country they live in today and the United States of the late-eighteenth century. Those who disapprove of the Revolution and the Constitution similarly recognize these differences. Specifically, Americans of all stripes are struck by how the country, its culture, and its Constitution have been fundamentally transformed since the late-nineteenth century. The United States in the twenty-first century is a managerial nation-state. Moreover, it has been so for more than a century; longer than it had been the decentralized federal republic as which it was founded. What explain this shift are changes that occurred long ago in the circumstances, demography, economy, and culture of the country. American Constitutional law has reflected these changes in the culture, as a century of court rulings has gradually transformed Madison's Constitution from a tool to constrain the national government and insulate local governments from it, to a tool that empowers the national government to supervise, guide, correct, punish, and restrict local governments. Successive generations of Americans have thus been born into a managerial state, and into a culture that understands liberty and equality differently than did Americans of the founding era. This transformation is dismaying for some and comforting for others, but it should allow American readers, students, and scholars to approach eighteenth-century America with detachment, as a distant and bygone historical civilization, albeit one that is still culturally relevant, meaningful, and instructive to them, such as ancient Rome or Biblical Judea.

What I propose in this book is that the American Revolution is best understood as a British event, one designed to safeguard traditional English liberties and preserve the existing status quo. I examine the Revolution through a British lens because I follow the lead of the colonists themselves, as the book's title indicates. On this method there is genuine disagreement among historians. Some historians believe their mission is to identify the hidden forces that moved people and events in the past; forces of which contemporaries were not aware, but were shaping their ideas and actions nonetheless. Other historians try instead to look at events through the eyes of people in the past, and to understand events as they themselves did; to record how contemporaries understood what they were doing, and why they were doing it. To my way of thinking, when we try to understand people and events in the past, we benefit more from channeling *their* understanding of their actions and beliefs, rather than identifying motivating forces that were hidden from them at the time, but which we can see (or think we see) from our own modern vantage point. These two competing approaches lead some historians to see the American Revolution as a story of change, and others (like myself) to see it as a story of continuity, in which the Revolutionists saw themselves as preserving the status quo, not challenging it.

An example of how one's historical method shapes one's understanding of the Revolution is the concept of class. A running theme in this book is "aristocratic resistance," a concept that describes the efforts of local governments – noble families in Europe, and elite-dominated colonial assemblies in America – to resist the concentration of power in central governments. In this framework, the American Revolution was an elite-led movement to resist change and preserve the decentralized structure of the British Empire. This characterization is a loaded one for modern readers, given how thoroughly we have internalized Marxian (or Marxist) assumptions regarding class and class conflict. Karl Marx's influence on the study of history, sociology, and economics has led most Westerners to conceive of elites and "common people" as groups with different and opposing circumstances, interests, sentiments, and allegiances. This is why modern observers routinely label elite-led conflicts like the American Revolution or the U.S. Civil War as "a rich man's war, but a poor man's fight." Even if this adversarial analysis of historical societies is accurate, it is important to remember that the concepts of class and class conflict are modern; they were foreign, as a general rule, to the minds of premodern people.

Certainly colonial Americans did not view their society in such adversarial terms. Elite families in early-modern England and America enjoyed support, deference, allegiance, and trust from below. Common folk in local communities saw the elite status of their social superiors as legitimate, and these elite families for the most part reflected the interests, fears, concerns, and values of their localities. This is why historians who use the modern concept of class to analyze colonial America clarify to their readers that contemporaries were unaware of the class dynamics that were shaping their ideas and actions; these dynamics are visible to the scholar in hindsight, but were hidden from contemporaries. By contrast, studying colonial America with *premodern* sensibilities regarding class allows one to understand this elite-led event as contemporaries themselves understood it – a communal resistance movement, rather than an elitist one.

Acknowledgments

This book reflects knowledge and sensibilities absorbed from other scholars over three decades of studying early-American history. I am grateful to the historians who had taught me, to those for whom I had worked as a teaching assistant, and to the many others on whose work I relied when conducting research and constructing my courses, lesson plans, and lectures. The material presented here reflects the findings, analysis, and insights of numerous teachers and scholars whose work has shaped my understanding of American history. At this point, I can no longer cite the sources of my convictions regarding colonial culture and society; I have absorbed so much from so many for so long, that I cannot tell where their thoughts and beliefs end, and where mine begin. I have listed their publications in the bibliography as a form of attribution, with apologies for failing to acknowledge specifically the ideas, findings, and interpretations which they will likely identify as their own in these pages.[1]

I thank my editors at Wiley Blackwell – Jennifer Manias, Niranjana Vallavan, Aneetta Antony, and Ajith Kumar – for their wise counsel on bringing this book to press, Katherine Carr for her sharp copy-editing, and Erica Charters, Tal Chet, Travis Bagley, Sophie Burton, Mike Campbell, Ralph Mitchell, David Smith, and Stuart Zenner for reading early drafts of the manuscript, in parts or in whole, and offering scholarly and editorial advice. I also thank my undergraduate students, who read the manuscript and provided insights and suggestions from a student's perspective; their critique was helpful in shaping the final product. Last, I am indebted to Chris Morris and Ben Wright for their sensible advice to drop academic jargon as much as possible (specifically with regard to Americanization and Anglicization).

---

1 Some sections dealing with colonial military history are based on or are drawn from my own publications on this topic. The sections dealing with the effects of Patriot manpower on American and British campaigning draw in part on David R. Smith's doctoral research on the "myth of the valiant few."

I am thankful to Yale University for admitting me into its graduate program many years ago and thus making possible my life in America and career in academia; I owe a special debt of gratitude to Associate Dean Ingrid Walsoe Engel, who went beyond the call of duty there on my behalf. Mostly, I am grateful to and for this country, which has welcomed me and has done so much for me.

About the Companion Website

This book is accompanied by a companion website:

www.wiley.com/go/Chet/ColonistsAmericanRevolution

The website includes the following supplementary material for instructors:

- About the Book
- The Value of History for Civics and Critical Thinking
- Experiences From the Classroom

Introduction

A Status Quo Revolution

> *The historian's understanding of past situations benefits greatly from the fact that he, unlike any contemporary observer, knows a good deal about the subsequent development. It is only in retrospect [...] that germinal forces, unnoticed or underestimated at the time, can be seen in their true significance. However, hindsight also has its dangers. Reading history backwards we are easily misled into postulating specific "antecedents" and "early phases" of phenomena which seem to require a long period of gestation; and we are almost inclined to distrust our records if they fail to confirm our expectations.*[1]
>
> —Karl Helleiner

Perhaps the most prominent theme in scholarship on early-American history is the formation of American identity – how (and therefore when) did American society become distinctively American, featuring uniquely American manners, sociology, sports, literature, religiosity, philosophical sensibilities, and politics. Most historians hold that life in colonial America gradually reshaped English settlers' habits, mores, values, and beliefs. What produced this cultural transformation, according to this view, were realities of life that were unique to America – slavery, racial diversity, ethnic diversity, the absence of a formal aristocracy, small governmental bureaucracies, and frontier conditions, such as cheap land, high wages, robust demographic growth, and class mobility. That is, the physical and social environment in America gradually reshaped the settlers' cultural traits, and the colonies thus drifted steadily away from their English cultural roots. Eventually, this process of Americanization produced the American Revolution.

---

1 Helleiner, K. (1957). The vital revolution reconsidered, *The Canadian Journal of Economics and Political Science* 23 (1): 1.

The Colonists' American Revolution: Preserving English Liberty, 1607–1783, First Edition. Guy Chet.
© 2020 John Wiley & Sons, Inc. Published 2020 by John Wiley & Sons, Inc.
Companion website: www.wiley.com/go/Chet/ColonistsAmericanRevolution

Other scholars – mostly specialists on colonial America – see the settlers as conventional Englishmen. These historians are generally skeptical regarding Americanization and the alleged cultural divide between colonists and Britons. They challenge the narrative of the colonies' centrifugal trajectory away from England's sphere of influence by tracing forces of Anglicization in America. Indeed, these scholars present the Revolution as a product of the colonists' *English* culture, and argue that the formation of a uniquely American identity took place not in the colonial era, but mostly after independence, in the nineteenth and twentieth centuries. To them, the American Revolution took place because of a sudden change in British imperial policy, not gradual changes in the identity and culture of American settlers.

U.S. History textbooks invariably deploy the first narrative – the narrative of Americanization – to explain the formation of American identity and the coming of the Revolution. Because they tell the story of the United States of America up to the present day, they trace the story of Americans' collective identity backward, to identify its earliest formation in the colonial era. With the benefit of hindsight, this framework identifies for students colonial antecedents of the Revolution – Mayflower Compact, Puritanism, Bacon's Rebellion, frontier culture, the Dominion of New England, Navigation Acts, rise of the assemblies, Zenger trial, Great Awakening, Albany Plan, Braddock's Defeat, Revenue Acts, and so on. By looking back to the Revolution from the nineteenth and twentieth centuries, these textbooks produce a storyline of English settlers becoming more Americanized by their physical and social environment; a story of growing distance and differentiation between settlers and mother country.[2]

What is obscured in this conventional account – and what is presented in this book – is the colonists' own understanding of the origins, causes, and ends of their Revolution.

What Was the American Revolution?

Colonial history is an awkward field of study because its focal point is not the colonial period itself, but the end point of that period – the Revolution. The Revolution is the black hole toward which all colonial-era developments

---

2 A famous contemporary example of this understanding of environment and culture is Michel Guillaume Jean de Crèvecoeur's *Letters from an American Farmer* (1782). Written by a French settler in America, *Letters from an American Farmer* set out to explain to Europeans what is an American. The answer provided is that an American is a European who has been transformed by the American environment: "Europeans submit insensibly to these great powers [of environment], and become, in the course of a few generations, not only Americans in general, but either Pennsylvanians, Virginians, or provincials under some other name. [...] The inhabitants of Canada, Massachusetts, the middle provinces, [and] the southern ones will be as different as their climates."

gravitate. One of the first to formulate such a historical narrative for colonial America was Thomas Paine, the radical pamphleteer who worked tirelessly to win American hearts, minds, and military volunteers for the Revolution in its earliest stages. Paine's *Common Sense* (1776) told American readers the history of colonial America in order to explain to them why it was both warranted and natural for the colonies to become independent. Offering natural-law justifications for rebellion and independence, as well as economic justifications, Paine conceptualized the relationship between Britain and its colonies as a mother–child relationship. Since the natural and desired end of such a relationship is maturity and independence, Paine contended that colonial status has a shelf life beyond which it becomes unnatural, abusive, and parasitic.

Following Paine's lead, historians (and U.S. History textbooks) have habitually presented the Revolution as a natural culmination of the colonial period. The idea conveyed in this narrative of colonial and Revolutionary history is that colonial rule was increasingly onerous and frustrating to settlers, and that this structural problem was resolved by independence. Students and readers thus absorb the understanding that by planting colonies across the ocean in 1607, the English government had set in motion the forces that inexorably led to independence nearly two centuries later; and that the impulse to separate was already there in embryonic form in 1607, consistently growing during the colonial era, as Americans pursued their own interests and formed their own identity. In the 1770s, that separatist impulse finally reached fruition when Americans' political self-determination and economic self-interest (a desire to lower tax and regulatory burdens, to print paper money, and to invigorate international trade and domestic manufacturing) brought this inherent tension between colonies and mother country to a point of rupture.

American separatism and rebellion seem like natural outcomes of colonialism in retrospect, but they surprised and perplexed contemporaries at the

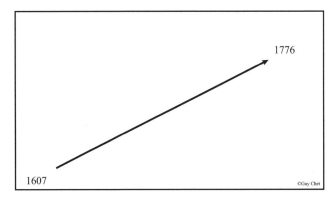

Figure 1 American independence as a gradual transformative process. © Guy Chet.

time. Even today, the fact that the stream of publications aiming to make sense of this rebellion increases from decade to decade suggests that the accepted narrative of the Revolution – the one first proposed by Thomas Paine over two centuries ago – fails to explain certain aspects of the Revolution. American settlers had perhaps the most comfortable living standards and *lowest* taxation rates in the Western world at the time; their trade was protected by the strongest navy in world history; their borders likewise were protected by the Empire; through London, they had access to the largest marketplace in the history of humanity; and the vastness of territory and limited reach of colonial governments combined to offer settlers an unprecedented degree of freedom of religious worship. For these British subjects to risk all these benefits by challenging the greatest military power in the world seemed to many – then and now – as an irrational, self-defeating, and ill-conceived undertaking.

Particularly mystifying are the leaders of this revolt – wealthy men from elite families, who risked not only their property, position, and lives, but also their families' status and possessions. These leaders of the rebellion understood the towering odds against them in confronting the naval, military, commercial, and financial might of the British Empire. They trembled at the prospect of war; they begged for both earthly and divine help to avert war, and then, after the war's outbreak, to avert defeat and death. Yet they felt compelled to press their resistance to Parliament and the king nevertheless. Could this expensive, demanding, and seemingly suicidal war really have been a tax revolt – one led by men who could easily afford to pay the new imperial taxes a hundred times over? Farther down the socioeconomic ladder, is it plausible that the 70 militiamen pointing their muskets at 700 heavily armed and well-trained redcoats on the Lexington Green (April 19, 1775) were pursuing an economic self-interest?

What explains these and other problems associated with the accepted interpretation of the Revolution is that the rebellion is widely understood as the final stage, or product, of a gradual change in American society and culture – a process by which colonists were transformed from Englishmen into Americans, from hierarchical monarchists to egalitarian republicans, and from dependent children (in Paine's formulation) to self-sufficient adults. But this narration of early-American history misrepresents colonial society and, therefore, also misrepresents the nature, direction, and purpose of the Revolution. American colonists were part of a culture that attempted to uphold the status quo and preserve established English customs, arrangements, and precedents. It was a culture governed by a conservative, backward-looking impulse. What sparked the conflict with Britain, therefore, was not the gradual transformation of Englishmen in America, but the transformation of the imperial government in London. This change in London's bureaucratic culture and constitutional beliefs explains why the imperial government found itself increasingly at odds with its provincial traditionalists.

The American Revolution had less in common with the revolutions of the modern age (the French Revolution and the republican and nationalist revolutions that rocked Europe and Latin America the nineteenth century), and much more in common with premodern constitutional crises in seventeenth-century England – the English Civil War (1642–1649) and the Glorious Revolution (1688). Rather than a tax revolt, a war of national liberation, or a revolt of the rising middle class, the upheavals of the 1760s and 1770s in British America were a revolt of an aristocracy – a conservative opposition movement, led by local elites, against constitutional reforms in the British Empire. This American resistance movement – like its seventeenth-century English predecessors – aimed to *preserve* the status quo, not to change existing political and societal norms.

Moreover, this provincial opposition movement was not a product of the colonists' Americanization; it was, in fact, a recognizably *English* response to governmental centralization and consolidation. The English aristocracy, seated in Parliament, had resorted to armed rebellion twice in the previous century in response to the centralizing reforms of Charles I and James II, which threatened not only the liberties of Parliament, as a governing national institution, but also the liberties of local governments (that is, the liberties of the landed aristocracy that controlled the machinery of local governance). Likewise, the families that sat in and controlled colonial assemblies in America opposed the centralizing reforms of the mid-eighteenth century, which similarly invaded the liberties and jurisdictions of the assemblies, and undercut the influence of these leading families in their local communities.

American Revolutionists were reacting to changes that the British had initiated in the imperial system in the 1750s and 1760s. This suggests that American separatism did not intensify gradually and constantly during the colonial era,

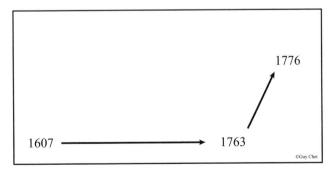

Figure 2 American independence as a reaction to abrupt change. © Guy Chet.

but was instead sparked during the decade that immediately preceded the War of American Independence.

And rather than envisioning a novel and untried system of government, the Revolutionists simply attempted to resuscitate the old system of "salutary neglect" by which Britain had governed its empire before the French and Indian War.[3] Thus, when the Revolutionists created a government for themselves (through the Articles of Confederation), they simply recreated the old salutary-neglect governmental system under which they and their forebears had lived before the French and Indian War: a weak and receding central government, shepherding powerful and sovereign local governments.

The Implications of the Americanization Debate

The implications of the Americanization debate are profound – were the culture, ideas, mores, and institutions of Revolutionary America created in America (products of unique conditions in America) or were they English imports? Did America Americanize English settlers, or did the settlers Anglicize their new environment, transforming America (through conquest, agriculture, trade, and civil engineering) into a place that could sustain *English* patterns of social and civic organization? Did the colonies grow increasingly alien to visitors and immigrants from England in the later-seventeenth and eighteenth centuries, or did America become more recognizably English as the frontier receded in the face of English settlement?[4] Was the colonial era characterized by centrifugal forces that drew the colonies *away* from Britain (as Thomas Paine explained in *Common Sense*), or

---

3 The term "salutary neglect" (that is, benign or beneficial neglect) was coined by Edmund Burke in 1775, as tension mounted between Parliament and American assemblies over the Tea Act, Boston Tea Party, and Coercive Acts. Burke used the term to describe and praise the historically light footprint of British governance in America, and to criticize Parliament's heavy-handed approach to imperial governance in the 1760s and 1770s. "Salutary neglect" is analogous to the more modern American term "states' rights" – it refers to a governmental structure that features strong local governments under a weak non-interventionist central government. Burke held that Britain's "wise and salutary neglect" of the colonies during the first 150 years of imperial rule produced populous, healthy, productive, and prosperous colonies, and a thriving and secure British Empire. Moreover, he pointed out that salutary neglect was consistent with Britain's imperial constitution. He thus chastised his colleagues in Parliament, charging that their American policies in 1773–1775 were not only unwise, but also unconstitutional and lawless.
4 As an approach to the study of American history, Americanization is associated with the scholarship of Frederick Jackson Turner (1861–1932). Turner was a part of the nationalist, nativist, Romantic movement that swept European and American intellectuals in the nineteenth century. As a scholar, he focused on uniquely American frontier conditions that produced uniquely American traits, identity, and culture, along with American independence, wealth, and power.

were the colonies instead increasingly drawn *toward* Britain's sphere of influence? Did the Revolution aim to enact change or to resist change – to establish new *American* customs and structures of government, or to preserve old *English* ones?

Looking back to the Revolution from the vantage point of the nineteenth and twentieth centuries lends credence to the Americanization thesis. By contrast, examining colonial America and the Revolution from the perspective of the colonists themselves supports opposite conclusions about the origins, nature, and purpose of the Revolution: the colonies were not propelled by forces of Americanization toward separation from the mother country over generations of colonial life. In fact, the colonial period saw effective *Anglicization* in America – the colonies were increasingly shaped by events and developments in England, and colonists were increasingly drawn toward the orbit of English politics, commerce, and culture, including political culture. Indeed, to the degree that American colonists during the Revolutionary era saw themselves as sharing an identity, values, and interests, they did so thanks to the transmission of English culture (goods, fashions, habits, ideas) to the American periphery.

The emergence of colonial separatism, therefore, was not a product of the gradual transformation of settlers from Englishmen into Americans. Rather, separatist sentiment materialized abruptly, in the decade preceding the Revolution, due to a constitutional crisis that impelled American assemblies toward a recognizably and self-consciously *English* form of resistance. This formulation casts the American Revolution as conservative and reactionary, rather than reformist or progressive. That is, those who led the colonial resistance movement did not aim to introduce novel arrangements to American society and government, but to preserve an inherited status quo against reformist innovations originating in London.

The American Revolution has long been associated with Europe's "revolt of the bourgeoisie" – republican revolts in the century following the American Revolution, led by Europe's "rising middle classes" against aristocratic privilege and in pursuit of political influence to match their growing cultural influence, wealth, and numbers. While European revolutionaries did draw encouragement from Americans' successful republican revolt, the American Revolution had more in common with revolts of the aristocracy in Europe than with these progressive and modernizing revolutions. The age of royal absolutism (the sixteenth, seventeenth, and eighteenth centuries) saw consistent and recurring aristocratic resistance, as kings tried to expand their powers, jurisdiction, and taxation schemes at the expense of their noble families. In response to such administrative centralization and concentration of power, aristocratic families tried to protect their inherited liberties from royal encroachment. At times they resisted through litigation, at times through political pressure, and at times through open military revolt. England saw two aristocratic revolts in the seventeenth century – the English Civil War (1642–1649) and the Glorious Revolution (1688). The American Revolution was a third such revolt – a political resistance movement led by American elites in defense of their ancient liberties and jurisdictions, which broke into open revolt in 1775.[5]

Terminology and Chronology of the American Revolution

This eighteenth-century understanding of the Revolution calls attention to two terms of trade – "liberty" and "revolution" – that modern readers must comprehend in their premodern usage if they are to understand eighteenth-century Americans' words, ideas, and actions. Liberty is the more difficult of the two terms, since it is as evocative and powerful in political discourse today as it was in the eighteenth century, yet its content is meaningfully different. In modern English, "liberty" and "freedom" are synonyms – one of Latin origin, the other Germanic. Terms like "free play" (in the field of mechanics), "free will" (in philosophy and religion), "free speech" (in civics), "free fall," and "sugar-free" indicate that "free" means "unburdened" or "unencumbered." For modern people, therefore, "freedom" and "liberty" in the political realm convey an absence of constraints by higher authority (such as parents, employers, masters, and rulers). When this modern meaning is applied to eighteenth-century America, the Revolutionists' complaints of their violated liberties ring as hypocritical, given the fact that the leaders of the Revolution were the rulers of their communities and imposed restrictive burdens on women, slaves, servants, Indians, the poor, religious minorities, apprentices, and various other dependent groups and individuals in their midst. A familiarity with the eighteenth-century meaning of "liberty," however, allows modern readers to understand why most contemporaries (on both sides of the Atlantic) did not see such rhetoric as hypocritical or inconsistent.

In Medieval Latin, *libertas* (from *liber*, or "free") conveyed the idea of an exclusive right to one's possessions – the right to tell others, including high government officials such as kings and magistrates, "this is mine; you cannot use it or take it." To be free, then, meant enjoying exclusive use of one's own property, possessions, office, or privileges. Politically, it meant that a ruler

---

5 The reference to the American Revolution as an "aristocratic resistance" is not literal – there was no legal aristocracy in the colonies. "Aristocracy" in the American context simply means the rich and powerful families that led their communities. Americans still use this term figuratively when referring to the families that have played leading roles in American economic, civic, and political life over the course of generations (for example, the Rockefellers, Roosevelts, Vanderbilts, Kennedys, Bushes, Gores, and the like).

could not simply take what belonged to those of his subjects who enjoyed such liberty (*libertas*). Indeed, medieval charters like the Magna Carta listed *libertates* (liberties) – particular privileges or reserved rights – granted to nobles, landed gentry, burghers, religious orders, commercial entities, and other individuals or associations. Thus, the liberties of the House of Commons (England's Parliament) were specific and legally defined privileges enjoyed by members of that legislature, such as immunity from arbitrary arrest, the right to free speech, and the like. Indeed, the eighteenth-century term was usually used in the plural ("liberties"), clarifying that liberty was understood not broadly, as it is today, but as a specific privilege explicitly articulated in law or custom. Like property, a liberty belonged to someone as a possession, meaning that the possessor had the right to defend his exclusive use of it, as a property owner has the right to exclude others from his or her property.

Thus, when English rebels (in the seventeenth century) and American rebels (in the eighteenth century) complained about violated liberties, they were not demanding to be freed from their ruler, as the modern usage of "liberty" would suggest. Instead, they were complaining that their government (the king or Parliament) had violated the law by infringing on particular privileges that belonged to them by law, grant, or established custom. The American Revolution should be understood in this context because what alarmed colonial elites, seated as they were in colonial assemblies, was that Parliament was taking over legislative powers that belonged exclusively to colonial assemblies, in violation of ancient custom, British law, and the imperial constitution. This was the liberty (*libertas*) about which they complained. When the War of American Independence broke out, rebel rhetoric regarding republicanism and natural rights certainly encouraged Americans to question the legitimacy of slavery and other forms of dependence in their societies; indeed, Americans were the first to voluntarily abolish slavery in their midst by law.[6] But Americans who viewed slavery negatively in the 1780s and 1790s saw it as a *moral* or *religious* wrong, not as a violation of legally established liberties.

The second term whose modern meaning leads modern readers to misunderstand colonial-era Britons and Americans is "revolution." By "revolution," moderns mean a fundamental, abrupt, and usually violent change in political institutions and political and social values. In the seventeenth and eighteenth centuries, however, "revolution" meant a 360° movement – a movement by which one *revolves*, or circles, arriving once again at the beginning point. This

---

6 The northern states abolished slavery during and immediately after the War of Independence. In southern states, the war prompted some slaveholders to emancipate their personal slaves, but the institution of slavery persisted. In the years that followed, the invention of the cotton gin revitalized and expanded slavery in the South. Abolition in the north led to the abolition of the Atlantic slave trade in 1807, and eventually launched a tense public debate over the future of slavery in the American West and South.

meaning persists still in the fields of mechanics and astronomy ("revolutions per minute," "the revolution of the Earth around the Sun"). Thus, when contemporaries referred to the Glorious Revolution of 1688 and the American Revolution as revolutions, they understood these events to be restorations of an older status quo; a return to a point of time in the past; a reset. Whereas today revolutions represent the rejection of established custom and its replacement with something new, original, and untried, in the seventeenth and eighteenth centuries, revolutions were understood to be conservative, designed to reestablish and preserve the old and venerated order. Indeed, the term "revolution" conferred legitimacy on the *seemingly* radical act of armed revolt against the government (in both 1688 and 1776) by calling attention to the fact that these movements were not radical, but traditionalist, anchored in law and ancient custom.[7]

Finally, just as the nature and purpose of the American Revolution can be obscured or skewed by misinterpreting eighteenth-century terminology, so can they be by misidentifying the Revolution's chronological limits. Studies of the American Revolution habitually cover two political peaks – the War of American Independence, which launched the Revolution, and the Constitutional Convention (or the ratification of the Federal Constitution), which allegedly completed it. In this telling of the story of independence, the Revolutionary project led to and was reflected in the second American Constitution. The first constitution – the Articles of Confederation – therefore receives fleeting coverage, as a faulty wartime stopgap that was addressed and perfected soon after. This framing of 1787 as the endpoint of the Revolution attaches to the revolt a meaning and purpose that nineteenth- and twentieth-century Americans identified in hindsight, but that the rebels themselves had not envisioned or endorsed. To them, the goals of the war were articulated in the 1781 Articles of Confederation and achieved in 1783, with military victory. For this reason, histories of the Revolution that wish to reflect the views and sensibilities of those who led and participated in the rebellion, ought to conclude their account in 1783, with the ratification of the first American constitution and the conclusion of the war.

The chronology of the Revolution, therefore, is itself contentious and loaded with interpretive judgment. Ending the Revolution with the ratification of a

---

7 When modern writers refer to the events of 1775–1783 as a revolution, they can clarify whether they are utilizing the term in its modern or premodern usage – whether they see this revolt as one that was designed to create something new, or to protect and enshrine something old. Those who are uncomfortable attaching the modern meaning of "revolution" to the American uprising against Britain can register their discomfort by capitalizing the word "Revolution." Whereas "American revolution" and "revolutionary" suggest to readers that this event was revolutionary in the modern sense of the word, "American Revolution" and "Revolutionary" are clinical terms that simply refer to the proper name of a given historical event, without offering judgment on its revolutionary or conservative nature.

novel and modernist constitution (the second American constitution) casts the Revolution as reformist and progressive, given that the Federal Constitution created a new structure of governance over the former colonies, invented new political institutions, and reflected a new conception of American nationhood. By contrast, ending the Revolution with the ratification of the first constitution presents the Revolution as conservative and backward-looking. The Articles of Confederation were a status quo constitution; a constitution that preserved the old salutary-neglect structure of government in British America and perpetuated it in the newly formed United States of America.

Both researchers and general readers benefit from an awareness of how terminology and chronology create analytical biases, shaping assumptions and expectations about history. When one uses the term "revolution" without considering the difference between its premodern and modern meanings, one is more likely to conceive of the Revolution as radical and reformist. Similarly, by casually accepting either 1607 or 1763 as the origin point of the Revolution, one subconsciously and unquestioningly internalizes a specific (and contentious) interpretation of the British Empire, of colonial society, and of American political culture. The same, of course, holds for the end point of the Revolution – uncritically accepting either 1783 or 1787 as the point of conclusion limits one's ability to consider a competing interpretation of the Revolution's origins, meaning, and purpose. Given the centrality of the American Revolution and the Constitution to current debates regarding American society, culture, economics, law, and politics, such historical awareness is also important for reasons other than history.

1

English Origins

To understand early-modern England and its colonies one must imagine a society without police. This is no easy task for modern readers, given the host of governmental enforcement agencies that currently hold jurisdiction over virtually every aspect of civic, economic, and private life. The absence of police shaped the daily lives of individuals in local communities, restricted the range of policy options available to rulers and legislators from the lowest to the highest levels of government, and informed the constitutional beliefs of both rulers and constituents. Indeed, this administrative reality in both England and America – the limited powers of coercion available to governments – was a running theme in the story of the American colonies and a dominant factor in the coming of the American Revolution. The overriding principle of Anglo-American society was self-government, and English communities saw the absence of coercive law-enforcement by an army or a police force as the manifestation of a free society, one in which constituents have a role in enacting the laws that govern them.

It is no surprise that this feature of American life was not uniquely American, but conventionally English. The customs, values, and beliefs of English settlers in America were shaped over centuries of English history. The sixteenth and seventeenth centuries were a particularly formative era in this respect, seeing the planting of England's first colonial enterprises in the New World, as well as the formation of key political habits and constitutional beliefs that traveled to America with the settlers.

The English Reformation

The Protestant Reformation, a formative process in the history of early-modern Europe and of New World colonization, had far-ranging and long-lasting ripple effects in England and its overseas possessions. In 1517, Martin Luther, a German

The Colonists' American Revolution: Preserving English Liberty, 1607–1783, First Edition. Guy Chet.
© 2020 John Wiley & Sons, Inc. Published 2020 by John Wiley & Sons, Inc.
Companion website: www.wiley.com/go/Chet/ColonistsAmericanRevolution

priest and theologian, challenged the pope's spiritual authority in the Catholic Church. His protest against corruption in the Church and demand for reform were a launching point for the *Protestant Reformation*. The differences between Catholicism and the various brands of Protestantism are numerous and subtle, but many of them emanate from a basic disagreement over the spiritual authority of the clergy, and of the pope in particular. Catholics see the pope as Christ's vicar, or substitute. As such, he possesses the spiritual powers that Jesus wields, including the keys to the kingdom of heaven. Protestants, on the other hand, see the pope as a man like any other. A related difference between Catholics and Protestants has to do with the means of salvation. In Catholicism, the Church has an essential role in individuals' salvation. Catholics cannot be absolved of the spiritual guilt accrued from sin without priestly intervention; that is, without receiving the sacraments – baptism, confirmation, mass, confession, last rites, and either marriage (for lay people) or ordination (for priests). Most Protestant Churches assert that only contrition can undo spiritual guilt. And no one – not even one's minister – has the spiritual power to usher one into the kingdom of heaven. Some Protestants go further still, holding that not even contrition can undo spiritual guilt. They see salvation as a divine gift that cannot be earned or initiated by humans through either contrition or good deeds.

One of the important features of the early Protestant Churches was that they were national, whereas the Catholic Church transcended national boundaries. This meant that a Protestant head of state was also the head of the reformed Church in that state. As important, it meant that Church taxes, gifts, and other revenues flowed from the king's subjects, through their local churches, to the king's treasury, rather than to the pope's coffers in Rome. Indeed, monarchs who converted to Protestantism habitually took possession of all of properties previously held by the Catholic Church within their territories – churches, monasteries, their treasuries, their lands, and the revenues produced from these properties. Naturally, the Catholic Church did not sit idly while Protestant kings and princes picked its pocket. Thus, the Reformation sparked a series of violent clashes in central and western Europe, referred to collectively as the Wars of Religion.

These developments reached England in 1534, when Parliament passed the Act of Supremacy. This law ended the pope's supremacy over the king within the English Church, declaring King Henry VIII to be the supreme head of the Church in England. England had had an uncomfortable relationship with the Catholic Church for centuries prior to the squabbles between Henry and the pope over the king's desire to rid himself of his wife. This was not unique – European monarchs did not appreciate the pope enriching himself off of their subjects and meddling in their affairs of state; namely, deciding who would receive powerful positions within a given state's ecclesiastical and civil administration. The Middle Ages were therefore rife with "investiture contests" – conflicts between monarchs and popes over who held ultimate authority over Church appointments within those monarchs' countries. In England, however, dissident voices enjoyed great freedom to criticize and challenge the Catholic Church. (Perhaps this was due to the sense of security and autonomy provided by the English Channel, or by England's great distance from Rome.) For example, despite vehement opposition from the Catholic Church, one of the earliest translations of the Bible from Latin into a vernacular language (the Wycliffe Bible) was produced in England in the 1380s.

When Henry VIII's marriage to Catherine of Aragon failed to produce male children, Henry sought an annulment of his marriage. When the pope (with strong guidance from Charles V, the head of the Holy Roman Empire) denied this request, the English court started tinkering with the idea of creating a national Church, in which Henry would be the spiritual leader. Converting to Protestantism would liberate him from tensions with the Holy See (the pope) over important appointments in the English Church, and it would allow him to control his own marital affairs. As important, it would allow Henry to take possession of all of the English property owned by the Catholic Church, which was the second largest landholder in England at the time, after Henry himself.

Parliament began debating this question in 1529, gradually granting greater powers over the English clergy to the king. Clergymen who refused to serve the king, were dismissed and either jailed or exiled. By that point, all money contributions from England to the Catholic Church (in the forms of tithes, gifts, bequests, bribes, and the like) had dwindled to a trickle. In 1533, with his first marriage annulled, Henry married Ann Boleyn, who was already pregnant with his second daughter, Elizabeth. The English Reformation was completed in 1534, with the Act of Supremacy, by which the English Church effectively separated itself from the Catholic Church and transformed England into a Protestant kingdom.

Henry was succeeded by Edward VI, his third child, born by his third wife, Jane Seymour. (English law did not bar females from the line of royal succession, but gave primacy to male children over their elder sisters.) During Edward's short reign (1547–1553), he and his advisers initiated reforms to turn the Church of England into a more thoroughly Protestant church, shaped by Calvinist theology. Edward died young, however, and was succeeded by his eldest sister Mary Tudor, Henry's first child (by Catherine of Aragon). Devoutly Catholic, Mary declared England to be a Catholic kingdom once again, and assertively went about converting churches back to Catholic practices – images and altars were returned, the Book of Common Prayer was removed, clerical celibacy was reimposed, and Eucharistic practices reaffirmed. Yet Catholic lands appropriated from the Church by Henry were not returned. Mary's restoration of Catholicism and her forceful campaign against Protestant leaders (which earned her the moniker "Bloody Mary") was short lived, ending with her death at the age of 42 in 1558.

She was succeeded by her younger half-sister Elizabeth I (1558–1603), widely considered to be the greatest monarch in English history. She repealed Mary's Catholic legislation and reinstated Henry's reforms, but did not revive Edward's more Puritan brand of Protestantism. Her reversal of Mary's policies led the pope to excommunicate her, putting a price on her head by inviting any interested party to overthrow or assassinate the queen with spiritual impunity. Despite this, Elizabeth managed to avoid assassination thanks to her considerable political skills, as well as a pervasive network of informants, spies, and secret agents. The Catholic plots on her life finally ended in 1587, when she executed her cousin, Mary Stuart (Mary Queen of Scots), who had found refuge in England following a successful uprising against her in her native Scotland. Elizabeth went on to subdue Catholics and fervent Protestants, both of whom destabilized her regime in their attempts to force her hand on religious matters and foreign policy.

Protestant agitators in England wanted a closer alliance with Protestant causes on the Continent, whereas Catholics supported a foreign policy that conformed to the interests of Spain and France, the major Catholic powers in Europe. But although Elizabeth aligned herself with rivals of France and Spain, she never went as far as her more radical Protestant constituents advocated with regards to both religious reforms at home and an anti-Spanish policy abroad.

New World Exploration, Settlement, and Trade

While Elizabeth remained cautious in her confrontations with Spain in Europe, this rivalry spurred her to support more aggressive anti-Spanish schemes in the Atlantic and the New World. Spain was the preeminent European power at the time thanks to the immense riches discovered in Central and South America. France and England began dabbling in New World exploration in the hope that they could hit pay dirt as the Spanish had. From the early stages of English exploration and colonization in the New World, English promoters looked longingly at the Caribbean, universally seen as the richest part of the Americas. Even before sugar established itself as the lucrative staple crop of the region, the association between hot climates and riches was firm in the minds of English leaders. They expected heat to produce not only rich crops, but also minerals, which were thought to be produced in the earth and drawn to the surface through the sun's magnetic power. Colonial promoters like Sir Walter Raleigh and Richard Hakluyt knew about the fabulous wealth of the Aztecs and Incas, which had rewarded Spain's early colonizing efforts, and they dreamed of an empire in the Caribbean that would allow England to rival the power of Spain.

But even though the English very much wanted a Caribbean empire to resist Spain's ascendance in Europe and the Catholic Church's Counter-Reformation, their environmental beliefs caused them to fear the effects of life in such a hot climate. They doubted whether English civilization could survive in such an alien environment. The history of English settlement there, under Elizabeth's successors, seemed to bear out both hopes and fears. Mineral wealth never materialized in the English West Indies, but once sugar plantations were established in Barbados in the 1640s, England's island colonies became far richer than any in mainland North America. However, the society these planters developed seemed outlandish by English standards. Ominous reports soon circulated in England about the sky-high death toll in the West Indies (due to tropical diseases), and about a society of great intemperance, violence, indulgence, and debauchery. Slavery quickly became the dominant feature of these colonies' labor system, and the slave population vastly outnumbered the free. Initial impressions suggested, therefore, that English society, culture, values, and religion did not transplant well to the Caribbean.

The Caribbean sugar islands became the economic center of England's emerging Atlantic economy. These plantations were fueled by continuous imports of slaves from Africa and North America (since workers perished quickly and routinely in these tropical environments) and by a steady supply of food and construction materials from North America and Europe (since every inch of arable land on the islands was used to produce sugar, rather than other necessities of life). Indeed, the success and growth of England's rice economies in the American South and its wheat economies in the northern colonies correlated with the success and growth of England's Caribbean colonies. Merchants who brought slaves, foodstuffs, and supplies to the West Indies sailed away with sugar, rum, and molasses (a dark brown syrup made from sugar cane), all of which were sold in West Africa (along with European firearms) in return for more slaves. These triangular trade routes (connecting England, the Caribbean, North America, and West Africa) illustrate the role of the American mainland colonies in the operation of England's Atlantic economy. In the seventeenth and early-eighteenth centuries, these mainland colonies were a backcountry support system for the Caribbean centerpiece of the English empire. The North American colonies were on the edge of European civilization, out of sight and mostly out of mind, as long as those sugar economies were being fed and supplied.

North America's peripheral role in the empire explains not only societal and demographic patterns of colonization there, but also the imperial government's habit of "salutary neglect" – the light imperial footprint in the mainland colonies, which allowed institutions of colonial self-government to take root there and gain cultural legitimacy and political dominance.

The first colony to be established successfully and permanently was Virginia (1607), followed by Plymouth and New Hampshire in the 1620s, Massachusetts, Maryland, Connecticut, Rhode Island, and Delaware in the 1630s, Carolina,

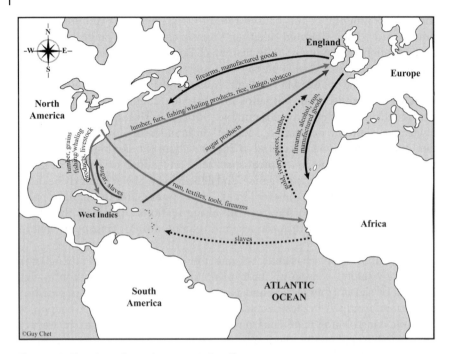

Figure 1.1 The triangular trade routes. © Guy Chet.

New Jersey, and New York in the 1660s, Pennsylvania (1681), and Georgia (1732). The method by which English colonies were founded and settled in the New World had originated in Ireland, in the sixteenth century. An individual investor or a company of investors (such as the Virginia Company or Massachusetts Bay Company) would obtain a royal charter from the court in exchange for money or services. The charter authorized a colony's proprietors to use military force to secure and pacify a given territory, to establish laws and regulations by which settlers would be governed there, to appoint office holders, and to sell land to settlers.

The Turbulent English Backdrop for New World Migration

Those petitioning the monarch for a colonial charter pointed out the Crown's interest in creating opportunities for a host of troubled and troubling people – such as Puritans, Quakers, Catholics, poor and unskilled laborers, and young men released from the army – to relocate from England abroad. Indeed, relocating to the edge of Christendom was an attractive option mostly for people who either had few prospects in England, or who felt threatened there. And in the seventeenth century, many in England found themselves in one of these two camps.

First, increasing numbers were being pushed off the land by the enclosure movement. Acts of enclosures were rezoning laws, which allowed the landed aristocracy to cultivate privately lands on their own estates that had previously been designated by custom as lands for common use. Each act of enclosure was an act of Parliament, a legislature populated by the same landed families that benefited from these rezoning laws. The enclosure movement was a long-term evolution in English agriculture and English law, starting in the sixteenth century and stretching into the nineteenth.

When "commons" (that is, common-use lands) were privatized and added to the privately held lots owned by a landed noble family, that family increased its agricultural production for the burgeoning urban markets in England and Europe. However, the farming families living on these estates lost access to supplemental sustenance previously provided by those common lands – grazing, fishing, trapping, collecting berries and timber, and the like. This meant that in estates in which commons were privatized and enclosed, each farming household could support fewer people. Consequently, these farming families gradually reformed themselves into nuclear families, since heads of household could no longer support unmarried siblings, grown children, and other members of the extended family. These peripheral family members were the people who migrated to England's growing cities, its crowded poor-houses, the armed forces, and the colonies. English literature from the early-modern period reflects great distress over this new phenomenon of a drifting population, with bands of criminals – "rogues and vagabonds" – in the countryside and on city streets.

The consistent growth of England's urban population was not solely a product of enclosures, however. Like the rest of Europe, England was experiencing steady population growth from the fifteenth century on, which became a population explosion by the eighteenth century. Thus, while enclosures allowed greater agricultural production to sustain England's growing population, they also allowed rural households to support smaller families. As England became more populous and wealthy – to a large degree because of enclosures and increased production for the marketplace and for export – it was also hit by an alarming increase in poverty, homeless, and criminality. The jails and poor-houses were full, and it seemed to some contemporary observers that enclosures were to blame, by introducing competition into formerly communal social structures. Specifically, these critics lamented the dissolution of the bonds that held English society together – the mutual obligations between the upper and lower classes in country communities, between neighboring families, and between members of the extended family itself.

This sense of crisis was manifested in the rise of utopian literature in the seventeenth and eighteenth centuries. One of the very earliest of this genre was

Thomas More's *Utopia* (1516), which describes a fictional well-ordered republic in which rulers govern skillfully and wisely, and the citizens are therefore happy, virtuous, reasonable, and productive. For More and his many followers, utopian fiction was a means by which to critique contemporary society and government, and to suggest solutions to contemporary problems. It is no surprise therefore that many narratives about America were utopian in character. Drawing on the literary fashions of the age, these narratives about exotic lands beyond the horizon offered target audiences observations about their own pressing problems, as well as attractive solutions. Colonial promoters naturally used utopian tropes in their promotional literature on America to attract English settlers and laborers to the colonies, to entice wealthy investors into buying shares in colonial companies (such as the Virginia Company), and to convince English monarchs to grant provincial charters and otherwise support colonization schemes in America.

With population growth, enclosures, rapid urbanization, rising criminality in the countryside and the city, and a growing sense that the bonds of society were dissolving, some Englishmen felt that immigration to the colonies offered better prospects than remaining in England. Additional incentives for emigration included the religious, political, and military upheavals in England in the seventeenth century. Catholics were living hard lives in England under Elizabeth, and even radical Protestants felt constrained under her reign.

When Elizabeth passed away (1603), English Catholics sighed with relief, but Protestants were gripped by fear because the heir to the English throne was James Stuart, King of Scotland and the son of the executed, and very Catholic, Mary Queen of Scots. Not only was James a foreigner, and the son of a Catholic conspirator against the beloved Queen Elizabeth, but he was not particularly cultured, and had a reputation for poor hygiene. While James I was a Protestant, many of his new English subjects suspected that he was a Catholic sympathizer and that he sought an alliance with Spain. The fear among the English aristocracy was that James might attempt to restore Catholicism.

By the time of James I's accession, much of the Catholic property nationalized by Henry VIII had been sold off to aristocratic families to finance Henry's and Elizabeth's military and domestic spending. If Catholicism were reinstated, some feared that the Catholic Church could reclaim these lands. Naturally, a large contingent of the landed elite was united in its opposition to this. James therefore met with suspicion from the start. And although he did attempt to reconcile with Spain, James understood his subjects' fears and suspicions, and made efforts to work with the country's leading families seated in Parliament. His was a successful reign, which ended with his peaceful death in 1625. (It was during his tenure that the colonies of Virginia and Plymouth were established in North America, as well as the Dutch colony of New Netherland, which England later captured in 1664.)

James I's son, Charles I, was markedly less humble and cautious. Unlike his father, who came to the throne very much aware of the unique limitations on the powers of English monarchs, and his own in particular, Charles saw himself as a conventional European monarch. He resented the presumptions of Parliament, and he alienated and defied it by promoting Catholics in his administration and establishing a closer relationship with Spain and France. Frustrated by Charles's policies and his high-handed demeanor toward his aristocracy, Parliament refused to vote for new taxes to fund his regime. Charles responded by dismissing Parliament and ruling on his own (without a Parliament) from 1629 to 1640. This period is known as "the personal rule," or "the eleven-year tyranny."

The personal rule ended because Charles was in dire need of funds. In 1640, his religious and domestic policies in Scotland sparked a successful rebellion against him in that kingdom, which was predominantly Presbyterian. When the rebellion spread to Ireland and threatened northern England, the king quickly reconvened Parliament, requiring them to fund an army for him. Yet his aristocrats were reluctant. They resented him, they did not trust him, and they wanted assurances from him that he would not return to the high-handed conduct that characterized his reign till then. Moreover, most of them were supportive of the Scottish rebellion. Parliament thus dragged its feet, and Charles refused to humble himself and acquiesce to its demands.

In short order, pro-Parliament riots in London impelled the King to flee the city (1642) and relocate his court to Oxford. In control of London, its harbor, and the populous and rich counties to the south, Parliament started forming and outfitting an army to fight the king in defense of the liberties of the English people and of Parliament, as the people's true representative. The English Civil War continued until the king was finally captured in 1647, and then put on trial and executed in 1649.

This was a radical turn indeed. Kings had faced rebellions before, and have even been executed, but as part of a coup led by some other claimant to the throne. In 1649, the king's subjects put him on trial and then executed him *legally*. Even more appalling, they then abolished the monarchy altogether and established a republic (the Commonwealth of England, and in time also Scotland and Ireland). This republic was headed eventually by Oliver Cromwell, a Member of Parliament and an officer in the Parliamentary army. After purging Parliament of uncooperative families, Cromwell established a military dictatorship, which promoted Puritanism in the Anglican Church. Under his iron rule, Parliament retained few of its traditional liberties and administrative powers.

In 1658, on Cromwell's death, Parliament reconstituted and reasserted its authority. Wanting nothing to do with republicanism after their harsh experience under Cromwell, the English aristocracy invited Charles I's son to return from exile and reclaim his father's throne as King Charles II (1660). The Restoration (that is, the restoration of the monarchy) is known as an era of restored stability and peace, following the military, political, and religious convulsions under Cromwell. As part of the Restoration settlement brokered between Parliamentary leaders and Charles II, the new king granted a general pardon to all those members of Parliament who had managed to survive Cromwell. The only ones who did not escape prosecution were the ringleaders who had orchestrated Charles I's execution. In all, roughly 20 were hanged or imprisoned for life.

Like his grandfather (James I), Charles II realized the limitations on the power of the English king and worked with Parliament, finding allies among more conservative factions. Radical Protestants and republicans were either driven out, or were politically isolated and kept in check. Like his grandfather, Charles II succeeded in stabilizing a volatile transition of power and strengthening the monarchy's financial and political standing.

Charles died without an heir and was succeeded by his brother, James II (1685). James was 52 at the time, and had served as head of the Admiralty (the Royal Navy) under his brother. Through his responsibilities in the Admiralty and through his commercial contacts, he became quite interested and involved in colonial affairs. Indeed, it was under his leadership of the Admiralty that England captured New York and New Jersey from the Dutch in 1664. (New Amsterdam was renamed New York in honor of James, the Duke of York.) Soon after ascending the throne, James started alienating the English aristocracy. First, he converted to Catholicism. Then he began following a policy of arbitrary monarchical power reminiscent of Charles I's. Avoiding consultations with the influential families in Parliament, James governed through royal prerogative – wielding power directly as king, rather than governing through his legislature. He levied taxes without Parliamentary approval and even violated Parliamentary law by elevating Catholics to positions of power in the Court, the army, civil administration, and the Anglican Church. His pro-Catholic leanings were evident in foreign policy as well, with attempts to broker an alliance with Spain.

Yet despite Parliament's frustrations with the king's transgressions, it was only on the birth of his son (who, the king proclaimed, would be raised Catholic) that Parliament acted against him (1688). The aristocracy's reluctance to rebel was understandable due to deep fears about unleashing the political and military terrors experienced during the English Civil War and its bloody aftermath. As important, James II was not a young man, and his heirs (by his first wife) were two Protestant princesses, Mary and Anne, who had married into the ruling families of Protestant powers in Europe (the Netherlands and Denmark, respectively). Moreover, James's second wife, Mary of Modena, had a long and dismal record of bearing babies who did not survive infancy. England's aristocracy could therefore expect Mary Stuart to claim the throne before too long. The birth of a healthy son thus came as a surprise to all, and as a great disappointment to the king's many critics in England. The royal birth was particularly disheartening to Mary and Anne, who – in the absence of a male heir – were next in line to the English throne.

Rumors spread quickly (in England, but also in the capitals of Holland and Denmark) that the child was actually born dead and replaced with another child – not of royal blood – who was smuggled into the queen's bedchamber in a warming pan. Royal births were affairs of state, with ministers and diplomats in the bedroom to witness the event and attest to the authenticity of the live birth. While there is no evidence that "the warming pan baby" (named James Edward Stuart) was indeed an imposter, rumor quickly spread in circles hostile to James that the king had perpetrated a fraud designed to continue his Catholic line, perpetuate his unpopular policies, rob his Protestant daughters of their birthright, and perhaps even effect a Catholic restoration in England.

In what is known as the Glorious Revolution (1688), Parliament invited Mary Stuart and her husband William – a powerful Protestant head of state, and the leader of a European military coalition fighting against Louis XIV's France at the time – to claim Mary's patrimony. Fearing the prospect of an Anglo-French alliance under James II, William agreed to risk a war in England. Moreover, he was desperate to add England's financial, naval, and military resources to his flagging military coalition against France. When he landed in southwestern England, William expected a major battle, but James was convinced that his Parliament's betrayal had infected his army as well. He therefore abandoned his army and fled to France, as William marched east to claim London.

Before William and Mary could ascend the throne, however, they were compelled by Parliament to sign a Bill of Rights (1689), guaranteeing the liberties of Parliament and of their English subjects. By this act, Parliament publicly asserted its supremacy over the king and became clearly recognized in England as the supreme power in a constitutional monarchy (that is, a monarchy in which the king's jurisdictions and powers are limited by law).

The Glorious Revolution was not the first time that Parliament had given or taken a crown. In 1649, Parliament took the crown from Charles I, along with his head. In 1660, it gave the crown to his son, Charles II. When members of Parliament invited Charles II to return to England, they struck a gentlemen's agreement with him. In return for his father's titles and lands, he promised to respect the jurisdictions and liberties of Parliament – to allow regular elections and sessions, allow Parliament to advise him on appointments and policies, and not arbitrarily arrest or remove members of Parliament. By contrast, the 1689 Bill of Rights was no gentlemen's agreement. It was not a promise by a particular king, but a binding and perpetual legal contract between the English Crown and the English people, as represented in Parliament. With the Bill of Rights, Parliament established its authority as the true representative of the English people, and as the ultimate source of political authority in England.

Questions for Discussion

1   What sentiments, beliefs, and principles commonly associated with the American Revolution were on display in England a century or more earlier?
2   Why were English kings and queens so limited in their power, compared to Continental monarchs?

Further Readings

Higman, B.W. (2010). *A Concise History of the Caribbean*. Cambridge: Cambridge University Press.

Israel, J. (1991). *The Anglo Dutch Moment: Essays on the Glorious Revolution and its World Impact*. New York: Cambridge University Press.

Turner, M. (1984). *Enclosures in Britain 1750–1830*. London: Macmillan.

Worden, B. (2009). *The English Civil Wars: 1640–1660*. London: Weidenfeld & Nicolson.

2

American Colonization

When students read about this period in English history, they do so quickly, as prelude and context to early-American history. What can get lost in this cursory reading of late-Tudor and early-Stuart England is that this turmoil was nearly continuous. Although life under Elizabeth and James I was not as violent and turbulent as it had been in the decades that preceded and followed, it was certainly not serene. And the destabilizing social and economic dynamics discussed in Chapter 1– enclosures, rapid urbanization, social and economic dislocation, rise in criminality, and religious strife – were constant throughout. So when presented with an opportunity to emigrate to New World territories that were idealized in the utopian promotional literature provided by these colonies' proprietors and managers, people who had limited prospects in England opted to give it a try. What is crucial to keep in mind is that they brought with them their political and religious sensibilities.

Transition from Direct to Representative Governance in Virginia

During the reign of Elizabeth, there was a failed attempt by Sir Walter Raleigh to plant an English colony in America. He established a settlement in Virginia (named in honor of Elizabeth, the virgin Queen), but the settlers were never seen or heard from again. The first plantation to be settled successfully was Jamestown, Virginia (1607). The second was Plymouth, near the Cape Cod peninsula (1620). There were some marked differences between the two colonies; most notably, the Plymouth colonists were more religiously homogeneous (Puritans), but this factor is often overemphasized since the first settlers there included many "strangers" alongside the pilgrim "saints." (Puritans referred to themselves as saints, and to other Protestants as strangers.) What was common to Jamestown and Plymouth was of greater

The Colonists' American Revolution: Preserving English Liberty, 1607–1783, First Edition. Guy Chet.
© 2020 John Wiley & Sons, Inc. Published 2020 by John Wiley & Sons, Inc.
Companion website: www.wiley.com/go/Chet/ColonistsAmericanRevolution

import to the English colonization project – both settlements could not sustain themselves independently. Their crops did not succeed, and their efforts at hunting, trapping, and fishing failed as well. Hunger and disease drove settlers in both colonies to consume not only their hogs, dogs, and horses, but also rats, mice, and snakes.

One of the Virginia settlers wrote that they were "driven through unsufferable hunger unnaturallie to eat [the flesh] of man, as well of our owne nation as of an Indian, digged by some out of his grave after he had leien buried three daies & wholly devoured; [one] slue his wife as she slept in his bosome, cutt her in pieces, powdered her & fedd upon her till he had clean devoured all her partes saveinge her heade, & was for soe barbarouse a fact and cruelty justly executed."[1] Such tales of extreme starvation were not the kind of stories that would attract more Englishmen to America. Indeed, the Council of Virginia dismissed this last incident as a scandalous misrepresentation. A pamphlet published by the governor's council explains that the man in question killed and dismembered his wife simply because he hated her. When her body parts were discovered, he used hunger as an excuse for what the authorities claimed was a crime of passion.

Yet evidence of starvation and disease was on display in the cemeteries of Jamestown and Plymouth. In Plymouth, the death toll rose so sharply in the winter of 1621 that settlers buried their dead at night to try to keep neighboring Indians in the dark about their depleting numbers. In Virginia, of the original 104 settlers, only 46 were still alive in September of 1607 (five months after settlement). Over the next few years, immigration and disease combined to keep the English population in check. The only thing that saved the English – in both north and south – was trade with neighboring Indians. Settlers exchanged clothing, textiles, tools, and alcohol for corn and meat. And although forbidden by the board of directors of the Virginia and Plymouth Bay Companies to trade firearms, they did that as well. Since Indians were purchasing firearms from French, Dutch, and Spanish traders anyway, the English ban made little sense to local settlers.

Rumors of starvation and disease in America reduced the value of shares in the Virginia and Plymouth Bay Companies. Moreover, such rumors made it that much harder to attract new immigrants to North America. To help place Virginia back on its feet, Deputy Governor (and Marshall of Virginia) Sir Thomas Dale instituted what came to be known as Dale's Code, which remained in force from 1611 to 1619. Serving under the absentee governor Thomas West (Baron De La Warr, or "Lord Delaware"), Dale oversaw a system by which settlers' lives and work were strictly controlled by Dale's officers. The death penalty was imposed for 25 offenses, including blasphemy, unlawful trade with Indians, adultery, rape, and theft, while lesser offenses were punished by whipping and mutilation.

---

1 Quoted in Spruill, J. (1938). *Women's Life and Work in the Southern Colonies*, 4–5. Chapel Hill: University of North Carolina Press.

While life under Dale's Code was oppressive in many ways, it was agriculturally and economically productive. By the late 1610s, thanks to the growing success of the plantation, Dale's Code was relaxed. Partly, this was done for the sake of recruiting – Virginia would be more attractive to English immigrants if its labor system and penal code were less draconian and more compatible with English habits and preferences. The most significant reason for the demise of Dale's Code, however, was the establishment of new settlements north of Jamestown. This geographic expansion (thanks to improved agricultural production) made it difficult for the authorities in Jamestown to maintain strict control over settlers' private lives, communal interactions, work, and trade.

This was a problem that would plague all levels of government in America – municipal, provincial, imperial, state, and Federal – until the twentieth century. Modern governments can marshal vast resources, coupled with communication and transportation technologies, to reach peripheral communities and exert real administrative power at a distance. Early-modern government bureaucracies were small, crude, and impoverished by comparison. They were too poor to obtain widespread compliance and too weak to coerce. While colonial or imperial officeholders could assert control within the vicinity of colonial capitals, they were constantly frustrated by their inability to gain reliable intelligence in peripheral communities and to exert real influence there.

The replacement of Dale's Code with representative government in Virginia (1619) can be seen as an attempt by the Virginia Company in London to deal with this challenge. Representative government created a cooperative or even symbiotic relationship between center (Jamestown) and peripheries, and thus fostered compliance in outlying settlements. Since it was beyond the capabilities of the colonial government to police a population that was expanding geographically and demographically – as Dale had done within the confines of Jamestown – the colony restructured its government on the basis of consent, rather than coercion. Following the English model, the Virginia Company hoped that when local communities in Virginia participated in legislation and tax assessments, they would cultivate compliance with provincial law. To accomplish this, the Virginia Company established procedures in 1618 for electing representatives for a House of Burgesses – two delegates from each town or plantation. This legislature met the following year to work with the governor and his council to enact laws for the colony.

Creating a Stable Society in the Chesapeake

The formation of representative government should be understood as an effort to establish a stable English society at the edge of English civilization; a society, indeed, that was recognizably *English*. Another component of this effort was the shipment of marriageable women to Virginia that same year (1619).

The recent success and prosperity of the colony, coupled with the promise of self-government, attracted more Englishmen to America. One problem made obvious by the growing number of male colonists was the sharp sex imbalance in Virginia. Because the competition for females was so fierce, the Virginia Company in London invested in a shipment of 90–100 young women to the Chesapeake. This was not a philanthropic act, but an investment – upon landing in Virginia, would-be husbands repaid the Virginia Company for their brides' voyage and other expenses. This scheme followed a similar venture, in which poor children were shipped to Virginia at the Company's expense and sold to settlers as apprentices (until they came of age).[2] This was the precedent for the development of indentured servitude as a colonial labor system. Indentured servants entered voluntarily into a contract by which they agreed to sell their labor and their freedom for a specified number of years. They were not slaves for life, and their children (if born during the parents' term of bondage) did not inherent the parents' legal status. However, indentured servants could be sold by their master to a third party for the remainder of the indenture contract.[3] There were similar arrangements in England, by which poor people contracted themselves to work for someone else to make money or pay off a debt, but these were short-term contracts, and the servant's contract could not be sold to another master.

Sending marriageable women to Virginia was certainly a profitable enterprise, but the Company's objectives went beyond immediate profits. Settling women in the colony would allow for its natural growth, but also, as Company Treasurer Sir Edwin Sandys pointed out, it would "make the men more settled & lesse moveable who [because of the shortage of women] stay there but to gett something and then return for England." Sandys worried that such instability undermined the sustainability and profitability of the colony. In 1621 and 1622, the Company shipped another 50 women in an effort to anchor the discontented bachelors to Virginia.

---

2 Being set to work as an apprentice as a young child was not uncommon in both England and the colonies. Children who were not supported by their parents (for example, orphaned or abandoned children, or children of unwed or indentured mothers) were apprenticed as early as two or three years old. In a society without government bureaucracies to care for children in need, apprenticeship gave families an incentive to take these children in and provide them with food, shelter, clothing, a Christian upbringing, and valuable laboring skills.

3 The term "indenture" refers to the contract itself. The would-be servant and would-be master signed a contract specifying the terms of the agreement – bondage, labor, years of service, terms of release, payment, and the like. The two parties then tore the contract, creating a pattern of indentations along the tear line. Alternatively, they could create two copies with matching indentures along the edges. Each party – servant and master – kept one part or one copy of the contract. At the end of the indenture period, both parties presented their document to a magistrate, who verified that the indentations matched and that each party had satisfied the terms of the contract.

Beyond these organized efforts early on, the Virginia Company continually urged women – young, marriageable women, that is – to emigrate from England, offering not only generous land grants but also advantageous matrimonial matches. In Maryland, similar measures met with resistance, since they allowed women to "vow chastity" (that is, to remain unmarried). The Maryland Assembly passed a bill in 1634 stipulating that if a woman remained single for seven years after receiving a land grant, she would forfeit that land to her next of kin. (The bill was vetoed by Lord Baltimore, the colony's proprietor and governor.)

Transition from Direct to Representative Governance in the North

Sex imbalance was not as pronounced in the northern colonies. These colonies attracted a lower proportion of indentured servants (an immigrant group that was predominantly male) and a higher proportion of intact families, which naturally produced roughly even numbers of male and female offspring. Yet these colonies experienced the same tensions evident in the South between direct governance and a growing and expanding population. Plymouth, the first English colony planted in the north, established a form of direct participatory government, with all citizens (freemen) of the colony having a seat in the assembly (the General Court). This body of freemen served as a legislature and high court, and also elected the colony's executive officers – the governor and his council (the "assistants"). This system of direct popular rule functioned well because the colony was small and compact – from 1620 to 1630, the colony grew from 100 to only 300 inhabitants. Ten years later, however, after the Great Migration, the colony reached 3000 inhabitants, settled farther afield in various towns and villages. This demographic development transformed Plymouth's General Court from a participatory assembly into a representative body. As was the case in Virginia's House of Burgesses, each township was charged with electing two representatives ("deputies") to serve on the General Court.

The same dynamics transformed the government in the Massachusetts Bay Colony, the largest and most dominant of the New England colonies. Settled nine years after Plymouth (1629), it quickly surpassed it in strength.[4] The first governor of Massachusetts, John Winthrop, ruled Massachusetts with an elected council of 12 officeholders ("assistants"), but without a representative legislature. The governor and his council made up the General Court, serving the province as a legislature, executive, and high court. Soon thereafter, though,

---

4 By the end of the seventeenth century, Massachusetts, which numbered roughly 60 000 at the time, would absorb Plymouth and its 7000 inhabitants.

attempts to raise taxes met with resistance from the towns, and with demands for the townships to have a greater voice in government. Consequently, the General Court changed in 1634 to include "deputies" – elected representatives from each of the towns (one or two per town, depending on the number of qualified voters in that town). Later on, tensions between the assistants and the deputies led to their separation – the assistants sat as an upper house, and the deputies as a lower house.

These early examples of provincial administration demonstrate that direct government – whether autocratic, like Dale's Virginia and Winthrop's Massachusetts, or democratic like Plymouth – could not command deference from a population that was growing demographically and expanding geographically. The tremendous growth rate of colonial populations forced colonial governors to choose between achieving their goals by force (with armed enforcers) or by consent. Since Dale and Winthrop did not have the resources or the manpower to coerce, they were left with only one option – the conventionally English practice of allowing local communities to participate in legislation and tax assessments through a representative system of government.

The evolution of representative government, then, was a product of the demographic growth and geographic expansion of the English population in the colonies (thanks to prodigious natural growth, buttressed by a steady flow of English immigrants). The replication of English civic organization in the colonies was thus a testament to the colonies' economic viability and maturation.

A Transatlantic English Civilization

Many studies of transatlantic migration encourage readers to conceive of the ocean as barrier between the Old World and the New. Once crossed, these accounts suggest, the Atlantic acted as a cultural divide, not only separating settler communities from their mother culture, but also initiating a cultural transformation – Americanization – in isolation from the mother culture. This narrative of colonial society suggests that the seeds of Revolutionary Era separatism were sown generations earlier, as English settlers crossed the Atlantic, settled in America, and thus began their gradual transformation into Americans. Yet there is strong counterevidence to this storyline – evidence of the continual Anglicization of the American environment, flora, fauna, and the settlers themselves. According to this storyline, the Atlantic Ocean did not separate and isolate the New World colonies from England. Rather, it increasingly integrated them into English civilization.

When historians move beyond the traditional focus on New England's Puritan communities, they encounter the migration stories of multitudes of "strangers" within New England, and of colonists farther south than New

England. These accounts indicate that settlers themselves did not see their departure from England as a rejection of England; they did not slam the door behind them as they left. They referred to themselves as English, they referred to England as "home," and they were never severely cut off from their families in England, or from English culture, politics, business, literature, trade, gossip, fashion, and the like.

A 1631 letter from John Pond – a young settler in Watertown, Massachusetts – to his parents back home sheds light on colonists' own understanding of their relationship with the mother country. (Readers who are in college, or have children in college, will recognize the letter's opening paragraph as one that precedes a request for the parents to send money.)

> Most loving and kind Father and Mother:
> My humble duty remembered unto you, trusting in God you are in good health [...]. I know, loving Father, and do confess that I was an undutiful child unto you when I lived with you and by you, for the which I am much sorrowful and grieved for it, trusting in God that He will so guide me that I will never offend you so any more, and I trust in God that you will forgive me for it, and my writing unto you is to let you understand what a country this new Eingland is where we live.

After describing the Indians, the terrain, climate, the livestock, the price of wheat, Indian corn, and butter, young John thanks his parents for sending him supplies by ship; supplies that were too expensive for him to buy himself:

> I humbly thank you for it. I did expect two cows, [...] because the country is not so as we did expect it. Therefore, loving Father, I would entreat you that you would send me a firkin of butter and a hogshead of malt unground [If] you of your love will send them, I will pay the freight. [And], loving Father, though I be far distant from you, yet I pray you remember me as your child, and we do not know how long we may subsist, for we cannot live here without provisions form ould eingland. Therefore, I pray, do not put away your shopstuff, for I think that in the end if I live it must be my living, for we do not know how long this plantation will stand, for some of the merchants that did uphold it have turned off their men and have given it over. Besides, God hath taken away the chiefest [man] in the land, Mr. Johnson [...].
> Here came over twenty-five passengers and there come back again [to England] four score and odd persons and as many more would have come if they had wherewithal to bring them home [England], for here are many that came over the last year, which [have lost their resources] so here we may live if we have supplies every year from ould eingland; otherwise we cannot subsist. [...]

So, Father, I pray consider of my cause, for here will be but a very poor being [without] your help with provisions from ould eingland. [...] I humbly thank you for your great love and kindness in sending me some provisions [...] I will plant what corn I can, and if provisions be no chaper between this and Michaelmas [...] I purpose to come home at Michaelmas.[5]

John Pond's letter to his father indicates that the Atlantic was not a barrier dividing colonists from England. It was instead a bridge that connected them to their families, businesses, news, and so forth. And it allowed them to return to England if things did not work out in America.

Modern American readers should keep in mind, in this respect, that as land-lubbers, they are predisposed to see the ocean as alien and hostile territory. But a maritime civilization like seventeenth- and eighteenth-century England viewed the ocean differently. Travel and communications by sea were faster, safer, and more dependable than by land. Indeed, as John Pond's letter illustrates, transatlantic traffic was the lifeblood of English settlements in the New World. And alongside new immigrants and trade, ships also provided settlers with news of the latest developments in England.

Indeed, throughout the seventeenth century, migration to and from North America was linked to the changing tides of English economics and politics. During the English Civil War, supporters of both sides came across seeking to escape hazards to life and property. However, there was also traffic going the other way – American settlers who supported Parliament against the king (or later on, supporters of Cromwell's "Puritan Revolution") returned to England to get involved in the struggle. The same happened following the Restoration – republicans, Cromwellian veterans, and radical Protestants left England for America, while others returned to England on the assumption that the restored monarchy would provide a measure of security, political and religious stability, and economic growth.

As John Pond observed in his private letter, every ship that brought immigrants to America, took others back to England. The driving force behind these waves of immigration and back-migration was security and economic opportunity. Indeed, this was true long before permanent settlements were established in North America – for at least 120 years before the *Mayflower* set sail, European fishing fleets were a common sight along America's northeastern coastlines, where crews would dock to wait out a storm, find food and water, or dry and salt their fish. The planting of permanent settlements in North America created a new draw for employable young men, but – as the managers of the Virginia Company discovered, and as statistics on

5 Quoted in Demos, J. (1972). *Remarkable Providences, 1600–1760*, 73–75. New York: G. Braziller.

back-migration confirm – these men were not predisposed to settling down permanently in America.

For male immigrants, coming to America was not a long-term commitment. Many came to make money in order to return to England and establish themselves there. Cheap land and high wages were the colonies' main draws. America represented an opportunity to get a fresh start by either escaping or repaying one's debts, escaping prosecution or family obligations, or grasping socioeconomic opportunities that were beyond reach in England. For some immigrants, though, the voyage to America was not a means to a desired end, but simply an adventure. They crossed over casually, knowing that they were not closing the door behind them; they could easily return home whenever they chose. Certainly, small groups of dedicated believers immigrated to America for religious reasons, seeing colonization as a Christian "errand into the wilderness," and intending to remain in America. But most people – in the seventeenth century as today – relocated for more mundane reasons.

Indeed, Puritan "saints" lamented that there were "strangers" among them, and that Atlantic traffic kept bringing more of them. And although religious leaders in Massachusetts tried to have immigrants screened for criminal records and religious affiliations, the directors of the Massachusetts Bay Company in London needed these people – soldiers, artisans, fishermen, servants, indentured servants, dockworkers, and other laborers – to make the colony a success. Englishmen were not clamoring to come to America; on the contrary, the colonial proprietors in London had to employ promoters and recruiters to convince Englishmen to go to America. The people in charge of the business end of these colonization enterprises could not afford to be picky about who they let in, even if they wanted to.

The result was that colonial populations were generally reflective of the middle and lower orders of English society, with significant portions of immigrants either free or indentured servants. In New England, like in the old country, roughly 25% of the working population were servants. In the southern colonies, where labor demands were higher, up to 50% of white immigrants were servants. Naturally, these people were recruited for their muscle and poverty, rather than their religious or moral character. Consequently, servants were often at the center of colonies' moral and disciplinary problems.

In New England, saints' moral alarm concerning strangers in their midst began as early as immigration did, on the boats coming across. The ships' logs record passengers being whipped and incarcerated for swearing, stealing, or worse (rape, public drunkenness, and assault). One of the first recorded hangings in Plymouth Colony was of a teenage servant named Thomas Granger, who was convicted of carnally abusing a mare, two calves, two goats, five sheep, and a turkey. Decent folk in New England and elsewhere complained about their children being exposed to "multitudes of idle and profane young men, servants, and others," but they could not stop the flow of people. Civic attempts to police the behavior of neighbors, parishioners, children, laborers, servants, and slaves represented an effort by governments of limited means and even more limited manpower to retain or regain control over populations that were growing numerically and expanding geographically.

What is striking in this persistent demand for order and for adherence to the values and customs of the community is the fact that this American reality was a mirror image of Old England. Migration to America formed part of a greater pattern of geographic mobility in England in the seventeenth century. Every decade from the 1630s on, England lost roughly 80 000 people due to emigration. Of the 550 000 who left England between 1630 and 1700, 378 000 left for the New World – 40 000 to New England, 116 000 to the Chesapeake and southern colonies, and 222 000 to the West Indies. But mobility *within* England was even more massive and widespread. This phenomenon – internal migration from one region to another – was a new development in early-modern England, one that was both a major cause and a symptom of the economic, religious, and political convulsions that roiled English society in the sixteenth and seventeenth centuries. It went hand in hand with the steady growth in England's overall population, from two million to over five million during this period.

The combination of demographic growth and high geographic mobility resulted in the disintegration of some rural communities, while urban centers formed and grew at a rapid pace. The demographic instability on display in American colonies was thus a feature of contemporary life in England as well, with inhabitants anxious to reestablish stable communities governed and policed by broad consensus regarding shared values, beliefs, and practices. Yet the continual mixing of populations that did not share bonds of kinship and history made this endeavor difficult, frustrating, and distressing.

Naturally, this held true for the colonies as well. In Virginia, the English population grew from 900 in 1620 to 85 000 in 1700. The New England colonies grew from 1800 in 1630 to 91 000 in 1700. During this period, New England's net gain from immigration was only 24 000. The rest of this tremendous growth the settlers accomplished on their own, by prospering and multiplying at a much higher rate than in England. This is attributed chiefly to high wages and cheap land, which allowed Americans to marry at a young age (early-20s for men, late-teens for women), whereas English grooms had to wait longer before they were in position to support a family. Travelers regularly reported on the early marriages and large families in every part of the American colonies. One such account declared that childless married women who transplanted to North Carolina became mothers soon after. Indeed, colonial promoters in England used the colonies' reputation for fertility and fecundity as an inducement for emigration, with pamphlets that celebrated English women in the New World as "great breeders."

Family records confirm these reports, especially in the northern colonies, where families with 10 or 12 children were quite common, and families with as many as 20 or 30 children were not unheard of (especially if one or two wives died during childbirth, allowing the husband to marry a younger wife, who continued producing offspring well into the father's old age). In the South, labor conditions created different demographic patterns. Until the 1690s, most of the population growth in the Chesapeake was the result of immigration. This was due, first, to unhealthy living conditions which were not conducive to breeding. Life expectancy in the Chesapeake colonies was 43 for men, and somewhat lower for women. Seventy percent of Anglos died before the age of 50. Additionally, the high demand for laborers in the South (in part due to low life expectancy there) depressed natural growth: 85% of all immigrants to the southern colonies arrived as indentured servants, the overwhelming majority of whom were men. Consequently, the sex ratio in the South became radically unbalanced. For example, Maryland numbered 600 colonists in 1650, including 200 females (30%). In 1704, the colony numbered 30 000, of which 7000 were female (20%). Having so few women in the South meant that fewer families were formed in these colonies, thus retarding natural growth.

Another result of the fact that so many southern immigrants were servants was that marriages occurred relatively late in life there. Men had to serve out their indenture contracts, and then earn enough to buy property or establish themselves otherwise before they could expect to find a wife. Women, as well, had to be free of their indenture before marrying.[6] Thus, the marriage age for women was roughly their mid-twenties, with roughly 10 years of childbearing potential behind them. Considering the rate of child mortality (30–50%, depending on region) and the low life expectancy for women in the South, ex-servants could usually be expected to bear only four or five children. Thus, not only were fewer families formed in the South, but families were smaller as well.

---

6 Despite this legal requirement, it was common for female servants to get pregnant while still under indenture (roughly 20% of female servants in a few representative counties in Maryland, for example, were brought to court for bearing illegitimate children). One can safely assume that this happened in many more cases that did not reach a court of law. The problem for the woman was that unless the father could buy the remaining time of her contract, she could not marry him (as she would if she were free). For female servants, therefore, sex represented tremendous risks – a fine, corporal punishment (lashes), and even additional years added to her indenture contract, to compensate her master for his trouble and for his lost labor during her pregnancy and maternity. Additionally, a servant mother could lose her child after it was weaned, unless she became free by then, since the courts bound these children in apprenticeships at a very young age so that the child would not be a burden on the master's household. Still, premarital pregnancies were common, especially among servants. The register of marriages and births in a study of colonial Maryland indicates that in up to 50% of recorded marriages in the seventeenth century, the bride was pregnant. This doubled the rate in England and in the northern colonies. This is understandable, as bridal pregnancies were much more common among servants and ex-servants. Since there were so many more of these women per capita in the South than in England or New England, one can expect to find higher rates of bridal pregnancies in the South.

The South still experienced demographic growth, though it was despite immigrant predominance over American-born Anglos (creoles), despite sex imbalance (a ratio of roughly 3:1), despite late marriages and small families, and despite early death. By the turn of the century, however, the sex imbalance began to correct itself, and southern colonies increasingly fell in line with northern demographic patterns. This too was a natural outcome of the patterns outlined above: since native-born women married younger and bore more children than immigrant women, the number of natives (creoles) soon eclipsed the number of immigrants. Moreover, because natural reproduction (unlike immigration) produced equal numbers of males and females, the sex imbalance began to even out as society began to grow naturally, rather than through immigration.[7]

Not only was the colonial population rapidly growing, especially toward the late-seventeenth and early-eighteenth centuries, but this burgeoning population was also constantly on the move – to and from England, to and from other colonies, and from town to town. The driving force behind this high rate of geographic mobility was the quest for economic opportunity, in the form of either farmland or urban employment.

This volatile demographic context explains the heightened civic and governmental anxiety about order, law, and social harmony in American towns. These communities were constantly bombarded by hordes of newcomers – strangers from across the ocean and from other colonies, counties, and towns; people from different socioeconomic backgrounds, with different traditions, different understandings of what behavior was acceptable and unacceptable; people that the local inhabitants did not know, and who naturally did not fit into the established local hierarchies, relationships, and customs. In the absence of police to enforce preexisting codes of conduct on newcomers, the arrival of new settlers continually challenged local customs, ideals, procedures, and institutions. This was evident at the earliest stages of settlement – for example, between saints and strangers in Plymouth – and intensified thereafter, as new arrivals from near and far joined American communities in greater and greater numbers.

Furthermore, free immigrants in American communities were joined by large numbers of unfree immigrants – apprentices, indentured servants, and slaves – who became part of their masters' households, which brought this clash of ethnic, religious, regional, and class cultures into settlers' very homes.

---

7 As southern and frontier communities became more demographically stable and conventional, women found fewer opportunities to find husbands. Thus, whereas few widows can be found in the death rolls and probate records of frontier communities, older women and widows tended to remain unmarried in more demographically conventional settlements, which featured a higher proportion of women. This dynamic affected the choices of younger women as well. Women who immigrated to America as servants arrived alone and were therefore free to pick their own matches. In more settled and conventional communities, however, more women were American-born and therefore had families nearby to influence their marital choices.

Questions for Discussion

1 What drew English men to the American colonies? What drew English women?
2 Why did English society in America grow so rapidly? And why was English society in the Chesapeake less stable (demographically and politically) than in New England?
3 In the absence of police forces, how did colonial populations police themselves?

Further Readings

Berkin, C. (1996). *First Generations: Women in Colonial America*. New York: Hill and Wang.

Cressy, D. (1987). *Coming Over: Migration and Communication Between England and New England in the Seventeenth Century*. New York: Cambridge University Press.

Konig, T. (October, 1982). 'Dale's Laws' and the non-common law origins of criminal justice in Virginia. *The American Journal of Legal History* 26 (4): 354–375.

Smith, D.S. (1972). The demographic history of colonial New England. *The Journal of Economic History* 32 (1): 165–183.

Spruill, J. (1938). *Women's Life and Work in the Southern Colonies*. Chapel Hill: University of North Carolina Press.

Zuckerman, M. (1978). *Peaceable Kingdoms: New England Towns in the Eighteenth Century*. New York: Norton.

3

African Slavery, White Supremacy, and Republicanism

Indentured servants in the South made up nearly half of the white population in the seventeenth century. African slaves, who were much fewer in number, were in some instances referred to as servants and in others as slaves in the early- and mid-seventeenth century, and the terms of their bondage as well were fluid. When the first African slaves arrived in the Chesapeake colonies, the practice of indentured servitude was simply extended to them. Since the expense of acquiring African servants was high, their terms of servitudes were longer than of English servants, but some Africans did outlive their periods of indenture or were otherwise able to purchase their freedom. Like English freedmen (that is, servants who outlived their indenture contracts), these black freedmen acquired land, accumulated property, sued their neighbors, passed their property onto their children, and in some cases even held minor public offices. This fluidity in the terms of black slavery came to an end in the latter half of the seventeenth century, as colonies enacted laws that standardized slavery as chattel slavery, a perpetual and hereditary condition that was distinct from indentured servitude and applied exclusively to Indians and blacks.

While slavery was a dehumanizing institution to modern observers, it is important to stress that Europeans definitely did consider both Africans and Indians to be human beings; that is, they were seen as having a soul and a degree of reason. This is why they were seen as appropriate targets for missionary work – they were humans, and therefore part of Christ's flock. Although modern people cannot conceive of such a thing as human property – the two terms seem contradictory by definition – premodern people, generally speaking, accepted the notion that human beings could lose their liberty and become others' property. Some societies through the ages saw enslavement as a matter of pure chance, unrelated to the slave's qualities as a person, whereas other societies viewed it as a necessary condition for people or peoples who did not have the mental or cultural maturity to govern themselves. In the case of Africans and Indians, some Europeans considered them to be akin to

The Colonists' American Revolution: Preserving English Liberty, 1607–1783, First Edition. Guy Chet.
© 2020 John Wiley & Sons, Inc. Published 2020 by John Wiley & Sons, Inc.
Companion website: www.wiley.com/go/Chet/ColonistsAmericanRevolution

children – creatures that had to be controlled and directed by their superiors, but who eventually could mature and acculturate into adulthood, equality, and freedom. Others, however, conceived of them as perpetual children, who would forever remain in their savage state and require direction and discipline from above.

Europeans' racial and white supremacist beliefs regarding Africans were shaped by the interactions of whites and blacks in Africa and the Americas, in the context of the transatlantic slave trade and New World slavery. Among historians of the United States, it is widely held that white supremacy developed – as an ideology, a legal regime, and a societal structure – in colonial Virginia in the late-seventeenth and eighteenth centuries. A minority position (one more in tune with scholarship on imperial and Atlantic history) is that American racial beliefs and race relations originated not in North America, but in Britain's Caribbean sugar colonies.

These competing theories are important not only for the study of American race relations and African American history; they shape one's broader understanding of the American founding. Specifically, these two conflicting narratives on race relations produce conflicting interpretations of the origins and nature of American liberty and republicanism: the Virginia model holds that Anglo-Americans' understanding of their political rights and liberties was inextricably linked to their experience of living in American slave societies. By contrast, the Caribbean model suggests that colonists' conception of liberty was formed in England, rather than in America.

The Virginia Theory Concerning Slavery, White Supremacy, and Republicanism

Slavery existed in North America before European settlement, as it existed in Africa before the Atlantic slave trade began, but the Atlantic slave trade changed both the scope and terms of slavery in America. The English mainland colonies, and later the United States, were a minor market for African slaves – of the roughly 10 million Africans transported to the New World, less than 5% (450 000) landed in North America. What was unique about the North American environment, however, was that it was virtually the only New World setting in which the African slave population increased by natural means. In the West Indies, slaves had an average life expectancy of six years. In North America, by contrast, they stood a much better chance of having children and seeing their children grow up. In most colonies, the natural growth rate of blacks – both Africans and African Americans – was similar to that of local whites. By the late-eighteenth century, blacks represented 20% of colonial society (roughly 500 000 of 2.5 million settlers at the time of the Revolution).

When Americans today think of American slavery, they visualize the plantation system of the early- and mid-nineteenth century – the American slave system in its "mature" form. That antebellum slave system was made up of white and black creoles (i.e. native-born Anglo-Americans and native-born African Americans) who operated within the sociopolitical context into which they were born and whose forms they knew and understood. But slavery in the colonial period was much more varied, with slaves, masters, and others experiencing slavery differently in different settings: frontier environments versus secure and economically developed communities, cities versus countryside, North versus South, upper South versus lower South, and small family farms versus large plantations. Slaves' health, life expectancy, family formation, group solidarity, and escape patterns varied depending on the setting and the era.[1] In urban settings, frontier environments, and on small family farms, slaves were able to gain a measure of control over their lives, schedules, and activities. They lived and worked in close proximity to whites and quickly learned the basics of the English language, Christianity, and other aspects of English culture. Whereas acculturation in such settings (north and south) took only a few years, the transformation of Africans into African Americans on large plantations (especially in the Deep South) was a lengthy process lasting up to a few generations.

When African slavery established itself in the Chesapeake in the mid-seventeenth century, Virginia was a frontier society. The unfree labor force was a mix of white, Indian, and African servants and slaves, and the terms of slavery and race relations were fluid and, for the most part, not codified. But as English settlements grew and expanded inland in the latter half of the century due to stronger demand for large tracts of land, the Chesapeake colonies' unfree labor force grew increasingly homogenous. Land owners exhibited preference for African slaves over Indian slaves and white servants, since Africans were more resilient to disease, had agricultural and technical skills that landowners prized, and were less likely to escape. Improved life expectancy further moved masters to invest in slaves who would serve for life, rather than servants who were bound for only a few years of service. Moreover, in the latter half of the seventeenth century English immigrants increasingly chose to indenture themselves in new colonies to the north, which offered better labor and living conditions.

---

1 Escaping Africans tended to run toward the backcountry and isolated swamps. They generally moved in groups that included women and children, despite the risk such groupings posed for a successful escape. Their purpose was to recreate communities free from white domination. But African American slaves (i.e. slaves born in America) generally escaped alone, usually with the hope of escaping *into* American society, rather than away. Moving toward the areas of heaviest settlement, they found refuge in thicker population centers, selling their labor to whites with no questions asked. Creoles' obvious confidence in their ability to integrate themselves into American society stands in stark contrast to that of Africans, who just wanted to flee from their Anglo-American world.

The law reflected this growing predominance of Africans in Virginia's unfree labor force. From the 1660s on, the law in Virginia specified that Africans were to serve for their entire lives and bequeath their legal status to their children. (The colonies of the Deep South were established with this principle – African chattel slavery – already in place.)

As improved living conditions allowed more and more white servants to outlive their terms of indenture, they found it increasingly difficult to advance in Virginia society. The fact that rich land-owning families bought large tracts of land on the interior meant that freedmen who wanted to buy land, establish farms, and start families had to move to the very edges of European civilization, practically in Indian territory, where they were subject to Indian violence. The only alternative was to remain in the more established and better protected regions to the south and east, as wage laborers on someone else's farm or plantation, an option not conducive to attracting a bride and starting a family.

If these growing numbers of free but landless whites had had a voice in the assembly, they might have moved the House of Burgesses either to subsidize secure but expensive land in the east, or to finance and deploy provincial troops on the periphery to safeguard frontier farms from Indian violence or even drive the Indians farther back. But since the landed elite dominated both the House of Burgesses and the Governor's Council, freedmen were unable to influence public policy on these matters. Frustration among frontier farmers and landless whites elsewhere in Virginia mounted, and in the 1650s and 1660s, Governor William Berkeley had to put down a few violent uprisings by poor or landless whites. Berkeley refused to hold elections to the House of Burgesses from 1661 to 1676, which enabled him and the landed elite to ignore the changing demographics in Virginia. Indeed, during this period, the House of Burgesses introduced property qualifications on voting rights, denying landless whites the vote.

These tensions erupted in 1675, when territorial disputes and escalating violence on Virginia's northern frontier led to Indian raids on English farms and villages there. Indian attacks intensified rapidly in the summer of 1675, resulting in roughly 300 English fatalities. The colony was in an uproar over the death and destruction visited upon frontier families, but also in fear that the violence would spread to the more established settlements to the south and east. Berkeley and the assembly faced great social and political pressure to react, and indeed, the assembly quickly voted to finance the recruitment of 500 provincial troops.

Fearing that establishing a strong English military presence on the northern frontier would provoke the Indians to respond, thus feeding the cycle of violence and making a bad situation worse, Berkeley did not use provincial forces to guard frontier settlements or attack Indian villages beyond the frontier. He instead deployed the troops short of the frontier battlefields, as protective garrisons (that is, defensive forces) in more secure and settled towns and plantations. Frontier families felt that they were used as a live buffer to protect wealthier and better-connected families to the southeast. Moreover, they found indignant supporters in some of those wealthier and better-connected planters, including Nathaniel Bacon, a member of the Governor's Council who in time came to lead this frontier movement. These supportive allies of frontier communities doubtless sympathized with them and shared their anti-Indian sentiments, but mostly they had a strategic difference with Berkeley and his allies in the House of Burgesses. They believed that Berkeley's non-confrontational response to Indian violence was a recipe for continued violence. Moreover, they feared that Berkeley's inaction in the north would encourage the Indians to expand their raids southward and eastward to Virginia's more settled, prosperous, and secure counties.

This assessment was not merely a matter of conjecture. That very summer, a local campaign of Indian violence in the small colony of Plymouth escalated into a major regional war involving numerous Indian tribes in New England (King Philip's War, 1675–1676). The war devastated Rhode Island, Connecticut, Plymouth, and Massachusetts, sparking fears among Bacon's supporters in Virginia that Governor Berkeley's response to Indian attacks on the frontier would exacerbate Indian attacks, rather than pacify the enemy. Moreover, they saw Berkeley's policy as exacerbating the bitter regional and class divide in Virginia politics.

The strategic debate between Governor Berkeley and Nathaniel Bacon quickly became a bitter personal and political feud, which resulted in Bacon raising a force of volunteers and leading it on an unauthorized and illegal campaign against Indian villages in northern Virginia. To diffuse regional tensions within Virginia society, Berkeley acquiesced to demands for new elections to the House of Burgesses. For its part, the House decided, in fear of violence from freedmen and frontier settlers, to lift all property qualifications on voting in the coming elections.

With the vote extended to all adult male citizens,[2] the 1676 election strengthened Bacon's base of support in the House of Burgesses, weakened the governor, and emboldened Bacon to demand a military commission. Although Bacon himself had been captured and forced to sign a confession, the election returns convinced Berkeley to deal with him gently. Berkeley not only pardoned Bacon, but also restored him to his seat on the council. Moreover, Berkeley signaled that he would consider granting Bacon a military commission to lead a campaign in the north.

---

2 By definition and by law, unfree people – both slaves and indentured servants – were not citizens.

When Berkeley eventually decided against it, Bacon's Rebellion turned from an Anglo-Indian war on the frontier to a regional and class war for control of the government of Virginia. Bacon led roughly 500 of his armed volunteers (recruited from northern and western frontier counties) southward to Jamestown to convince the assembly to recognize – and pay – his volunteers as government troops. Additionally, he sought from the legislature a military commission to raise and lead more troops against the Indians in the north. The Burgesses were convinced by Bacon's armed militiamen to accede to these demands. In a confrontation between Berkeley's and Bacon's armies, Berkeley's force dissolved, leaving him on the run and Bacon in charge of Jamestown. Bacon promised to eradicate the Indian menace, discontinue trade with the Indians, end corruption in high places, and halt unjust taxation. To his troops he promised all the Indian plunder they could carry.

But before attacking the Indians in the north, Bacon led his mostly northern and western troops against wealthy pro-Berkeley planters in Gloucester County, killing some and plundering their estates. Berkeley, who matched Bacon promise for promise (including the promise of plunder from pro-Bacon families), also promised freedom to indentured servants who would rally to his flag. But with Bacon in control and on the ascendance, Berkeley failed to draw sufficient numbers, as his supporters were terrorized by Bacon's men. Bacon then led a successful campaign against the Indians in the north, providing his men with plunder and slaves.

At the height of his power, however, Bacon fell ill with dysentery. After his death (October 1676), regular forces arrived from England and assisted Berkeley in restoring his government. He returned loyalist property that had been plundered by Baconites to its rightful owners. Additionally, he executed a number of Bacon's supporters, but most were pardoned in an effort to heal the sectional and class divisions that produced this civil war. This project continued under Berkeley's successors, Governors Culpepper and Effingham, who took a hard line against populists, but put an end to the legal proceedings against Bacon's followers. They also took care to pacify that segment of society – servants, freedmen, and poor whites generally – that had fueled Bacon's Rebellion.

Servants were granted certain legal protections regarding living and labor conditions, including the outlawing of corporal punishment for white servants. While it was a combination of factors that led to the decline of indentured servitude in Virginia following Bacon's Rebellion (including better employment opportunities opening up at the time for poor English immigrants in new colonies like Pennsylvania, New Jersey, and New York), there is no doubt that white servants and freedmen demonstrated in the 1660s and 1670s that they were a destabilizing and dangerous element in Virginia society. Planters were wary of importing more of them, especially after 1676, when they wielded more political power in Virginia, and enjoyed more liberties and protections. Africans proved to be less threatening toward the planter elite than poor whites. The rebellion therefore signaled the end of indentured servitude in Virginia, and placed an even higher premium on African slaves. From 1702 on, not one indentured servant was brought to Virginia.

Many American historians hold that white supremacy (the ideology, as well as the legal and social system that institutionalized it) established itself in America following the Virginia model. They see this as a reflection of Virginia's economic, cultural, and political leadership in British America. According to this narrative (articulated most famously by Edmund Morgan), authorities in Virginia aimed to bond rich planters and poor whites by creating racial rivalry within the underclass, between white and black laborers.[3] In the decades following Bacon's Rebellion, free Indians and blacks in Virginia were forbidden by law from employing white servants; the legislature enacted a punishment of 30 lashes for blacks (enslaved or free) who struck a white person; sexual relations between whites and blacks were outlawed; and masters were forbidden from manumitting (freeing) their African slaves without special permission from the government. Thus, these historians claim, white supremacy was manufactured, or at least deliberately exacerbated, to create a sense of community among whites – racial division between whites and blacks was used to heal a preexisting class division among whites and create the seemingly strange relationship between slavery, liberty, and republicanism in America.

According to this narrative, the Virginia assembly elevated poor whites' economic, legal, and social standing because the white underclass proved to be so deadly during Bacon's Rebellion. Economic subsidies for freedmen facilitated the formation of a society of large and small planters united in their economic interests, and a republican ideology conferred on white Virginians shared civic responsibilities and a shared stake in maintaining the existing social order. Meanwhile, a growing caste of slaves separated from society by racism and fear of slave revolts eased tensions between rich and poor whites, generating among them a sense of civic cohesion through their construction of a shared racial antipathy. Most important, this narrative holds that Virginia's mix of African slavery, Anglo-American liberty, and white supremacy became the model for the American colonies more broadly, shaping Americans' political ideology – specifically on race, liberty, and self-government – in the Revolutionary era and beyond.

---

3 Critics of Morgan's highly decorated and influential 1975 book (*American Slavery, American Freedom: The Ordeal of Colonial Virginia*) point to its Marxist framework highlighting class over race, but also to the possible distorting influence of mid-twentieth-century racial politics (specifically, southern race relations in the 1950s, 1960s, and 1970s) on colonial scholars of that era.

The Caribbean Theory Concerning Slavery, White Supremacy, and Republicanism

The Virginia theory suggests that Anglo-American liberty and white supremacy were (i) intertwined with one another and (ii) local products of race relations in North America. By contrast, the Caribbean theory denies both. It contends that both liberty and white supremacy were imports to North America, from England and the West Indies respectively. Moreover, the Caribbean theory holds that English liberty and white supremacy were not intertwined, but simply coincided wherever Englishmen settled in the New World. As Englishmen, settlers carried with them wherever they went an ancient, precolonial attachment to English liberties and representative government. As settlers living among enslaved Africans, they also developed racial fears and a commitment to white supremacy.

For scholars who adhere to the Caribbean theory, white supremacy and harsh slave codes were not a clever strategy of white elites to "capture" the allegiance of poor whites, but an outgrowth of genuine fear by all whites – slaveholders and non-slaveholders alike – about life in the midst of enslaved black majorities. These fears were most pronounced and most influential in the Caribbean sugar colonies, where the racial imbalance was greatest. This Caribbean approach to American race relations demotes Virginia from its position of cultural leadership in the South and in British America generally. Instead of seeing the Virginia model of race and politics replicated in other colonies to its north and south, the Caribbean theory presents Virginia as following a pattern established in the colonies of the Deep South (the Carolinas), which themselves were satellites of Caribbean colonies.

The intimate connection between the British West Indies and the colonies of the lower South is well known. Nevertheless, the sudden and artificial separation of 13 mainland American colonies from the West Indies in 1776 creates in the minds of students and scholars alike a framework that retroactively connects the mainland colonies to one another. This Americanist framework obscures the American South's Caribbean connection throughout the colonial period. It obscures, for example, the fact that for much of its colonial existence, South Carolina exhibited socioeconomic and cultural patterns that corresponded more closely to those in the Caribbean colonies than to those in the mainland colonies to its north. The Caribbean theory, therefore, restores the wealthiest and most populous English colonies – the sugar colonies of the West Indies – to the heart of the American South.

For 10 years after its settlement in 1627, Barbados (like earlier colonies in Virginia and Bermuda) concentrated largely on tobacco culture, though it also began producing cotton and indigo in the 1630s. From the beginning, Barbados was a reasonably successful producer of staples for the English market. This success drew large numbers of English immigrants to it and initiated a land

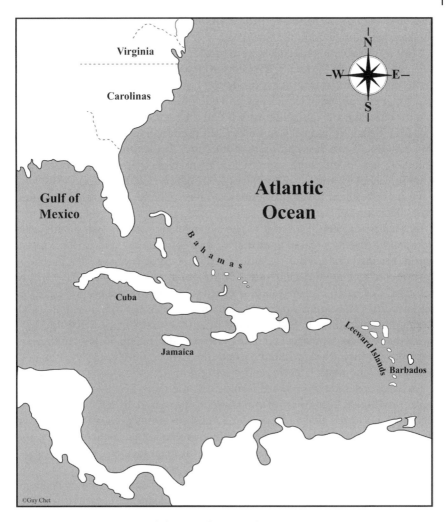

Figure 3.1 The West Indies and deep South. © Guy Chet.

rush that, within a decade, resulted in the occupation of virtually all arable land in both Barbados (166 square miles) and the nearby Leeward Islands (four islands covering 251 square miles).

Like Virginia, Barbados was a for-profit business venture, with most immigrants being single male indentured servants, used for tobacco, cotton, and indigo production. Just as competitive, exploitative, and materialistic as early Virginia, Barbados experienced a rapid concentration of wealth, as the society polarized into small groups of proprietors and a mass of servants and free laborers. With a work force of mostly single men who worked hard and died young, Barbados and the Leeward Islands became notorious for their riotous and abandoned lifestyles.

Most of these early tendencies were further enhanced by the gradual rise of sugar cultivation in Barbados, the Leeward Islands, and Jamaica from the mid-1640s on. The profits from sugar production were tremendous, but so were the investments required in land, labor, and equipment. The fact that sugar was so capital-intensive and labor-intensive led to the further concentration of property into the hands of the few families wealthy enough to purchase the laborers and equipment necessary for mass production. At the same time as they were amassing larger and larger estates for themselves, these plantation owners were replacing white servants and free white laborers with African slaves, who were more resilient to tropical diseases, more reliable as workers, and more cost effective.

By the early 1650s, as a result of the sugar revolution, Barbados achieved a population density greater than that of any comparable area in the English world, except London. But the introduction of African slaves into Barbados contributed to a rapid decline of the white population, as many whites either returned to England or migrated to other colonies where there were greater opportunities to acquire land and avoid an early death. From 30 000 in 1650, the number of whites in Barbados fell to 20 000 in 1680, and 15 000 in 1700 (with the African population climbing from roughly 800 to 50 000). In the seventeenth century, it was without a doubt the richest, most densely populated, and most economically developed English colony.

As Barbados and the Leeward Islands became more heavily African and as sugar production became more intensive, profits soared. By 1660, the wealth of Barbados exceeded that of any other English overseas possession. However, this tremendous wealth did not turn Barbados into a stable or safe society, and many of the plantation owners fled the tropical sugar factories they had established to settle back in England as absentee proprietors.

The model established in Barbados and the other sugar colonies was one of a slave-powered plantation system, stratified social structure, great disparities in wealth and lifestyles, high ratio of blacks to whites, high ratio of men to women, high levels of absenteeism among the wealthy plantation owners, and heavy mortality among workers. This model was successfully transplanted to the much larger colonies of Jamaica and Carolina, both settled in the second half of the seventeenth century. Like the Leeward Islands, these colonies followed the Barbados model and eventually became successful plantation colonies, though not as quickly as Barbados. By the 1750s, South Carolina and Jamaica were two of the three richest and most economically important British colonies (along with Virginia).

Indeed, Carolina was not simply modeled after Barbados; it was established virtually as a Barbadian colony, with over half of the whites and over half the Africans who settled there during the first generation (1670–1690) coming directly from Barbados. The white Barbadians who resettled in Carolina included some members of the planter elite and some servants and free laborers, but the great majority came from the small planter families – families owning roughly 10 acres and up to 20 slaves. In the context of the great concentration of land and wealth in Barbados, these families found it increasingly difficult to compete with larger plantations. They instead chose to sell out and relocate with their families and slaves to Carolina, where land was not as scarce and competition not as stiff. Another group that helped settle and establish the new colony were Barbadian merchants, who saw an opportunity to become planters there.

All these white Barbadians brought with them not only their experience and wealth, but also the social and cultural system that had been so dominant on the islands over the preceding 40 years. Carolina, for example, was the only mainland colony that began its existence with a pronounced preference for African slave labor and a significant number of African slaves among its original settlers. For at least a generation, the colony functioned effectively as its West Indian founders had intended – an adjunct to the Barbadian economy. Carolina developed a vigorous grazing economy, and in return for Barbadian slaves and sugar products, it sent large quantities of beef, pork, corn, lumber, naval stores, and Indian slaves to Barbados, the Leeward Islands, and Jamaica. The West Indies remained the leading importer of these Carolina goods in the eighteenth century.[4]

However, just like early on in Barbados, early Carolinians searched avidly for a profitable agricultural staple that would do for their colony what sugar had done for Caribbean colonies. Early experiments with tobacco and indigo were reasonably successful, but it was not until the successful introduction of rice in the 1690s that the colony's planters found a crop that was sufficiently profitable to justify the investment in a massive plantation system along the Barbadian model. And rice did indeed transform South Carolina as sugar had done in Barbados. Rice exports grew steadily, from 1.5 million pounds in 1710 to almost 20 million pounds in 1730. By 1770, rice accounted for 55% of all South Carolina exports, with indigo coming in second at 20%.

Although the wealth generated by rice and indigo planters in Carolina was substantially smaller than that of their counterparts in the West Indies, it far exceeded that of any other settler population in the mainland colonies. Per capita wealth in South Carolina's Charleston district in the 1770s was an astonishing £2337, more than four times that of people living in the tobacco areas of the Chesapeake and nearly six times greater than that of people living in New

---

4 Carolina was not wholly dependent on trade with Caribbean colonies. It also found markets for its produce by provisioning pirates and privateers who operated in the Atlantic, preying on Spanish, French, Dutch, and English shipping. Indian tribes to the west were another market, which supplied South Carolinians with deerskins that brought handsome profits in England.

York City or Philadelphia. Like West Indian planters, wealthy proprietors chose to flee the appalling health conditions on their plantations (which recorded the highest death rates in British North America), choosing instead to reside in Charleston or in London.

During the early-eighteenth century, rice, indigo, naval supplies, foodstuffs, and deerskins brought in the capital necessary to acquire the almost wholly African slave labor force that gave South Carolina such a close resemblance to the West Indies. The black population grew from 2500 in 1700 to 40 000 in 1730, to 75 000 in 1770. Already by 1710 there were more blacks than whites in the colony, and by 1720, blacks outnumbered whites by almost two to one; a much higher ratio than any other mainland colony at that point, or at any point until the early-national period. The ratio rose further to 2.5 to 1, where it remained for the rest of the colonial period. It is important to keep in mind that this ratio reflects colony-wide populations; in certain counties, the ratio of blacks to whites was as high as 9 : 1. Although the racial imbalance in Carolina was never as stark as in Barbados and Jamaica, it did turn the Carolina Lowcountry into what one Swiss contemporary described as "more like a Negro country"[5] than a settlement of Europeans.

Until the 1720s, South Carolina's black population was able to grow by natural means, but with the intensification of rice production in the eighteenth century, and the consequent mass importation of Africans, slave demographics took on a West Indian turn, with death rates outstripping birth rates (at least until the 1750s and 1760s). Whereas increased life expectancy and family formation among blacks in the Chesapeake, middle, and northern colonies facilitated the formation of an African American identity and culture there, the high ratio of Africans to African Americans, of men to women, and of blacks to whites in the Deep South undermined it.

The early connections – demographic, economic, and cultural – between the British West Indies and the Carolinas intensified in the eighteenth century. Although the stream of immigrants from the West Indies had dried up, South Carolina still imported directly from the Caribbean colonies 70–85% of its sugar products (sugar, molasses, and rum). In return, it exported to the islands up to 20% of its rice crops, as well as other exports. This steady flow of goods, as well as the commercial and social correspondence between trading partners and relatives, brought with it news, gossip, business opportunities, and ideas regarding society, culture, fashion, race relations, agriculture, and even architecture. (The veranda, or front porch, which was first developed in the West Indies, appeared almost simultaneously, around 1735, in most of the North American colonies engaged in West Indian trade.) The *South Carolina Gazette* often

---

5 Wood, P. (1996). *Black Majority: Negroes in Colonial South Carolina from 1670 through the Stono Rebellion*, 132. New York: Norton.

reprinted items from island newspapers, and vice versa. Especially interesting to South Carolinian readers was news of the frequent slave uprisings in Jamaica and other sugar islands, along with the graphic descriptions of violence perpetrated against Englishmen and their womenfolk.

Because of the proximity of Spanish Florida and French Louisiana, as well as many powerful Indian tribes to the south and west, South Carolina (and later, Georgia) already lived with a persistent threat of attack, just like the similarly vulnerable Caribbean colonies. Additionally, the large numbers of enslaved blacks in the rural rice-growing areas also presented the colonies of the Deep South – like those of the West Indies – with a potentially dangerous domestic enemy, especially in wartime. To address this threat, South Carolina enacted a harsh slave code. Based on that of Barbados, it was the most draconian of the slave codes of the mainland colonies.

The strong Caribbean influence on the lower South clearly shaped race relations and labor practices there, and sustained cohesive civic bonds among whites. These bonds thickened in the context of a hazardous disease environment, threatening foreign powers, domestic threats to life and property, mutual interests, and a shared *Caribbean* culture that was shaped by life as an enclave of English civilization in the midst of "African savagery." These attitudes and the racial practices they produced undoubtedly resonated in other slave societies to the north of the Carolinas, especially in plantation economies such as Virginia's, where the racial demographics were at least somewhat similar, giving rise to racial fears among whites, a sense of cultural supremacy of whites over blacks, and social and political solidarity among whites.

The Implications of the Virginia and Caribbean Models

Situating the Deep South in the cultural orbit of Barbados and Jamaica, rather than that of Virginia, reflects the economic, demographic, and military realities of the colonial era. By contrast, historians who present Virginia as a leading force in shaping the racial culture of the Deep South anachronistically project Virginia's post-Revolutionary leadership in the South onto the colonial era. The Virginia-centered explanation for the formation of American ideas on race, liberty, and republicanism therefore reflects the vantage point, experience, and interests of modern Americans, who look back on the colonial era with a continental orientation, rather than an Atlantic one. The Caribbean approach, by contrast, is truer to the Atlantic vantage point, orientation, and interests of contemporary colonists – both black and white – who understood and experienced British America, and the South in particular, as an integral part of a regional system centered in the West Indies.

From this perspective, the leading factor in shaping colonists' racial ideas was not class divisions among whites, but fear of black violence and slave resistance. By the same token, this approach presents colonists' attachment to English liberty, government by consent, and representative government as an English inheritance – an English import – rather than a product of American slavery.

Questions for Discussion

1 Why did the terms of African slavery and of race relations in America grow harsher over time?
2 How does the debate on the origins of English settlers' racial beliefs (the Virginia model vs. the Caribbean model) relate to the debate on the origins of white Americans' beliefs regarding their own political liberty, representative government, and government by consent?

Further Readings

Berlin, I. (1998). *Many Thousands Gone: The First Two Centuries of Slavery in North America*. Cambridge: Harvard University Press.

Burnard, T. (2002). *Creole Gentlemen: The Maryland Elite, 1691–1776*. New York: Routledge.

Burnard, T. (2015). *Planters, Merchants, and Slaves: Plantation Societies in British America, 1650–1820*. Chicago: University of Chicago Press.

Ekirch, A.R. (1987). *Bound for America: The Transportation of British Convicts to the Colonies, 1718–1775*. Oxford: Clarendon Press.

Galenson, D. (1981). *White Servitude in Colonial America*. Cambridge: Cambridge University Press.

Galenson, D. (1985). *Traders, Planters and Slaves: Market Behavior in Early English America*. Cambridge: Cambridge University Press.

Morgan, E. (1975). *American Slavery, American Freedom: The Ordeal of Colonial Virginia*. New York: Norton.

Wood, P. (1974). *Black Majority: Negroes in Colonial South Carolina from 1670 through the Stono Rebellion*. New York: Knopf.

4

The Glorious Revolutions in England and America, 1688–1689

The Glorious Revolution of 1688 was a seminal event in the political and constitutional history of both England and its colonies, highlighting the longstanding (precolonial) English attachment to liberty and self-government. What produced this dedication to self-government in England, as well as in its New World settlements, was the history and culture of England, not uniquely colonial practices (such as slavery) on the peripheries of English civilization.

The Glorious Revolution enshrined the supreme political authority of constituents, as represented in their legislatures, and reaffirmed traditional jurisdictional boundaries between the central government and local communities. Its practical effect was to insulate local ruling bodies – in the empire, within England, and within colonies – from central governments. In America, it enshrined "salutary neglect" as the governing principle of imperial administration. It thus set the stage for later constitutional conflicts between colonial assemblies and Parliament over the imperial constitution and English law, following Britain's efforts to centralize imperial governance in the 1760s and 1770s.

The Military Origins of the Glorious Revolution in America

The Glorious Revolution in America followed immediately on the heels of, and mirrored, the Glorious Revolution in England. However, it was not merely a ripple effect of the coup that took place in the mother country. Rather, it sprang from causes – some imperial, some regional, some internal within several colonies – which can be traced to American military and diplomatic affairs in the preceding decade.

The traditional understanding of American military history (popularized in the nineteenth century by Romantic authors like James Fennimore Cooper and

The Colonists' American Revolution: Preserving English Liberty, 1607–1783, First Edition. Guy Chet.
© 2020 John Wiley & Sons, Inc. Published 2020 by John Wiley & Sons, Inc.
Companion website: www.wiley.com/go/Chet/ColonistsAmericanRevolution

Francis Parkman) is that over the course of the colonial era, English settlers were Americanized – they unlearned the conventions of European warfare and instead adopted "American tactics." Rather than rely on large static formations to offer massed defensive fire (European tactics), colonists adopted Indian methods of small open-ordered formations that utilized offensive tactics and individual movement, concealment, and marksmanship. This storyline fits into a much broader narrative of Americanization, according to which life in America's physical, economic, social – and military – environment transformed Englishmen into Americans. This storyline is used to explain not only the formation of Americans' national identity and their eventual desire to separate from their mother country, but also their ability to best professional British troops on American battlefields during the War of Independence.

The notion that European warfare was outdated, or at least ill-suited for American conditions, has gained greater prominence since the late-1960s, when French and American military debacles in Vietnam seemingly demonstrated the superiority of guerrillas over regular troops. Yet there is no evidence that the American colonies doubted the efficacy of, or sought to revise, English military or tactical doctrines. Their military manuals, training, and actions in the field indicate that they remained committed to the accepted principles of European warfare – massed deployment of troops, massed and coordinated fire, and defensive tactics.[1] Despite their European orientation, however, the degeneration of colonial military forces over time – a decline in professionalism, combat experience, training, and readiness – led to a decline in their ability to execute their Old World military doctrines in battle situations.

Most English settlers in America had little or no prior military experience. The fledgling colonies therefore recruited trained and experienced English soldiers to train and command their military establishments. A study of battlefield engagements between colonists and neighboring Indians in New England reveals that under the leadership of these European veterans, English forces

---

1 See Beattie, D. (1986). The adaptation of the British Army to wilderness warfare, 1755–1763. In: *Adapting to Conditions: War and Society in the Eighteenth Century* (ed. M. Ultee), 56–83. Alabama: University of Alabama Press; Chet, G. (2003). *Conquering the American Wilderness*. Amherst: University of Massachusetts Press; Pargellis, S. (1936). Braddock's defeat. *American Historical Review* 41: 253–269; Pargellis, S. (1933). *Lord Loudoun in North America*. New Haven: Yale University Press; Steele, I.K. (1969). *Guerrillas and Grenadiers*. Toronto: The Ryerson Press. For the more traditional view, espousing the emergence of "American tactics" during the colonial era, see Eames, S.C. (2011). *Rustic Warriors*. New York: New York University Press; Dederer, J.M. (1990). *War in America to 1775*. New York: New York University Press; Ferling, J. (1981). The New England soldier: a study in changing perceptions. *American Quarterly* 33: 26–45; Grenier, J. (2005). *The First Way of War*. Cambridge: Cambridge University Press; Leach, D.E. (1958). *Flintlock and Tomahawk*. New York: The Macmillan Company; Malone, P. (1991). *The Skulking Way of War*. New York: Madison Books; and Starkey, A., (1998). *European and Native American Warfare, 1675–1815*. Norman: University of Oklahoma Press.

employed conventional European tactics and were rewarded with battlefield victories and strategic advantages that paved the way to territorial expansion. The Battle of Mystic (1637), for example, helped the English and their Indian allies break the power of the Pequot Indians, and opened Connecticut for inland settlement. However, colonists failed to replicate such tactical victories when the military commanders of the first generation were replaced by a new generation of local officers who were not European veterans. In King Philip's War (1675–1676), therefore, Indian war bands enjoyed great success against towns and villages throughout New England. In the towns and in the field, English forces were repeatedly surprised or drawn away from their defensive positions. They were thus unable to use massed fire to repel Indian attackers (although on the rare occasions when they did, they were usually successful).

The degeneration of colonial military establishments was a product of provincial governments' limited financial resources. Limited and inconsistent funding resulted in small field forces and inadequate provisioning. Moreover, provincial officers lacked practical experience in combat and command, and did not have strict authority over their men. And the troops were civilians – strangers to serious military training, to military life, and to combat. Because of these structural deficiencies, provincial troops could not be relied upon to perform their assignments, act in concert, and commit themselves to the tactical defense, all of which required discipline, patience, and faith – born of experience – in one's commander, comrades, and training.

The English won King Philip's War despite repeated battlefield failures thanks to attrition. The long war exhausted the resources of their poorer rivals, making Indian villages and war bands more susceptible to English attacks over time. This victory cost the New England colonies dearly – roughly one thousand fatalities (over 2% of the total English population), the destruction of 13 settlements, and crippling property damages. Proportionally, it is considered the bloodiest war in American history.

Addressing New England's Military Vulnerabilities: the Covenant Chain and the Dominion of New England

Both King Philip's War and Bacon's Rebellion were seen at first as mild local disturbances in 1675, but in 1676, both metastasized into lengthy, large-scale, devastating wars. The haplessness of colonial armed forces in New England and Virginia signaled to imperial administrators in America and in London that English colonial possessions in America were militarily vulnerable. To address this, Charles II quickly forged an alliance (the Covenant Chain, 1677) with the Five Iroquois Nations, an Indian confederacy that represented the chief military power to the west of the colonies, from the St. Lawrence River to modern-day western Pennsylvania. In these negotiations, Charles II was represented by Sir Edmund Andros, the governor of New York and senior royal governor in America.

This alliance was critically important in shaping Anglo-Indian relations in North America, but it also determined the course of Anglo-French relations in America. Anglo-Iroquois diplomatic and trade relations drew the English colonies into the preexisting rivalry between the Iroquois and their traditional enemies to the northwest – tribes of the Great Lakes region, such as the Ottawas, Pottawattamies, Sacs, Foxes, and Sioux. The French in Canada, as allies and trading partners of these "upper Indians," were similarly drawn into this historic regional Indian rivalry, and through it, into friction with the English.

While the colonies of New France and New England were commercial rivals in the great fisheries in the North Atlantic, and although England and France were historic enemies, the French settlements on the St. Lawrence were still quite far from the northernmost English settlements in the late-seventeenth century. Nevertheless, relations forged with Indian partners and allies north and south of the St. Lawrence drew European settlers into preexisting Indian rivalries and sparked violence across the broad frontier between New England and New France. By the early 1680s, shortly after the signing of the Covenant Chain, settlements in northern New England were absorbing violent attacks from Indian and French raiding parties from the north.

Given the grave concerns in London over the colonies' military vulnerability following King Philip's War only a decade earlier, the Board of Trade (a board of commissioners charged with reporting and advising the king's cabinet, or Privy Council, on colonial trade) devised a plan to defend the northern and western frontiers. It called for the unification of all the northern colonies, from New Jersey to Massachusetts, into one super-colony, the "Dominion of New England." James II implemented this plan soon after he took the throne in 1685. Founded in 1686, the Dominion of New England grew gradually, as one colony after another was absorbed by royal decree into the new colony. In the process, James II dissolved colonial borders, dismantled colonial legislatures, and eliminated colonial bureaucracies. James named Edmund Andros, the former governor of New York, as the governor of the new colony. The Dominion of New England was established without a legislature, allowing the governor to rule through his council, which acted as executive, legislature, and high court.

The Dominion of New England reflected a judgment in the Board of Trade and the king's Privy Council that the administrative and political fragmentation of the northern region of English North America into seven separate colonies undermined effective governance there. Disputes among neighboring colonies over military policy, recruitment, and funding during King Philip's War were seen by many as the key factor in the colonies' failure to suppress the rebellion in its early stages. Moreover, economic competition between neighboring colonies encouraged the rampant smuggling and illegal trade in the region's burgeoning

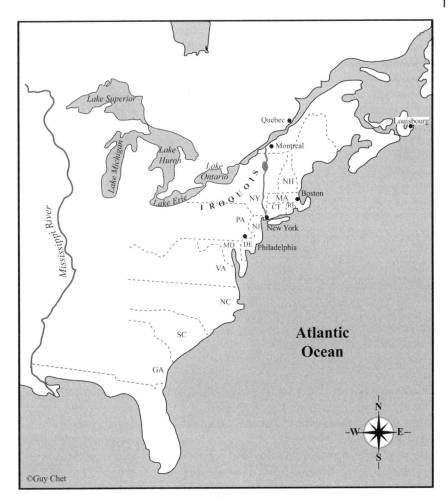

Figure 4.1 The Anglo-French-Indian frontier. © Guy Chet.

port towns. Imperial officials saw the failure of the colonies to elevate above local interests and act in concert – in the face of Indian attacks on land, and smuggling and piracy at sea – as a symptom of the dominance of the assemblies in colonial politics. The fact that colonial governors were financially dependent on their assemblies made them more attentive to the local and commercial interests of their constituents than to the imperial priorities of their king. Thus, smugglers and pirates traded openly without fear of prosecution, frontiers were left unprotected, and intercolonial competition prevented regional cooperation.

Royal officeholders viewed legislatures – Parliament and colonial assemblies alike – as bodies in which legislators tried to bend public policy (and public spending) to serve the parochial and private interests of elite families in the townships and localities. Just as James II and his circle resented initiatives in Parliament to shape or direct the policies of his government, so did they resent the ability of colonial legislatures and courts to undermine imperial policies such as the Navigation Acts and other trade restrictions. The Board of Trade and the Crown saw colonial governors as political weaklings, who for that reason were unable to pursue the common good, as it was understood by imperial officials in London. Instead, governors acquiesced to the narrow interests of their local elites, who wielded power through the assemblies.

By unifying the northern colonies and dissolving their legislatures, James eliminated what imperial administrators identified as the twin causes of the region's military, maritime, administrative, and commercial dysfunctions. To address these dysfunctions – military insecurity on land and lawlessness at sea and port – James II concentrated broad powers in Governor Andros's hands. Without interference from representative assemblies with competing regional interests, Andros was to secure the increasingly hot northern frontier, enforce England's unpopular trade laws, collect unpopular taxes, and prosecute popular smugglers and pirates who bolstered local economies in New Jersey, New York, and the New England colonies. Not surprisingly, this centralization of administrative power earned Andros the enmity of the colonies' leading families, as well as many others below them.

Colonial Opposition to the Dominion of New England

James II's policies in North America mirrored his governing philosophy and agenda in England. His penchant for governing through royal prerogative (the king's authority to enact law on his own, without authorization from Parliament, or even in violation of Parliamentary legislation) triggered aristocratic resentment and fear of arbitrary government. Like Charles I and Cromwell before him, James saw centralized control and prerogative power as more effective and pragmatic tools for governance, ones more reflective of the general needs of the country. Members of Parliament in England and members of colonial assemblies saw things differently; they were agents of local government and saw the general needs of the country as an aggregation of the needs of local communities. They therefore saw centralized power as arbitrary and injurious to local communities.

Like James II himself, Edmund Andros encountered suspicion and ill-will among his constituents even before assuming the reins of government in the Dominion of New England. The radical and controversial restructuring of the governments of the northern colonies created great anxiety among English settlers, attached as they were to the principle of government by consent. Leading families were outraged over their loss of influence over public policy and public finances in their respective colonies, and citizens of the townships were anxious over the removal of their elite representatives from the levers of power in the halls of government. Thus, English subjects on both sides of the Atlantic saw James II and Edmund Andros as hostile to representative government and the notion of government by consent.

James II created the Dominion of New England and structured it as he did explicitly to liberate the governor from the oversight and influence of local elites. Working without a representative legislature made the governor of the Dominion more accountable to the English government in London than to local constituents and their representatives. Indeed, New Englanders immediately noticed Andros's independence and his preference for prerogative, or arbitrary, power. He worked with the Royal Navy, customs officers, and regular troops to clamp down on smuggling and the profitable trade with pirates. Whereas settlers had succeeded – through their legislatures – in bending past governors to their will and keeping them from strict enforcement of imperial trade laws, Andros was insulated from such influence from below. Thus, when news of the Glorious Revolution in England arrived in America, early in 1689, Andros's constituents capitalized on the opportunity to remove him from office and reverse his reforms.

When the news arrived from England, Andros was on campaign along the northern frontier. In response to ongoing Indian attacks in New Hampshire and Maine, Governor Andros had outfitted a force of 700 men and led it north. He left redcoats and provincial soldiers along the way to reinforce defenders in frontier settlements and forts. When he returned to Boston (April 1689), he learned not only that King James had been deposed, but that his own absence had allowed his political enemies to orchestrate a coup against him as well. Andros was arrested and dispatched to England in a show of allegiance to the new regime in England. The old colonial charters were quickly reinstated, old boundaries reestablished, and the colonial assemblies reconstituted.

The Rise of the Assemblies and Return of Salutary Neglect After the Glorious Revolution

The Glorious Revolution in America brought to a halt Stuart attempts – dating back to the Covenant Chain – to increase and deepen England's direct involvement in American affairs; efforts that culminated in James II's commitment to consolidate, centralize, and streamline colonial bureaucracies in the northern colonies. But even though the colonies of the Dominion of New England reverted to their pre-1685 state, there were changes. As in England, where the Glorious Revolution restored and then enhanced Parliamentary authority, so the American assemblies not only regained their traditional dominant position vis-à-vis governors in colonial politics, but also entrenched and sanctified it. In New York, for example, there was no assembly before the founding of the

Dominion of New England, but after the Glorious Revolution in America, an assembly was constituted and secured its rights with a new charter from the Crown. In Massachusetts, a new royal charter (1691) extended voting rights to all property holders, rather than to members of the Congregationalist Church alone. In Maryland, the Glorious Revolution had religious and economic overtones, since most of the rich, established planter families were Catholic, while most laborers and indentured servants were Protestants. When news of the Glorious Revolution reached America, Protestant crowds removed Catholic officials appointed by Lord Baltimore, the colony's proprietor. As was the case in the New England colonies, the removal of Catholics and other James II loyalists was a signal of allegiance to the new regime of William III, who was engaged at the time in a fierce war against the Catholic powers of Europe and against Catholic conspirators within the British Isles.

The Glorious Revolution in America was characterized by the same dynamics as the Glorious Revolution in England. It was a drastic response by agents of local government – local elites representing their communities in legislative assemblies in both England and America – to the strengthening of the executive under James II. Specifically, Parliament and colonial assemblies responded to the increased commitment of James II and of his governors in America to liberate themselves from the oversight and limits that their legislatures imposed on their powers. The administrations of James II in England and of Edmund Andros in America expanded the power and independence of the Crown. In the Glorious Revolutions, local elites on both sides of the ocean, long accustomed to a great degree of self-government and non-intervention by central authorities, rose to restore, safeguard, and enhance their local jurisdictions.

The English aristocracy launched the 1688 Revolution to defend their liberties in Parliament and in their localities. Accordingly, William III halted and reversed James II's centralizing policies, thus restoring and enshrining the administrative dominance of aristocratic families in local government. These same dynamics played out in the colonies as well – William III withdrew from the activism of Charles II and James II in colonial administration. If James attempted to curtail salutary neglect by enhancing England's role in colonial governance, William III's accession signaled a return to salutary neglect as the empire's structural framework and governing philosophy.[2]

---

2 One could argue that in some respects, William shared James II's ideas of centralized governance in the English Empire. He converted Maryland into a royal colony, dictated to Massachusetts the terms of a new royal charter, and enhanced the role and powers of the Board of Trade. Nevertheless, he also restored to colonial assemblies and courts their powers and jurisdictions, and even enhanced them. This restoration of powers allowed colonists to exercise their traditional liberties and shape their own domestic and commercial policies under the later Stuarts (William and Anne), and even more so under their Hanoverian successors (George I, George II, and George III).

The Glorious Revolution in America, therefore, should not be understood as an early manifestation of American discomfort with English or monarchical rule. Like the English aristocrats who orchestrated the Glorious Revolution in England, American assemblies in 1688–1689 were neither opposed to monarchy nor alienated from England. Rather, they were simply opposed to King James II's encroachment on their liberties and local jurisdictions. In fact, removing James II's loyalists was not a rebellious or confrontational act on the part of American assemblies in 1689, after William III was already crowned as the new king of England. It was a sure way to simultaneously reverse James II's centralizing reforms and curry favor with the new king and with Parliament. Just as Parliament supported William with the expectation of reciprocity (that is, with the expectation that William would sign and abide by the Bill of Rights), so the American assemblies made a show of loyalty and support for the new regime in England with the understanding that this measure would be noticed and reciprocated.

Indeed, the new regime in England – both king and parliament – accepted and blessed the dissolution of the Dominion of New England, acknowledged local elites in the colonies as partners in its global struggle against James II's foreign and domestic supporters, retreated from James II's approach to imperial governance, and acquiesced to the political dominance of colonial assemblies over provincial governors.

A Contest Between Medieval and Modern Visions of State

The contest between central governments and local elites was not unique to England, to America, or to the early-modern era. The Middle Ages and Renaissance saw regular and consistent friction between European monarchs and noble families over the proper limits of royal power and aristocratic liberties (*libertas*). These conflicts were triggered by royal efforts to centralize their bureaucracies; that is, to establish direct governing authority (including the right to collect taxes and fees) over all the territories and all the inhabitants in their kingdoms. Driven by sharp increases in the cost of waging war, kings committed themselves to increasing their tax revenues, which included not only increasing the tax burden on their noble families, but also collecting revenues from their nobles' clients and tenants. This was a cyclical dynamic, since enhanced tax revenues allowed kings to enlarge and modernize their armies, which they then used to further pressure and intimidate local noble families into greater administrative, economic, and financial concessions. This process of royal centralization was the primary characteristic of the "age of absolutism," which saw gradual increases in the administrative, economic, and military power of the monarch, at the expense of the security, autonomy, and power of aristocratic families in local government.

This development was a departure from the decentralized medieval kingdom, structured as it was along a set of feudal obligations toward one's superior (patron). The medieval state was made up of local noble families who ruled their private estates independently. These aristocratic rulers governed their local estates directly and completely – regulating commerce as they saw fit, appointing officials of their choice, imposing and collecting taxes and fees, administering justice, and conducting wars against their neighbors independently or in concert with other noble rulers. However, these noble families owed their king (typically the largest landholder in the country) certain services – military support and hospitality (or cash in lieu of these). In exchange, they received royal recognition and protection of their titles, lands, and possessions. The feudal kingdom was essentially a salutary-neglect kingdom – it featured powerful local rulers (the landed aristocracy, who were the rulers of their private estates) under a weak central government. The king ruled his private estates fully, like any other nobleman, but he had little to no jurisdiction beyond these estates. He did not wield direct governmental power over his aristocrats' lands and tenants.

Throughout the Middle Ages, frustrated kings tried to change this state of affairs to gain some direct power on the local level by bureaucratically penetrating the noble families' jurisdictions. Powerful kings were able to expand their bureaucracies and install administrators to collect fees and taxes beyond their private estates. By contrast, weak kings were prevented from doing so by vigilant local ruling families, who aggressively safeguarded their *libertas* – their jurisdictions, possessions, and privileges of possession. They paid their debts to their sovereign (in taxes, service, and hospitality), but they ably thwarted kings who tried to establish a measure of direct governance within their estates.

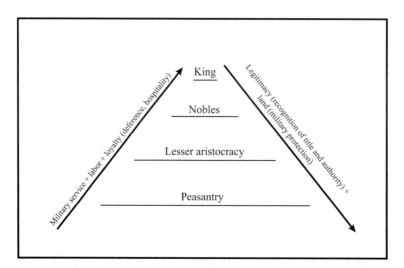

Figure 4.2 The feudal system. © Guy Chet.

Aristocratic families had a clear view of their liberty to govern in the localities, and could point to custom and common law to validate their view of a decentralized medieval state. Nevertheless, in the long run, they were fighting a losing battle. The 500-year period from the end of the Middle Ages to the dawn of the twenty-first century has seen the continuous growth of central governments and a consistent expansion of their jurisdiction within local communities. Indeed, the diminution of local governing bodies and their subjection to national governments has been the central and defining characteristic of the transition from the medieval state to the centralized modern nation-state.[3]

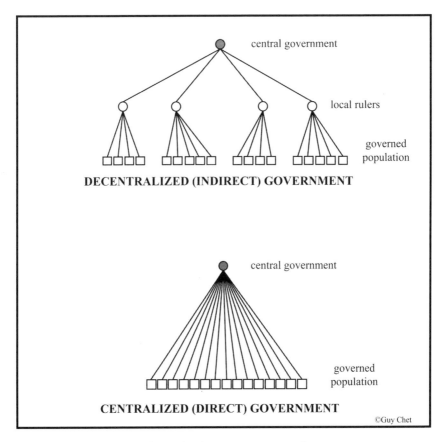

Figure 4.3 Decentralized and centralized governance. © Guy Chet.

_____

3 Historians have offered various explanations – military, bureaucratic, cultural, financial, economic, sociological, and environmental – for this shift toward the modern nation-state. Like the process of state centralization itself, this debate is ongoing.

Contemporaries in the intervening period, from the sixteenth to the nineteenth centuries (the early-modern era, or age of royal absolutism), recognized that this process of state centralization, or state building, was novel and portentous. Centralized governance therefore faced persistent resistance from local ruling elites – aristocratic families and free cities in Europe, regional French *parlements*, the English Parliament, and colonial assemblies in America. In most cases, this aristocratic resistance took the form of peaceful and political obstruction of royal designs, but sometimes it broke into violent clashes on the battlefield. This aristocratic resistance to centralization explains the English Civil War, the Glorious Revolution, the Glorious Revolution in America, and the American Revolution.

Indeed, the English habit of representative government had its origins in such opposition to centralization. Parliament's founding document is Magna Carta, signed in 1215 by King John, the infamous English monarch chronicled in the legend of Robin Hood. In the Magna Carta John promised his nobles that he would recognize, respect, and uphold their ancient liberties (their legal privileges as peers of the realm). Specifically, he promised not to arrest them arbitrarily, deny them *habeas corpus*, disallow them a jury trial, or levy new taxes on them without their consent. Moreover, he agreed to submit his conduct on these matters to monitoring by a representative council of nobles. King John made these concessions not out of magnanimity, but out of weakness and desperation. His failed wars in France had impoverished his treasury, leading him to unilaterally demand higher feudal contributions from English noble families. Indeed, the legend of Robin Hood portrays its hero as an aristocrat whom King John had arbitrarily dispossessed. When opportunity presented itself, the frustrated and resentful nobles mounted a joint rebellion to defend their traditional liberties – the ones articulated in Magna Carta – against the king's violations. When he could no longer resist them, he assented to their demands. Ever since then, as more Englishmen came to be represented in Parliament, English Parliaments have tried to hold their kings to the assurances recorded in the "Great Charter."

Aristocratic Resistance to Centralized Governance

The origin story of Magna Carta, as well as Magna Carta's history after 1215, indicate that aristocratic resistance – the contest between local elites and the central government – was a persistent feature of English life from the Middle Ages through the early-modern era. The liberties for which English and Anglo-American rebels fought in 1642, 1688, and 1776 were not new rights, but medieval liberties, anchored in ancient custom and recorded in common law. To safeguard these liberties of local governments, local elites in England and in its New World colonies formed representative assemblies whose function was to monitor, supervise, and curtail the power of the chief executive (i.e. the king or colonial governor).

On occasion – during the English Civil War, Glorious Revolution, and American Revolution – these assemblies' habitual and longstanding political resistance to bureaucratic centralization escalated and flared into violence and open rebellion. But it is essential to keep in mind that these rebellions were reactionary, aiming to preserve the inherited medieval status quo, rather than to introduce changes to the governmental system. For example, while the English Civil War and American Revolution became republican movements over time, they did not begin with a republican agenda. Only in time did the rebels address their concerns by abolishing monarchy.[4] Like the aristocratic uprisings of 1215 and 1688 (which were monarchical from start to finish), the rebellions of 1642 and 1776 were sparked not by an ideological or principled objection to monarchy, but by distress regarding a central government that was expanding its jurisdictions at the expense of local ruling bodies and wielding unchecked, arbitrary power in the localities. All these rebellions aimed to accomplish a common end – to reverse the concentration of power in the central government by restoring power to local governments. In America (in both 1689 and 1776), this meant a return to the old status quo of salutary neglect, an imperial system that mirrored England's domestic administrative structure – strong local governments under a weak central government.

Written Constitutions

Since administrative centralization violated ancient liberties and customs that were long-observed but unwritten, English and Anglo-American rebels insisted on writing them down, producing the Magna Carta (1215), the English Bill of Rights (1689), the 13 state constitutions drafted during the War of American Independence, the Articles of Confederation (1781), Federal Constitution (1788), and American Bill of Rights (1791). These documents all functioned as constitutions. That is, they explained how the government was constructed, or *constituted*. They clarified how governmental power was organized and wielded – they drew jurisdictional boundaries between local and central governments, and explained which institutions of the central government wielded which powers.

Written constitutions were a striking feature of English (and Anglo-American) political culture, inviting scholars and students to consider why those rebels felt obliged to write down, publish, and disseminate what beforehand were

---

4 Even after the battles of Lexington and Concord, Ticonderoga, and Bunker Hill, the American delegates at the Continental Congress still addressed King George III as their king and referred to themselves as his faithful subjects (for example, in the Olive Branch Petition).

unwritten liberties enjoyed by local communities and unwritten rules restricting central governments. What are written constitutions designed to do? Why write down on paper the way a government is structured, or constituted? After all, many societies in history had – and have – a clear understanding of the structure (that is, the constitution) of their government without articulating it in a unitary written legal document. Citizens can understand how their government functions without reading it in a written constitution because living in a given political community familiarizes them with its unwritten codes – the duties and boundaries of each branch of government, the duties and boundaries of the central and local governments, various limits imposed on governmental authorities, the government's relationship with the Church, administrative procedures for the government, criminal procedures, and so forth.

The written constitutions of 1215, 1689, 1776–1780, 1781, 1787, and 1791 reflect an English and Anglo-American distrust that *unwritten* rules and norms against centralization were sufficient to prevent the future concentration of power in central governments. Indeed, every single provision found in these written constitutions – from the Magna Carta to the American Bill of Rights – reflects the experience of past violations of that very provision. These written constitutions therefore mark the revolts that produced them as conservative and backward-looking. The administrative order articulated in each of these constitutions was not a new order, but an older, more archaic, more decentralized order that had been challenged and violated by the central government. For example, the first constitution of the United States of America simply articulated the imperial constitution, or structure, of the British Empire – before the Revolutionary Era, the British Empire had been governed by the principle of salutary neglect, and the United States under the Articles of Confederation was constituted as a salutary-neglect republic.

Transforming unwritten rules and customs into a written document with the force of law was designed not merely to end and reverse existing abuses, but also to explicitly prevent future attempts to change the way the government operated. A society's unwritten rules function as a "living constitution" – a set of rules that evolve and adapt to the changing values, beliefs, and preferences of future generations. By contrast, written rules subject future generations to the values, beliefs, and preference of previous generations in perpetuity; or until they are repealed or replaced by new written rules.

A medieval dictum of English law (attributed to Henry of Bracton) explains that law is not power, but a restraint on power ("the bridle of power"). This understanding of law informed Englishmen's understanding of liberty. "English liberty" referred to the legal principle of *libertas*, conveying the notion that free people are governed by knowable and predictable laws, rather than by their rulers' arbitrary will. The growing power of legislatures in England and in the English diaspora reflected a commitment by English elites to use the law to restrain the power of the executive (i.e. of the king and his various bureaucracies). Written constitutions helped Englishmen and Anglo-Americans subject their government officials to the laws that they themselves enacted, thus instituting – in the words of the Massachusetts state constitution – "a government of laws and not of men."

Questions for Discussion

1   Why was the Dominion of New England so offensive to colonial elites? Why was it offensive to non-elites?
2   If representative government and government by consent are indeed the values of medieval aristocracy, how did they become the hallmarks of modern democracy?

Further Readings

Chet, G. (Summer 2007). The literary and military career of Benjamin church: change or continuity in early American warfare. *Historical Journal of Massachusetts* 35 (2): 105–112.

Ferling, J. (1981). The New England soldier: a study in changing perceptions. *American Quarterly* 33: 26–45.

Greene, J. (1992). The glorious revolution and the British empire, 1688–1783. In: *The Revolution of 1688–1689* (ed. L. Schwoerer), 260–271. Cambridge: Cambridge University Press.

Henretta, J. (1972). *"Salutary Neglect": Colonial Administration under the Duke of Newcastle*. Princeton: Princeton University Press.

Sosin, J. (1982). *English America and the Revolution of 1688: Royal Administration and the Structure of Provincial Government*. Lincoln: University of Nebraska Press.

5

The Imperial Wars

The Glorious Revolution drew England into William III's preexisting European war against Louis XIV's France (the War of the Grand Alliance, or Nine Years War). By the same token, it drew England and France into the ongoing cycle of violence in North America. Although violence had already flared between England's North American colonies and New France during the decade between the Covenant Chain and Glorious Revolution, the formal declaration of war in Europe intensified this regional conflict. From 1689 on, French authorities augmented their support for Indian attacks on English frontier towns. They not only provided their Indian allies with weapons, munitions, and supplies for independent raids, but at times also led joint forces of French and Indian troops into New England. The collapse of Governor Andros's regime in the Dominion of New England created favorable conditions for these French and Indian raids, as the defensive forces that Andros had deployed along the northern frontier dissolved just as the French war effort intensified.

The War of the Grand Alliance was the first in a series of global wars between France and England (alongside allies on both sides). Historians of colonial America refer to these wars collectively as "the imperial wars" to distinguish them from local or regional wars in America, such as the Powhatan Wars, Pequot War, Bacon's Rebellion, King Philip's War, Tuscarora War, Yamasee War, Cherokee War, and Lord Dunmore's War. The imperial wars comprise the War of the Grand Alliance, known in America as King William's War (1688–1697); the War of Spanish Succession, known in America as Queen Anne's War (1702–1713); the War of Austrian Succession, known in America as King George's War (1744–1748); and the Seven Years War, known in America as the French and Indian War (1755–1763).

Diplomatic, strategic, and administrative reforms under Charles II and James II – from the Covenant Chain to the Dominion of New England – were a response to frustrations with the performance of colonial military forces in previous local conflicts. The Glorious Revolution ended James II's imperial

The Colonists' American Revolution: Preserving English Liberty, 1607–1783, First Edition. Guy Chet.
© 2020 John Wiley & Sons, Inc. Published 2020 by John Wiley & Sons, Inc.
Companion website: www.wiley.com/go/Chet/ColonistsAmericanRevolution

reform program, with the new regime of William III signaling the return of salutary neglect as the empire's governing constitutional principle. Nevertheless, because colonial forces remained small, poorly trained, unprofessional, and not particularly accomplished in the field during the early imperial wars, the eighteenth century saw incremental increases, from one war to the next, in Britain's direct military involvement and leadership in American warfare. The last of these wars – the French and Indian War – was a thoroughly European war, funded mostly by the British treasury, led mostly by British administrators and commanders, and fought mostly by British troops.

In hindsight, the Crown's growing role in military defense and territorial expansion in America can be understood as ushering the imperial reforms of the 1760s and 1770s, which sparked the American Revolution. Just as the colonies increasingly gravitated toward England's sphere of military influence in the eighteenth century, so the British government was increasingly drawn into colonial administration by its unprecedented degree of military spending, administration, command, and combat in America. During the French and Indian War, Britain's national debt nearly doubled from £74 million to £132 million. By the end of that war, therefore, North America was no longer peripheral in the empire's strategic and economic policy; at that point (1763), it represented a major investment of British resources. Britain therefore initiated a series of policies to protect its investment. These postwar policies represented not simply a financial plan for the British treasury to recoup its losses and pay its war debts, but a coherent program of imperial reform designed to produce effective centralized management of British possessions, including effective tax collection in American ports. This reform program centered on extending imperial jurisdiction over and within colonies, expanding the customs service, improving law enforcement, and gaining control of provincial bureaucracies and courts.

The intercolonial cooperation and solidarity that these imperial reforms sparked in the 1760s and 1770s stand in sharp contrast to the consistent intercolonial and regional discord exhibited by colonists during the imperial wars. Indeed, this wartime disunity among and within colonies calls into question the notion that the colonial era saw the emergence of an American identity, and that this sense of American nationhood produced the American Revolution.

Intercolonial Friction During the Imperial Wars

Because the dissolution of the Dominion of New England returned military and civil administration to colonial governments and local authorities, King William's War (1688–1697) was characterized by the very same problems that had hampered English military operations a generation earlier, during King Philip's War (1675–1676). Regional cooperation between colonial governments was rare and clumsy; provincial forces suffered from poor financing, poor logistical support, manpower shortages, and high turnover rates. Moreover, forces in the field and local garrisons (that is, defenders stationed in forts and towns) received little training, exhibited poor discipline, and were inexperienced in combat. As was the case in King Philip's War, therefore, English forces were repeatedly surprised and ambushed, both in camp and in the field. English settlements thus remained highly vulnerable to Indian attacks, driving families to abandon their homesteads and leading to the near-depopulation of English settlements along the northern frontier.

King William's War and Queen Anne's War did not feature large-scale battles and campaigns, but were instead a continuous series of small-scale local raids. Efforts by Massachusetts governor William Phips to address his colony's military deficiencies through better logistical, strategic, and tactical cooperation with neighboring colonies were unsuccessful. Given that French and Indian raids did not penetrate south of Massachusetts, the legislatures of Rhode Island, Connecticut, and New York were reluctant to contribute money and men to military operations in distant territories along the Massachusetts frontier (modern-day Maine, New Hampshire, and western Massachusetts). Moreover, Phips's efforts to create a regional strategy and regional policymaking were reminiscent of Governor Andros's mission, and therefore triggered institutional suspicions and resistance in these neighboring colonies.

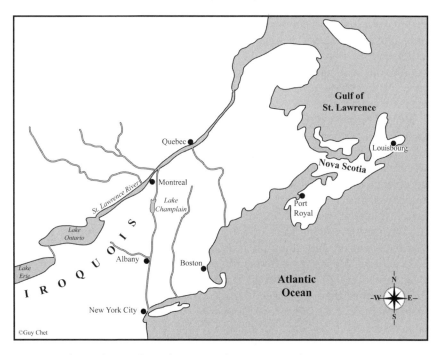

Figure 5.1 The Anglo-French North American frontier. © Guy Chet.

Governor Joseph Dudley, Phips's successor, followed up on this effort during Queen Anne's War (1702–1713). Like Phips, Dudley repeatedly clashed with neighboring governors to the south over their wartime responsibilities toward Massachusetts and New Hampshire. Unlike Phips, however, Dudley succeeded in cajoling and bullying his neighbors into supporting his military initiatives by using influential connections in London to involve British administrators in strategic and logistical planning.

Dudley was an unpopular figure within Massachusetts and beyond. This unpopularity had its roots in the Dominion of New England. Dudley had served on Governor Andros's council and was jailed and expelled with Andros during the Glorious Revolution in America. While in England, he rehabilitated his reputation with the new regime, and in 1702, with the backing of influential friends in London, he replaced Phips as the new royal governor of both Massachusetts and New Hampshire. Dudley's wartime responsibilities as joint governor of the entire northern frontier led him to revive Andros's attempts to create a comprehensive military and diplomatic policy for the entire region. This, along with his personal history with New England's social and political elite, made him an unpopular figure there once again.

Instead of begging neighboring governors and legislatures for help, as Phips had done, Dudley influenced Queen Anne to instruct these provinces to contribute funds, supplies, and troops to Dudley's operations in the north. Orders dealing with logistical support – from the mobilization and transport of men and supplies to the establishment of supply depots – were issued in London, rather than Boston. Agents of the imperial government also led diplomatic negotiations with allied Native powers like the Iroquois Confederacy, and the queen pledged both naval and military forces for Dudley's offensive operations against New France. Such joint Anglo-American operations increased the funds and number of men at Dudley's disposal, and also provided him with experienced, disciplined, and dependable troops – British soldiers and sailors.

To support the operations of provincial forces under his command, Dudley created a new provincial bureaucracy – a hierarchy of commissary officers appointed by Dudley – to purchase and manufacture equipment, firearms, munitions, and provisions. He established a central supply depot in Boston, as well as a frontline supply depot in Maine. The creation of a more efficient and professional logistical infrastructure for provincial forces allowed Dudley to recruit and maintain a larger army, but it also exacerbated tensions with the Massachusetts assembly. His new bureaucracy was filled with loyal appointees who owed their commissions to him personally, allowing Dudley (rather than the assembly) to distribute patronage in the form of government contracts for provisioning the army and providing other logistical services, such as construction and transportation. Dudley thus built a network of powerful allies in both London and Boston, which allowed him to prosecute the war effectively. In doing so, however, he sparked accusations in Boston and neighboring colonial capitals that he was attempting to revive Andros's tyrannical centralization.

Indeed, Dudley did create a coherent regional policy reminiscent of the Dominion of New England thanks to his joint command of Britain's two front-line colonies, administrative reforms, coordination with British military and naval forces, and staunch support from Queen Anne. Thus, the New England colonies were finally in a position to translate their demographic and logistical advantages over their French and Indian rivals into military advantages in the field. In this respect, Queen Anne's War marks a transition in colonial military history. King Philip's War and King William's War highlighted the military limitations of colonial governments and the poor soldiery of colonial forces. The eighteenth century saw colonial governments addressing these shortcomings – amateurism and inexperience among officers and men, poor training, small military establishments, limited resources, and a tradition of intercolonial discord – by increasing their reliance on British funding, British logistical support and coordination, and British forces.[1]

Regional Friction Within Colonies During the Imperial Wars

The primary challenge facing colonial governments was their inability to protect frontier settlements from attack. Given that the Anglo-Iroquois alliance insulated New York and Pennsylvania from enemy hostilities, the region that absorbed all attacks from the north stretched from western Massachusetts, through New Hampshire, to northern Massachusetts (modern-day Maine). The first line of defense there were the few small English forts along the New England frontier. Since the forts were insufficient to seal off the English

---

1 Assessing the martial competence of American colonists was a contentious topic in the colonial era, and it remains so among colonial and imperial military historians to this day. The narrative of Americanization presents North America as an exceptional military environment that challenged the accepted and time-tested rules of European military science. Thus, according to the Americanization thesis, American settlers learned to shed European military conventions, preferring a more offensive and pragmatic (less formalized) form of warfare that highlighted individual movement and concealed and accurate fire. Although this theory regarding an "American way of war" has gained the ascendancy among modern historians, it clashes with a broad consensus among provincial and imperial military authorities in the seventeenth and eighteenth centuries. Unlike modern historians, contemporaries saw evidence that the hallmarks of European warfare – positional warfare, mass deployment, defensive tactics, and coordinated fire – were quite effective in the North American environment and against mobile forces in the field. See D.J. Beattie, "The Adaptation of the British Army to Wilderness Warfare, 1755–1763"; G. Chet, *Conquering the American Wilderness*; Pargellis, "Braddock's Defeat"; S.M. Pargellis, *Lord Loudoun in North America*.

countryside, and since the territory between them was too vast to patrol effectively, enemy raiding parties could regularly and easily penetrate New England's porous first line of defense.

The primary factor limiting the effectiveness of the forts and the ranger units patrolling the frontiers was financing. To block enemy access to English settlements, the governments of Massachusetts and New Hampshire would have had to invest heavily in constructing more forts, deploying more men, and creating an effective supply and transport system to serve these far-flung garrisons and forces in the field – building roads, bridges, and supply depots, as well as contracting suppliers, wagon drivers, boatmen, and the like. Because such a financial commitment was beyond the capabilities of these colonies, French and Indian forces were able to advance undetected deep into English territory, repeatedly catching English towns unprepared for defense.

The second line of defense were provincial garrisons placed within the frontier towns themselves, to bolster civilian defenders. Although effective in protecting the inhabitants when attacked, maintaining defensive garrisons in all frontier towns was costly. Colonial governments preferred instead to invest their limited resources in offensive expeditions against French forts and Indian villages, fields, and fisheries. Offensive campaigns were more cost-effective than defensive deployment of troops as garrisons in the towns because provincial forces on campaign were usually employed (that is, paid) for relatively short periods of time. By contrast, defensive garrisons were stationed for longer terms, in some cases year-round. Moreover, the investment in defensive garrisons paid off only on the rare occasions in which they were actually attacked, whereas offensive operations in enemy territory held the prospect of preventing Indian raids and shortening wars by convincing Indians to abandon the war effort. Limited financial resources prevented colonial governments from pursuing both strategies simultaneously – deploying garrisons in the towns crippled offensive campaigns against the enemy and vice versa.

Although offensive campaigns compromised the security of frontline settlements by drawing defensive forces from them, the nature of representative government dictated that the policy preference of the more populous, prosperous, and secure townships on the interior won out over that of frontier communities on the peripheries. These dynamics of Indian policy in New England mirrored those that had produced Bacon's Rebellion in Virginia. The result was that Indian raiding parties repeatedly attacked the edges of English territory, inflicting a heavy toll (in casualties, captives, and property losses) on towns such as Northampton, Hadley, Hatfield, Deerfield, Springfield, Haverhill, Kittery, York, and Wells. These devastating attacks impelled families to leave their homes, seeking shelter and security farther to the south and east. But since the depopulation of the frontier threatened the more populous, productive, and secure counties on the interior, measures were taken to maintain an English presence on the frontier. During King William's War and Queen Anne's

War, the Massachusetts General Court offered frontier communities tax benefits. Along with this carrot, however, the legislature also wielded a stick in the form of strict prohibitions against the evacuation of frontline communities. By law, families that deserted their homes without authorization from the provincial government could forfeit their property.

When recurring attacks nevertheless threatened to drive locals from their homesteads, the provincial government deployed garrisons and patrolling ranger units to reinforce local militia. These measures, however, were short lived. For example, after the infamous 1704 attack on Deerfield, Massachusetts – in which 160 residents were either killed or taken into captivity – the assemblies of Massachusetts and Connecticut voted to fund provincial troops to serve as garrisons in Deerfield and nearby towns. By the next campaigning season, however, those garrisons were gone.

Such regional tensions *within* colonies mirrored the intercolonial tensions between frontline colonies (Massachusetts and New Hampshire) and colonies shielded from Indian violence by their interior position (Rhode Island, Connecticut, New York, New Jersey, and Pennsylvania). Just as frontier communities in Massachusetts tried to extract military resources and financial support from communities farther removed from Indian violence, so too did frontline colonies. This problem – the divergent circumstances and priorities of different northern colonies, and the divergent interests of local populations within them – had been on full display during King Philip's War, with disastrous results. The Dominion of New England represented an attempt to address this critical strategic weakness of the northern colonies by doing away with representative government in them. Andros's government was to assess the interests and needs of the Dominion of New England as a whole, rather than allowing local circumstances and interests to shape regional policymaking. The Dominion's dissolution reestablished the old status quo, including the old state of intercolonial wartime fragmentation, discord, and rancor.

Colonial Solidarity and Mutual Support After the Imperial Wars

In 1774–1775, when Britain penalized Massachusetts for the Boston Tea Party with the Coercive (or "Intolerable") Acts, frontier settlers in western Massachusetts stood shoulder to shoulder with the people of Boston in fierce opposition to British policy. Moreover, other colonies immediately declared their support for their fellow colonists to the north, and joined them in opposition to Parliament. Such colonial solidarity stands in sharp contrast to the long history of regional and intercolonial disunity, competition, and friction during the regional and imperial wars of the seventeenth and eighteenth centuries. When settlers in Massachusetts were being killed, raped, dispossessed, and taken into Indian captivity during King Philip's War, King William's War and Queen Anne's War, colonies to the south were consistently uncooperative, reluctant to lend material support, and fearful of being drawn into the circle of violence themselves. Yet when those same Massachusetts settlers were subjected to administrative and financial disciplining by Parliament in 1774–1775, other colonies rushed to lend support, despite the real prospect of suffering similar harsh treatment at the hands of Parliament.

Some scholars solve this puzzle by arguing that in the intervening years between Queen Anne's War and the Revolutionary Era, the settlers grew to see themselves as *Americans*; they developed a sense of nationhood thanks to various long-term developments, such as geographic mobility, demographic, and economic integration, shared experiences, and the Great Awakening. Thus, when Britain targeted colonists in Massachusetts in 1774, other Americans were moved by a sense of kinship and solidarity to see the cause of Massachusetts as the cause of all Americans. In the 1770s, that is – unlike during King William's War and Queen Anne's War – the welfare of Americans in Massachusetts was of personal concern to fellow Americans elsewhere. So much so, that it moved them to risk incurring Parliament's wrath, Parliamentary disciplining, and even war.

Other historians explain the novelty of intercolonial solidarity in 1774 not as a product of change in American sensibilities and sentiments, but a product of the same kind of local self-interest on display during the early imperial wars. According to this view, it was not solidarity and concern for the wellbeing of fellow Americans in Massachusetts that moved colonies such as New York, Virginia, and South Carolina to rise up in opposition to the Intolerable Acts in 1774–1775. Rather, it was these colonial assemblies' recognition that Parliament's imperial reforms – from the Sugar Act, through the Stamp Act, to the Coercive Acts imposed on Massachusetts – threatened their own liberties. Their support for Massachusetts was thus an act of self-interest and self-defense, rather than of sentimental solidarity and altruism.

In the context of this debate, it is worthwhile to consider the difference between the threats posed by Indian violence and those posed by Parliament's Sugar Act, Stamp Act, Townshend duties, Tea Act, Quebec Act, and Coercive Acts. Indian violence during the imperial wars victimized frontier communities on the periphery. By contrast, British legislation in 1763–1774 victimized eastern populations and economies generally, and colonial assemblies in particular. Whereas Indian attacks in one colony did not threaten the inhabitants of other colonies, a Parliamentary assault on the liberties of one colonial government was understood as an assault on the imperial constitution, and thus a threat to all colonies.

Questions for Discussion

1 Why did wars create or intensify internal divisions within and among English colonies?
2 Did these internal divisions – both within and among colonies – represent the failure or success of representative government in the colonies?

Further Readings

Leach, D.E. (1973). *Arms for Empire: A Military History of the British Colonies in North America, 1607–1763*. New York: The Macmillan Company.
Leach, D.E. (1974). *The Northern Colonial Frontier 1607–1763*. Albuquerque: University of New Mexico Press.
Peckham, H. (1964). *The Colonial Wars 1689–1762*. Chicago: University of Chicago Press.
Steele, I.K. (1969). *Guerrillas and Grenadiers: The Struggle for Canada, 1689–1760*. Toronto: The Ryerson Press.

6

From Deference to Suspicion

What strikes observers of the brewing conflict between colonial assemblies and Parliament in the years following the end of the French and Indian War (1763) is the suspicion with which colonists viewed the actions and intentions of the imperial government. While some scholars understand this suspicious view of government as conventionally English, others see it as uniquely American – a product of American conditions and of colonial (rather than English) history. Indeed, the origins of American political ideology is at the forefront of the debate on the origins of American identity and culture. Both camps acknowledge currents of both Americanization and Anglicization in colonial America, but differ on the question of which cultural force was stronger: was American colonial culture essentially English, or was it distinctly American by the time of the Revolution? Were those traits that were uniquely American central to American culture or merely peripheral? An examination of colonial political culture reveals that colonial America was like England, only more so. Rather than creating a different or new political ideology, life in America confirmed and strengthened English political beliefs into entrenched convictions.

Cato's Letters

Many studies trace Americans' political ideology – their attachment to representative government, government by consent, separation of powers, checks and balances, civil liberties, rights of property, rights of conscience, and the like – to John Locke (1632–1704). A contemporary of the Glorious Revolution, Locke was a staunch promoter of its legality and justice, and became one of the greatest and most eloquent prophets of representative government and of capitalism, the two hallmarks of Anglo-American political culture.

The Colonists' American Revolution: Preserving English Liberty, 1607–1783, First Edition. Guy Chet.
© 2020 John Wiley & Sons, Inc. Published 2020 by John Wiley & Sons, Inc.
Companion website: www.wiley.com/go/Chet/ColonistsAmericanRevolution

Yet Locke's philosophical treatises on human nature and human government were not accessible to the average English reader. Like modern Americans, Anglo-American colonists received their political and moral philosophy not directly from philosophers, but second-, third-, or fourth-hand, from journalists and other opinion-makers (including policymakers), through various media. One of the means by which Locke's doctrines on moral and political philosophy became popular in England and its colonies was a series of 144 public letters – "Cato's Letters" – published by John Trenchard and Thomas Gordon in the *London Journal* between 1720 and 1723. These were letters of criticism against the government of George I, and primarily against the king's chief minister Robert Walpole, who dominated British politics from the 1720s to the 1740s. Indeed, Gordon and Trenchard published the letters anonymously due to fear of retaliation by Walpole's government. Their choice of pen name – Cato, the tragic defender of Rome's republican virtues – cast Walpole as a would-be tyrant; a modern-day Julius Caesar.

Robert Walpole rose to power under King George I, the first monarch of the Hanoverian dynasty, which followed the Stuart line after the death of Queen Anne. George was at heart a Continental monarch. He did not speak English, he spent much of his time in his German principality (which he governed as an absolutist monarch), and he did not understand Britain's quirky political system. Early in George's reign, Walpole – a minister in the king's council – guided the Court and Parliament safely through the turbulent waters of the South Sea Bubble (a financial crisis and political scandal that rocked Britain in 1720–1721). Consequently, he won the king's full trust and support. Thereafter, Walpole came to dominate British politics through the liberal distribution of bribes, a vast network of domestic spies, and extensive royal patronage – the creation and distribution of paying jobs in the court, civil service, Church, army, and navy as gifts to influential families in British politics. Moreover, he cemented his influence in Parliament by corrupting the electoral process through both electoral fraud and gerrymandering. His efforts to create a large and reliable majority for the king in Parliament were further facilitated by the repeal of the Triennial Act (which mandated Parliamentary elections at least once every three years) and its replacement with a Septennial Act (forcing elections after seven years). Whereas frequent elections intensified partisan politics and helped expose corruption in high places, longer terms for members of Parliament had the opposite effect, allowing members of Parliament freedom to pursue advantageous relationships with Walpole.

Walpole thus reduced the heat and intensity of British politics. Because the real political arena of debate and negotiation shifted from Parliament to Walpole's offices, Parliament became more of a rubber stamp than a contentious deliberative body. Walpole smoothed over differences between camps by handing out political gifts to potential opponents, transforming them into friends and allies. After the violent political turmoil of the mid- and late-seventeenth century – from the Civil War through the Glorious Revolution and the two long wars it sparked – many Britons, especially propertied families, welcomed the lull that Walpole managed to establish in the political arena.

Walpole's challenge in maintaining this pacific political system was money. His vast network of patronage and graft was expensive. Although he always had a supportive Parliament, populated by his many friends and dependents, to vote for new or higher taxes, the money itself had to be collected from British constituents. Thus, as Parliament kept raising taxes to pay Walpole's bills, Britons increasingly felt that they were cut out of the political process. They could sense that their representatives in Parliament were not enacting *their* will, but Walpole's. That is, in the eyes of growing numbers of British constituents, political corruption was turning political representation and the principle of government by consent into a sham.

In "Cato's Letters," Gordon and Trenchard criticize Walpole's government, and the political class more broadly, for its betrayals. In doing so, they outline the correct principles that should guide the government of a free people. These essays were wildly popular in England, despite the government's attempts to suppress them. They were as popular and influential in the colonies – reprinted and quoted widely in colonial papers and pamphlets, and sold as bound copies. Virtually half the private libraries in the American colonies contained bound volumes of Cato's Letters.

Cato's Lockean Ideas on Human Nature and Human Governments

In contemplating the ideal government for Britain, "Cato" starts with two premises regarding human nature. The first is that all men are born free, are equal by nature, and possess some degree of reason. By stressing that all men have both the right (freedom) and the capacity (reason) to decide their own actions, Cato challenges the notion that God or nature had selected an aristocracy to rule the rest of society. Instead, Cato asserts, nobles and kings are, by nature, no different from their tenants – free, equal, and rational. The second premise that guides Cato's reasoning concerns human motivation. He insists that human beings are selfish by nature: because people are rational, they are governed by self-interest, not altruism (self-sacrifice). These two assumptions about human nature were not universally accepted at the time, and they remain contested today, but they form the basis for Cato's observations on society, and on the nature and purpose of government.

Cato explains that because humans are free and rational, they have the ability and the capacity to act on their innate selfishness. The result is theft, fraud, abuse, assault, rape, and murder: it is self-love that guides humans, who therefore "adopt or reject principles, just as these principles promote or contradict their interest and passions." In striving to fulfill their interests, "there is nothing so terrible or mischievous, but human nature is capable of it." And while priests and moral teachers try to teach self-restraint and altruism, only "fear and selfish considerations can keep men within any reasonable bounds." Only self-interest (that is, fear of punishment) can prevent anti-social behavior.

The challenge for any government, according to Cato, is to create conditions that would restrain constituents, thus transforming them from the selfish and predatory creatures they are into peaceful, cooperative, and productive citizens. In this framework, as Cato explains, the government acts as a mechanism that artificially synchronizes people's private and public interests – when one fears governmental punishment for crimes, one's self-interest (self-preservation) aligns with the community's interest (peace, security, productivity).

The ideal government, Cato instructs, promotes both the public interest and individuals' self-interest – it prevents egregious crimes like theft and assault, while allowing constituents to otherwise pursue their wants and desires freely. Given that people pursue their private interest by pursuing wealth ("Happiness is the effect of independency, and independency is the effect of property"), governments can maintain this delicate balancing act by dedicating themselves to the protection of property. Such a government serves the interests of individuals (that is, it allows people to pursue their self-interest by protecting them against theft, fraud, and assault), while also serving the interests of society.

Yet Cato warns readers that this solution – a powerful government that will punish and deter criminals – cannot solve the problem of human nature. In fact, it creates a worse problem than the one it fixes. After all, the people who populate the government – rulers, legislators, bureaucrats, tax collectors, police officers, prosecutors, judges – are as human as their constituents. They are as rational, self-interested, and anti-social as anyone else, but their authority provides them with greater opportunities, means, and temptations to abuse, dispossess, and otherwise take advantage of their fellow-citizens.

This is the main problem that Cato addresses regarding governance. With Walpole's regime in mind, Cato reminds his readers that when they use the government to protect themselves from predatory neighbors, they expose themselves to much greater threats from predatory people wielding governmental power. Thus, because only "fear and selfish considerations can keep men within any reasonable bounds," Cato recommends mechanisms by which constituents can surveil, control, intimidate, and punish government officials – from local judges and custom officers to kings and queens.

For Cato, Britain's mixed government of limited (or balanced) monarchy featured exactly such mechanisms – government by consent, political representation, the rule of law, and civil liberties (freedom of speech, freedom of conscience, *habeas corpus*, trial by jury, and the like). It was these very means of accountability that Walpole's varied corruptions were undermining, according to critics like Cato. Cato described limited monarchy as the ideal blend of republican liberty and monarchical authority, stability, and peace. He encouraged readers to see accountability in government as the guarantor of English liberty, and to see Walpole's regime as paving the way toward the kind of political subjection on display in France and other absolutist monarchies in Europe.

A Shift from Classical to Modern Republicanism; from Deference to Suspicion

Political theorists identify such discourse on accountability in the seventeenth and eighteenth centuries as a meaningful departure from classical republican ideology. In classical republicanism – that is, in classical Greece and Rome – rulers were expected to govern justly out of a sense of justice, decorum, and altruism (public service). This is the reason public offices in classical Greece and Rome were not salaried positions. These posts were considered public honors, rather than jobs; members of the leading families served without pay, volunteering their services and their resources to their fellow-citizens.[1] By contrast, the modern republican ideology that was forming in Europe in the early-modern era reflected a more cynical view of human nature. Since, as Cato explains, humans cannot be selfless, a political system that depends on officials' selflessness is bound to produce corruption and oppression.

Both classical and modern republican thought, therefore, stems from the recognition that unchecked, governmental powers are dangerous weapons against society. The classical mentality trusted the officeholder's virtue and civic mindedness to keep the awesome powers of government in check. It thus sought to entrust public offices only to the virtuous. For those – like Cato – who

---

1 This issue came up after the American Revolution, in a vehement debate over whether service in the new national government should carry a salary. Benjamin Franklin and Thomas Jefferson, among others, ardently opposed the motion, claiming (in keeping with classical republicanism) that turning places of honor into places of profit would invite the wrong sort of people into public life, thus subverting the republican political and social system. They warned that the formidable powers of government cannot be entrusted to people who seek private gains from public offices. These posts should instead be held by those intent on selflessly serving the interests of their fellow citizens. The classical system of unsalaried government posts (*honores*) was itself a kind of ethical filter. It allowed only men of wealth and social standing – men who did not have to work for a living – to hold positions of great power. Their social standing ensured that they had a record of virtue, altruism, and civic spirit among their neighbors and communities; and their wealth insulated them from temptations that might corrupt an official of more modest means. Opposing Jefferson and Franklin on the issue of salaries, John Adams warned against blocking men of moderate resources from government service. He charged that the classical idea of public officials disinterestedly serving the people had always been a myth. He argued that since self-interest is a natural and unconquerable human trait afflicting rich and poor alike, it must be incorporated into the political system. He insisted that for the sake of transparency and accountability, public officials should receive and must accept honest payment for their service.

held a more modern and bleaker view of human nature, such efforts are futile since no one can elevate above selfishness and private interest. And since no one can be trusted with the governmental power, all public officials must be subjected to vigilant public oversight, control, and punishment. After all, as Cato insists, moral and religious education cannot produce true virtue in human beings; only "fear and selfish considerations" can intimidate people with power from abusing their power. Only fear of exposure and punishment can move naturally anti-social creatures to wield power ethically and responsibly.

The solution offered by modern republican ideology to the problem of government – that is, abuse of governmental power – reflected a political mentality that had gained credibility in Britain, and even more so in British America. This mentality espoused a dark view of human nature, leading its adherents to assume that people with power will abuse it. This belief was the practical implication of Cato's philosophical premise that all people are by nature free, equal, rational, and selfish.

The Demographic, Economic, and Cultural Sources of the Politics of Suspicion

When historians explain American colonists' embrace of modern republicanism, they usually tie it directly to public criticism of Walpole's regime in Britain. After all, criticism of Walpole circulated in the colonies, just as it did in Britain, through newspapers and other publications, including Cato's Letters. Thus, British and American histories identify Walpole's regime as a spark that agitated and motivated social critics who espoused and promoted modern republicanism. Having witnessed, under Walpole, the failure of the moral and political framework of classical republicanism, these social observers and political thinkers concluded that classical republicanism failed to take human nature into account. Walpole's corruption of public officials moved them to call for mechanisms of popular surveillance and control over officeholders.

It is inaccurate, however, to describe this shift from classical to modern republicanism merely as a reaction to the overt corruption of public life under Walpole. First, this growing suspicion of the intentions and motivations of public officials predated Walpole; Walpole's regime simply gave credence to such suspicions. Additionally, the transition from politics of deference to politics of suspicion was not exclusively British, although it certainly was entrenched earlier and deeper in Britain than in Europe. Moreover, this shift in mentality was more rapid and thorough in America – farther away from Walpole's reach – than in Britain.

The true engines of this change in political beliefs and sensibilities (from classical to modern republicanism) were broad societal, economic, demographic, and religious developments in the early-modern era. In medieval and

Renaissance Europe (including England), communities were small, stable, and homogenous. This kind of social, religious, political, ethnic, and class setting bred a common understanding regarding the inner working of a given community – how to behave in public, how to behave in private, how to organize family life, how to live together, how to use common lands, how to use private lands, how to work the land, how to display deference to superiors, how to display concern for inferiors, how to treat one's neighbors, how to sell and buy goods and services, and so forth. Because members of a local community were born into a social and cultural environment that was demographically stable and homogenous, they absorbed its values, customs, and arrangements organically. They lived out their lives in that same environment, alongside neighbors who shared their sensibilities and habits.

Communities such as these produced a basic and implicit trust in their local public officials. Because Church elders, town office-holders, magistrates, judges, and sheriffs shared the circumstances and sensibilities of their neighbors, constituents had good reason to assume that their leaders shared their understanding of right and wrong, decent and indecent, fair and unfair, the common good, and the law. By contrast, in the seventeenth and eighteenth centuries, increasing demographic instability and heterogeneity in these communities had a contrary effect on trust and deference toward officeholders.

Communal unity, homogeneity, and consensus were disrupted by several developments associated with the early-modern era – economic and population growth increased internal migration, enclosures and urbanization led to the decline of some communities and the rapid growth of others, and religious strife broke up church communities. These developments brought into close physical proximity families from different backgrounds, different regional traditions and habits, different allegiances to the locality, different understandings of the common good, and different beliefs regarding morality, religion, justice, and law. In such increasingly pluralistic settings, without a broad consensus on community values and interests, inhabitants could not maintain faith that a local elder, mayor, judge, or sheriff shared their values or interests. In a community characterized by increasing regional, ethical, religious, ethnic, and cultural diversity, constituents had good reason to fear that a judge or sheriff belonged to a group other than their own. Thus, trust and deference (the hallmarks of classical republicanism) were increasingly replaced with a suspicion and apprehension toward people wielding political power (the hallmarks of modern republicanism).

In other words, the result of the growing diversity within communities was a growing fear that leaders were partisans; that they felt allegiance to a certain faction within the community – the Protestants or the Catholics, the rich or the poor, the east-siders or the west-siders, the older established families or the newcomers – rather than the community as a whole. Thus, the result of demographic growth, geographic expansion, economic growth, commercial expansion, class mobility, resettlement, urbanization, and religious diversity was a shift from politics of trust and deference to politics of suspicion.

These developments were slow and gradual, and one cannot pinpoint where or when they began and ended. What can be identified, however, is that in communities that were small, stable, and homogeneous, local inhabitants could find the old classical beliefs about human nature and human government credible. In communities that grew demographically, expanded geographically, and became more heterogeneous and less stable, classical beliefs became less credible and the tenets of modern republicanism became more credible. In such communities, constituents grew more receptive to the notion that their leaders did not serve the common good and did not share their interests, values, and understanding of the law. Thus, local experiences (like enclosures, internal migration, and urban living) combined with national experiences (such as Walpole's corruption, James II's arbitrary rule, and Cromwell's tyranny) to make people more skeptical of the classical mentality, and more receptive to the cynical modern understanding of human nature.

This explains the increased demand for political representation in the early-modern and modern eras. In the context of the classical mentality, premodern people saw factions (in the court, legislature, town hall, local church, or any other civic association) negatively, as destructive to communal unity and cooperation. But in the context of an increasingly heterogeneous community containing different groups with different circumstances, interests, and values, early-modern people began to suspect that internal factions were at the very least necessary, to ensure the integrity and honesty of officeholders. As Cato explained, when constituents cannot count on officeholders to share their particular view of the common good, the only antidote to corruption, abuse, and partisanship in high places is an opposition that monitors and questions public officials' every move.

The utopian literature of the age was itself a feature of this new mindset. It reflected the growing pluralism in English society (in the Church, first and foremost), and it encouraged readers to envision different ways of organizing public life and various ways of conducting oneself in society. This social commentary joined the more explicit critique offered by political philosophers, pamphleteers, and opposition writers such as Cato. These genres encouraged audiences to question the moral authority, and even the moral integrity, of those wielding political power in the state, the Church, the courts, and the localities. The result was a political culture struggling with the challenge articulated by Cato – how to maintain a government powerful enough to protect individuals from their selfish and predatory neighbors without exposing them to even greater abuse from selfish and predatory government officials.

A Political Philosophy Learnt Practically, Through Daily Experience in Local Communities

The English were forced to confront this conundrum repeatedly in the seventeenth and eighteenth centuries. It was at the forefront of national politics under Charles I, during the English Civil War, under Cromwell's dictatorship, in the Restoration of 1660, the Glorious Revolution of 1688, the Hanoverian succession, and the two Jacobite revolts at the dawn and eclipse of Walpole's era. But this conundrum stirred local communities even more viscerally and more consistently, irrespective of national politics. When one examines social organization, civic institutions, criminal procedures, and political habits in British communities throughout England, Scotland, and British America, it is apparent that they all reflect a driving fear that people with power will abuse it. The common theme, therefore, in local government (in municipalities, courts of law, local churches, and other civic associations) was an effort to disperse power; to prevent its concentration in one person, one group, or one institution.

The British did not adopt this apprehensive and cynical view of human nature and human government because of utopian literature, political publications like Cato's Letters, or philosophical treatises such as John Locke's. Rather, what produced their political mentality was the experience of their local lives in communities characterized by demographic growth, geographic expansion, and increasing diversity. Wrongs suffered at the hands of central governments (for example, Cromwell's dictatorship or colonial governors' military policy on the frontier in the face of Indian violence) further reinforced the worldview that British constituents had absorbed in their localities. Literary works and political tracts of the age merely reflected this change in English mentality; they did not produce it.

In America, economic, demographic, and sociological conditions made this shift in mentality (from classical to modern republicanism) more rapid and thoroughgoing than in England. American communities were even more unstable than English ones – the demographic growth rate in the colonies (both natural and through immigration) far outstripped that of England, as did economic growth; religious, ethnic, and racial diversity were greater; and geographic and class mobility were more extensive by a wide margin. As a result, distrust of public officials, factionalism, and a demand for popular control of government through representation were even stronger features of politics in America than in England. In his path-breaking study of Dedham, Massachusetts, Kenneth Lockridge traced this transition from classical to modern republicanism in a single American community.[2] Over the course of two generations,

---

2 Lockridge, K. (1970). *A New England Town: The First Hundred Years: Dedham, Massachusetts, 1636–1736*. New York: Norton.

Dedham grew demographically, expanded geographically, grew increasingly stratified socioeconomically and religiously, and thus developed various internal divisions. These fissures transformed Dedham from a homogeneous and unified community that envisioned itself as a family and trusted its leaders, to a splintered community that started suspecting – and then was convinced – that elders in the town and the church were partisans, promoting the interests of their own families, neighbors, and allies.

Dedham, Massachusetts

The founders of Dedham were aware of the threat that economic success and demographic growth posed to the communal character of the town. They therefore allotted land on the town's periphery slowly, and in small patches, but to no avail. Population growth and geographic expansion put an end to Dedham's physical unity, and therefore also to the communal bonds that had united the townspeople. The peripheral communities at the edges of the original village were populated predominantly by newcomers, who were generally younger, poorer, and less connected to the original families and the church. Moreover, whereas the original families all lived within walking distance of the town square, the meetinghouse, and the church, the new populations on the peripheries were too distant – in some cases up to 10 miles away – to experience the communalism of the original town and benefit from the services it provided. For example, militia patrols did not extend far beyond Dedham's original confines; peripheral settlers found it difficult to participate in church services and town meetings; and various other services provided by the town and the church were inaccessible to those living far away.

   This state of affairs produced growing resentment among peripheral residents whose taxes, tithes, and militia service were accruing to the benefit of the more established and wealthier families in the original town, and not to the growing populations on the outskirts. Recognizing that they were subsidizing the communalism enjoyed by people in the original township, the outlying populations attempted to create in their own locales a communal experience modeled on that of the original town. They established local civic and political institutions – churches, patrols, magistracies – that were autonomous from those of the original town. The heated disputes over these attempts of secession from the original town transformed political life in Dedham – from town meetings that were few and far between, led by the heads of leading families ("selectmen"), and characterized by general deference to the leadership, to more frequent and lengthy sessions that were acrimonious – even violent – and in which the leadership, authority, integrity, and legitimacy of the established elite was repeatedly challenged.

Because they opposed the autonomy or secession of outlying communities, the selectmen were viewed by growing numbers of their constituents as betraying their trust; they were increasingly seen as promoting the narrow interest of their own locality, families, neighbors, and economic partners. This acrimony and suspicion reflected the fact that the old community had disintegrated into a number of separate communities that were divided geographically and therefore also economically, socially, ecclesiastically, and culturally. In this context, these various constituencies insisted that only one of their own could legitimately represent them.

This drama repeated itself in numerous American settlements, including in the very settlements that seceded from Dedham to create their own townships. Driven by widespread availability of cheap land, explosive demographic growth, and high rates of geographic mobility, the local communal dynamics on display in Dedham shaped the political mentality of American settlers. It was these realities of daily life in American villages and towns – rather than tracts on political and moral philosophy – that explain the rapid shift from a classical to modern republican mindset among English settlers.

From Classical to Modern, from Trust to Suspicion, from Communalism to Capitalism

This shift in the settlers' thinking on human nature and human government went hand in hand with a shift in their economic beliefs, from a precapitalist ideology that promoted communalism to a thoroughly capitalist mentality that valued and encouraged competition.

What preceded capitalism in the West was the village economy. The economic model that explains the village economy is termed a "moral economy." This term conveys the contrast between the capitalist and precapitalist ethical code of conduct. The implication of this term is not that capitalism is, by comparison, *im*moral, but rather *a*moral. That is, in capitalist societies people believe that the way individuals interact with one another in the marketplace should not be dictated by interpersonal moral obligations to family or friends, but by impersonal market forces – supply, demand, and competition. Thus, a grocer is not obligated to set a lower price for relatives, friends, neighbors, and co-religionists and a higher price for strangers. By the same token, these friends and neighbors are not obliged to buy from the grocer, but are free to buy from his competitors, at a lower price. Both grocers and consumers accept that the price of goods fluctuates according to supply, demand, competition, and the self-interest of both seller and buyer, as grocers try to make a profit or minimize losses. By contrast, in a moral economy – a village economy – the community tries to subjugate market forces and the self-interest of individuals to one's moral obligations to the community. It expects both sellers and buyers to be civic minded and altruistic in the marketplace, by elevating their communal obligations to friends and neighbors over their own self-interest. In this communal setting, the capitalist code of conduct – treating neighbors and strangers alike in the marketplace, maximizing profits, minimizing losses, sellers competing with other sellers, consumers competing with other consumers – violates the moral code of the village economy.[3]

The moral economy, like classical republicanism, sees private interest and internal competition as a threat to the community. The incompatibility of this economic code of conduct with the capitalist ethos was articulated perfectly in colonial Massachusetts in 1639, during the famous trial of Robert Keayne. Historians use this trial to highlight the growth of competitive (that is, capitalist) economic practices in New England, as well as the moral opprobrium this triggered.

Robert Keayne, who kept a shop in Boston, had earned a reputation – first in England and then in Massachusetts – for selling his wares at a high price. He was taken to court and charged with taking too high a profit. He was convicted of this offense and fined £200. His detractors demanded a harsher punishment, but most of the magistrates called for more moderate censure because there was no statute setting the proper profit margin in trade. Moreover, Keayne was not the only offender – other merchants in Massachusetts and elsewhere also raised the prices of their commodities when they could. But Keayne's ordeal was not over when the court case concluded. Following his conviction and censure in court, he faced the prospect of excommunication by his church, where he tearfully acknowledged "his covetous and corrupt heart," but also offered explanations for several of his actions. These explanations Keayne offered in his own defense prompted the Reverend John Cotton to give parishioners moral instruction regarding their commercial conduct in the marketplace by listing the "false principles" that had informed Keayne's misguided actions:

1) That a man might sell as [high] as he can, and buy as cheap as he can.
2) If a man lose by casualty of sea [...] in some of his commodities, he may raise the price of the rest.
3) That he may sell as he bought, though he paid too [much and] the [price] be fallen.
4) That, as a man may take the advantage of his own skill or ability, so he may [take advantage] of another's ignorance or necessity.

---

3 The postcapitalist, or Marxist, critique of capitalism was primarily economic. Karl Marx argued that capitalism was wasteful. Writing in an age of capitalist ascendance (the latter half of the nineteenth century), Marx predicted that capitalism would crumble under its own weight naturally because competition creates overproduction, cycles of boom and bust, economic and financial instability, and downward economic mobility for the middle classes. By contrast, the *pre*capitalist critique of capitalism was primarily moral: seventeenth- and eighteenth-century critics charged that competition, free enterprise, and maximizing profits were corrosive to the social and ethical bonds that held traditional communities together.

Cotton's list provides modern readers with an outline, in contemporaries' own words, of the governing principles of the moral economy. In short, they convey the idea that private profit – driven by supply, demand, and competition – is injurious to the community.[4] In order to protect members of the community from these market forces, and to maintain the character of the community as a community (rather than just a collection of individuals who live together but are not morally accountable to one another), the populace must set limits on private profits from trade *within* the community.

Even though Western societies no longer operate within the strictures of the moral economy, modern people can still find functioning moral economies in their own lives. The most conspicuous and effective moral economy is the family. Economic interactions within a family – selling a car to a sibling, offering a loan to one's son or daughter, picking an assisted-living facility for a parent – are expected to be governed not by considerations of self-interest and maximizing profit, but by interpersonal bonds of moral obligation. Commercial interactions within the family are designed to promote communal harmony, not competition, cost cutting, and profit. Indeed, when a person interacts with a family member as one would with an outsider – that is, using the family member's need to sell high or buy low – the offender usually faces the kind of criticism and sanctions Robert Keayne did in his community, including the prospect of excommunication. Moral criticism and social penalties are the methods by which a community (for example, a family) educates its members about the rules of the moral economy.[5]

What these examples from both the seventeenth and twenty-first century reveal is that communalism (a culture that constrains self-interest and competition) and capitalism (a culture that allows and looks favorably on competition, self-interest, and private profits) are forces that undermine one another;

---

4 The moral economy conveys an "organic" view of society – understanding society to be an organism of sorts. Rather than merely a collection of individuals, the citizenry of a given community is seen as forming a single political body. According to this view, competition within the "body politic" is destructive to it, just as competition between different organs within one's physical body is destructive to the body.

5 Even in the broader society, the contours of the precapitalist moral economy can become visible, especially in times of crisis, such as wartime or the aftermath of natural disasters. In the wake of devastating hurricanes or floods, after the attacks of September 11, 2001 and during World War II, when market forces produced higher prices for gasoline and other commodities, many Americans shelved their capitalist mentality and pressed retailers to keep prices low. This was accomplished by publicly shaming "price gougers," filing lawsuits against them, or initiating government-imposed price controls. At such moments of stress, when forces of war or nature threaten the integrity and cohesiveness of a society, even capitalist societies resurrect elements of the moral economy as part of an effort to highlight, celebrate, and reinforce communal bonds. In such circumstances, what is usually seen as "turning a profit" is denounced as "profiteering," and what is regularly identified clinically as "raising prices to levels the market would bear" is castigated as "price gouging."

as one strengthens, the other declines. The more a family operates along capitalist principles, the less it functions as a family. And the more an economy functions like a family or commune, the less capitalist it is.

The Progress of Capitalism in America

Keayne's trial and Dedham are two case studies that shed light on a question that has long preoccupied scholars of American culture, economics, and politics – why did Americans embrace capitalism so quickly and so thoroughly. Some have explained that capitalism took root and flourished in America because Americans were particularly receptive to new laissez-faire economic theories that sought to liberate individuals from the constraints of the moral economy. But the story of colonial America is not a story of a mad rush to escape the moral economy and embrace capitalism. Instead, numerous community studies reveal that Keayne's neighbors in Boston and the people of Dedham were typical in their commitment to the rules of the moral economy.[6] However, these communities were not sufficiently strong and cohesive to punish and discourage the proliferation of competitive (capitalist) practices within them.

The history of colonial society reveals that village communities attempted to maintain the communal bonds among their members by curbing competition among members of the community and "correcting" anti-social behavior like "profiteering" and "price gouging." Just as English nobles enclosing common lands faced sharp criticism, and at times violent retaliation, from their tenants for putting private interest ahead of their neighbors' welfare, so did American offenders like Robert Keayne. By the same token, when newcomers tried to set up shop in an established village community, they faced resistance from local residents who saw them as a threat to the livelihood and welfare of local service providers (blacksmiths, millers, storekeepers, doctors, and the like). In the context of these English and American moral economies, free enterprise and the maximizing of profits – whether in the form of enclosures, establishing competing businesses, or raising prices in times of scarcity – were regarded as a breach of trust and an assault on the bonds of mutual assistance uniting the community.

---

6 See, for example, Gross, R. (1976). *The Minutemen and Their World*. New York: Hill and Wang; Boyer, P. and Nissenbaum, S. (1974). *Salem Possessed: The Social Origins of Witchcraft*. Cambridge: Harvard University Press; Demos, J. (1970). *A Little Commonwealth*. Oxford: Oxford University Press; Greven, P. (1970). *Four Generations: Population, Land, and Family in Colonial Andover, Massachusetts*. Ithaca: Cornell University Press; Steffen, C. (1993). *From Gentlemen to Townsmen: The Gentry of Baltimore County, Maryland, 1660–1776* Lexington: University Press of Kentucky; Tillson, A. (1991). *Gentry and Common Folk: Political Culture on a Virginia Frontier* Lexington: University Press of Kentucky.

What prevented communities in England and America from perpetuating their premodern and precapitalist way of life was demographic and social change. A moral economy can form and survive only in a small, intimate, homogenous, and stable community, one governed by consensus and traditions produced over generations. In the context of such demographic and social stability, bonds form between families over generations. It is these relationships that inform inhabitants about their varied moral obligations to one another, creating webs of loyalty and mutual assistance and establishing shared norms for private and public behavior. Moreover, only such a tight-knit community can impose and enforce *informal* sanctions – such as gossip, shaming, shunning, and violent vigilantism – to effectively police those who break these norms and fail to live up to their moral obligations toward their neighbors.

By contrast, in a town that is growing demographically and expanding geographically, inhabitants cannot share the same living circumstances (geographically, sociologically, and economically), nor can they share the same history and anthropology, nor a broad consensus on what is ethical and unethical. Because the population is too large and diverse to form an intimate and cohesive community, it cannot use those informal communal means effectively to punish neighbors for ethical transgressions.

These were exactly the conditions that undermined and challenged local moral economies in England. And if local communities in England could not stave off for long the advance of capitalist practices and beliefs, they were virtually powerless to do so in America. American society was even more unstable than England's – not only was its natural growth rate astounding by any historical and modern standard, American villages and towns were also hit by successive waves of immigrants from other towns, other colonies, from England, and from Europe. What accounted for these was strong and consistent economic growth, due to an abundance of land (that is, cheap land) and scarcity of labor (high wages). British America was a society on the move, experiencing legendary demographic growth, geographic expansion, geographic mobility, and socioeconomic mobility (that is, class mobility).

In England, the gradual shift to the capitalist ethos (and modern republicanism) involved violent social and political convulsions, including bread riots, enclosure riots, and banditry. But in the colonies, this transition was much quicker, smoother, and more thorough. From the start, two factors worked against the small moral economies established by the early settlers – factors that were stronger in America than in England. First, all these communities were newly formed; none featured family relations and alliances dating back generations. Moreover, every generation brought about a massive turnover in the demographic make-up of American towns, because of the staggering rate of growth and geographic mobility in the colonies. American towns, therefore, quickly lost the preconditions for communalism – small size, demographic and social stability, a shared history, and shared circumstances, interests, and values. Thus, American communities were even less stable and less cohesive than English ones.

Already in the first generation after settlement, one can identify fissures forming in American moral economies, especially in rapidly growing towns. Hence, only a decade after the founding of Boston, Mr. Keayne's neighbors took him to court, having failed to dissuade him from his competitive practices by informal and unofficial means. Moreover, Reverend Cotton's efforts to teach Bostonians the unwritten rules of their moral economy indicate that locals were not united by an ethical consensus on how to conduct themselves in the marketplace.

The second factor working against American moral economies was that communal cooperation and mutual assistance were not as essential in America as in England, since the opportunities for economic independence and social advancement were greater in America. At the time of the Revolution, England's population was more than double that of the 13 colonies, but was concentrated in a territory roughly the size of Pennsylvania. This made land expensive and wages low, giving English elites – wealthy farmers or merchants, local gentry, or local and national bureaucrats – various means of informal influence in their communities. By offering patronage (in the form of gifts, services, contracts, commissions, and jobs), they built reciprocal relationships of allegiance and support with families below them on the socioeconomic ladder. In America, however, the combination of vast territory, cheap land, and high wages made patronage and mutual assistance less critical for advancement, and therefore less effective at bonding families to one another. Numerous immigrants landing in America with less than nothing – as indentured servants – could and did, within a decade or two, become independent landowners. In England, this kind of socioeconomic climbing could take generations.

The moral economy offers the carrot of mutual assistance for those residents who observe its rules, while offering transgressors the stick of communal disapproval and disciplining. In America, both the carrot and the stick were smaller – American settlers could advance their socioeconomic status on their own to a much greater degree than their counterparts in England; and American communities were less capable than English ones of resisting, discouraging, or punishing those who pursued private interest over communal unity and harmony. The result, therefore, was a society that drifted more quickly, thoroughly, and permanently away from the ethics and social organization of the moral economy, and toward the competitive practices, moral beliefs, and politics that define capitalist societies.

What makes Dedham more than an anecdotal local story, then, is that it exemplifies the tension between an emerging capitalist economy and the precapitalist peasant economy (and peasant values) that preceded it. Likewise, it illustrates how the village economy's classical republicanism gave way to the competitive, capitalist mindset of modern republicanism. Case studies like Dedham show that English settlers transitioned from a premodern economic and political mentality to a modern one not by conscious deliberation and choice. They were not convinced to do so by John Locke, Montesquieu, Cato, Bernard Mandeville, or Adam Smith. Instead, it was their daily experience in their local villages and churches that incrementally changed their philosophical, economic, and political sensibilities. Although they tried, English settlers failed to create, sustain, or enforce the social bonds and obligations on which the moral economy and classical republicanism depend. This failure in numerous villages and towns throughout colonial America should be understood in the context of unprecedented demographic, geographic, and economic growth and mobility. During the first century of English colonization, the colonies' white population grew to roughly 400 000. From 1720 to 1776, it grew to over two million. Settlements proliferated rapidly up and down the eastern seaboard and into the continent's interior. Not surprisingly, the economic output of these colonies grew over 85-fold from 1650 to 1776.

Thus, local communities once governed through politics of trust and deference were quickly transformed by their own success. With natural growth, waves of immigration, geographic expansion, and class mobility challenging local customs and social arrangements, these moral economies' homogeneity, unity, and consensus gave way to pluralism and competing interests. Local politics reflected this transformation, as these towns soon became characterized by the politics of factionalism, suspicion, and opposition. What colonists read in Cato's Letters and other political tracts did not drive these changes in economic and political culture, but merely confirmed what settlers already perceived in their own lives. Indeed, their local experiences made them receptive to Cato's accusations against Walpole and lent credibility to his philosophical claims regarding human nature and the nature of human government.

When, on rare occasions, these colonists' provincial governments intruded into their local village lives (for example, in times of war), those assumptions and fears about government that had been forming locally were applied outward, to the provincial capital. On rarer occasions still, when the imperial government made its presence felt in the localities (in the 1760s and 1770s, for example), these same suspicions and fears were directed toward London. It was mundane daily life in the localities – in churches and militias, on juries and patrols, and in dealings with municipal governments – that warned American settlers that people with power will abuse it. It was local experience, therefore, rather than longstanding bitter experience with monarchy or imperial rule, that shaped the colonies' guarded and distrustful attitude toward the British government in the 1760s, and led them into rebellion in the 1770s.

Questions for Discussion

1 Why were English communities in America so susceptible to the twin ideologies of modern republicanism and capitalism?
2 Do modern republicanism and capitalism indeed reinforce one another?
3 Were American colonists' philosophical and political sensibilities conventionally English or uniquely American?
4 How did English people acquire their philosophical beliefs and political mentality?

Further Readings

Bailyn, B. (1962). Political experience and enlightenment ideas in eighteenth-century America. *The American Historical Review* 67 (2): 339–351.

Bailyn, B. (1970). *The Origins of American Politics*. New York: Vintage.

Boyer, P. and Nissenbaum, S. (1974). *Salem Possessed: The Social Origins of Witchcraft*. Cambridge: Harvard University Press.

Greene, J. (1986). *Peripheries and Center: Constitutional Development in the Extended Polities of the British Empire and the United States 1607–1788*. Athens: University of Georgia Press.

Gross, R. (1976). *The Minutemen and Their World*. New York: Hill and Wang.

Lockridge, K. (1970). *A New England Town: The First Hundred Years: Dedham, Massachusetts, 1636–1736*. New York: Norton.

Pole, J.R. (1983). *The Gift of Government: Political Responsibility From the English Restoration to American Independence*. Athens University of Georgia Press.

Rahe, P. (1992). *Republics Ancient and Modern: Classical Republicanism and the American Revolution II: New Modes and Orders in Early Modern Political Thought*. Chapel Hill: University of North Carolina Press.

Reid, J.P. (1989). *The Concept of Representation in the Age of the American Revolution*. Chicago: University of Chicago Press.

7

The Road to Revolution

The road to the Revolution was short – the change in the transatlantic relationship between colonies and mother country was sudden, it came late in the colonial period, and it reflected policy changes taking place in London, rather than changes in the identity or character of the colonists in America. In the 12 years that preceded the war (1763–1775), Parliament and the Crown led an imperial reform movement, aiming to change the way Britain governed its empire. This change in Britain's approach to imperial governance had its roots in the years between the outbreak of King George's War (1744) and the end of the French and Indian War (1763). Colonial opposition to this imperial reform had its roots in traditional English sensibilities regarding self-government, law, and the imperial constitution.

The Interwar Years

Britain had increased its military involvement in North America during Queen Anne's War (1702–1713). British military investment of men, supplies, energy, and political and financial resources increased further in King George's War (1744–1748), and further still during the French and Indian War (1755–1763). During the interwar years, small-scale violence with neighboring Indians continued in both the northern and southern colonies. When hostilities between France and Britain broke out in Europe, these local quarrels, vendettas, and border disputes intensified, as the French, Spanish, and British escalated military spending and military operations in America.

The major North American campaign of King George's War was a joint Anglo-American operation (provincial troops supported by a strong British fleet) against Louisburg, the strong French fort at the mouth of the St. Lawrence River. France had constructed this stronghold after losing Port Royal, its naval base in Nova Scotia, during Queen Anne's War. Since 1713, Britain's

The Colonists' American Revolution: Preserving English Liberty, 1607–1783, First Edition. Guy Chet.
© 2020 John Wiley & Sons, Inc. Published 2020 by John Wiley & Sons, Inc.
Companion website: www.wiley.com/go/Chet/ColonistsAmericanRevolution

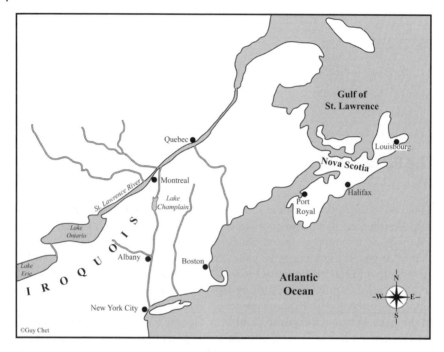

Figure 7.1 Louisbourg and the St. Lawrence river. © Guy Chet.

occupation of Nova Scotia and Newfoundland, and its naval dominance in the North Atlantic, posed a challenge for the French fishing industry in the region. Even more important, it threatened the supply lifeline for Quebec and Montreal (upstream on the St. Lawrence River) in any future war. The strong fortifications in Louisburg – the strongest on the eastern seaboard at the time – countered these British advantages and provided a safe harbor for the large Canadian fishing fleet. Yet Louisburg fell to an army of provincials in the summer of 1745, thanks to an effective siege by Britain's Royal Navy.

At the end of King George's War, peace negotiations returned Louisburg to French hands. Although the only significant accomplishment of the war was reversed at the negotiating table, the capture of Louisburg shaped the diplomatic and military developments that produced the next war (the French and Indian War) 10 years later. The loss of the sole French stronghold at the mouth of the St. Lawrence posed a mortal threat to all of New France during King George's War – it allowed Britain to block virtually all incoming supplies to French forces, allies, and civilians as far west as the Great Lakes. After the war, Britain further strengthened its position in the Gulf of St. Lawrence by constructing a strong naval base in Halifax and settling large numbers of disbanded soldiers in Nova Scotia to help pacify the conquered French and Indian populations there.

Recognizing that in a future war, the British would likely again capture Louisburg and blockade the St. Lawrence, the French government initiated a vigorous and costly fort-construction project in the Great Lakes and along the Ohio and Mississippi Rivers, connecting Canada with French Louisiana. This western supply route from the Gulf of Mexico was to replace the St. Lawrence as Canada's lifeline should the British navy again seal the mouth of the St. Lawrence to French shipping.

This French effort to establish a military presence and Indian alliances in the West was a desperate attempt to adjust to France's logistical and strategic weakness in the east; a weakness on full display during King George's War. Although British authorities – colonial and imperial – did little to counter or impede this French military and diplomatic buildup in the West, they did notice it with growing concern. In June of 1754, Britain's Board of Trade convened the Albany Congress – a meeting of imperial officials and delegates from the colonies – to shore up Indian alliances in the West and coordinate colonial

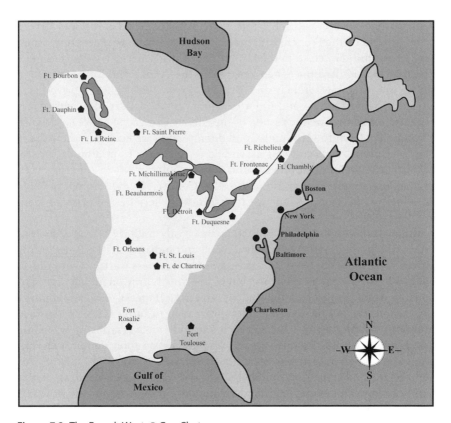

Figure 7.2 The French West. © Guy Chet.

defenses. Under the leadership of Benjamin Franklin, the Congress adopted the Albany Plan, a blueprint for a union of colonies (the United Colonies of America) under a chief executive (President-General of the United Colonies) and a council of delegates representing each of the colonies. According to the Albany Plan of Union, this central governing body would be empowered to deal with matters of regional defense, Indian relations, intercolonial trade, and westward expansion. And it would have the authority to tax American settlers to finance its operations.

Anglo-American Relations During the French and Indian War (1755–1763)

That same summer, Lieutenant Governor Robert Dinwiddie of Virginia commissioned Lieutenant Colonel George Washington to uphold the British claim to the forks of the Ohio (the location of modern-day Pittsburgh, Pennsylvania) and construct a fort there. Washington's force was driven from the field by the French, who built their own fort there (Fort Duquesne). This minor military clash in the far reaches of the American wilderness was the spark that ignited the Seven Years War (the French and Indian War) – a global war that saw French and British forces fighting in India, Africa, Europe, the West Indies, and America. Following the failure of Washington's expedition and the anemic results of the Albany Congress – a weak promise of neutrality from the Iroquois Confederacy, and a rejection of the Albany Plan of Union by all colonial assemblies – George II appointed General Edward Braddock as Britain's Commander in Chief in North America, with instructions to take possession of the Ohio Country. In the summer of 1755, Braddock led his troops to the western frontier, where he and many of them met their death.

Although the British faced humbling and costly military setbacks such as Braddock's in the early stages of the French and Indian War, the British army proved to be quite effective and successful at wilderness warfare. They did so not by adopting "American tactics," but by applying European military conventions to campaigning and fighting in America. Imperial officials, military administrators, and field commanders were able to bring Britain's logistical superiority to bear against their French and Indian adversaries by extending British military infrastructure – roads, bridges, forts, supply depots, and supply trains – deep into the western, northern, and southern frontiers. This bureaucratic and logistical groundwork allowed the British to deploy and sustain large forces in enemy territory, creating military engagements in which they enjoyed overwhelming superiority in men, munitions, and provisions. Their enemies were thus forced to either attack the strong British positions at a disadvantage, avoid battle altogether by abandoning the field, or surrender. By 1760, Britain had conquered the trans-Appalachian West and all of New France. By 1763, it also took possession of Spanish Florida.

The man who built the army's logistical system – in London, in the administrative centers of British North America, and on the frontiers – was General John Campbell, Earl of Loudoun. During his two-year tenure as Commander in Chief (1756–1757), Loudoun devoted himself to the gray administrative and financial details that many commanders (and many military historians) find tedious, but are indispensable prerequisites for effective large-scale campaigns. The army signed long-term contracts with suppliers in London, built three central supply depots in America, contracted the services civilian surveyors, road builders, carpenters, wrights, boatmen, and wagon and sled drivers to create a secure and reliable transport system connecting the central supply depots to the front lines. Loudoun secured these supply routes with forts, strong garrisons, and military escorts for the supply trains.

While in the long run Loudoun's efforts paid off, in the short run they won him the enmity of colonial elites. More accustomed to working within a military hierarchy than with civic leaders and politicians, Loudoun was notoriously imperious in his dealings with provincial assemblies. They, in turn, were uncooperative and purposefully slow to respond to his orders, demands, and threats. They compared him to Edmund Andros and Joseph Dudley for his effort to create and direct a regional policy, upending the preexisting order by which each colony devised its own policies and directed its own administrative and military affairs.

In time, Prime Minister William Pitt removed Loudoun from his post. Pitt's correspondence with provincial legislatures was respectful and deferential, and he greased the wheels of provincial bureaucracies with generous subsidies from the British treasury. The assemblies grew more cooperative as a growing portion of their military expenditures (on provincial troops' wages and provisions) was paid with British funds. By the late-1750s, Pitt's military spending started bearing fruit on both land and sea. Britain's control of the Atlantic allowed it to transport to America a large well-supplied army, while denying New France vital supplies, munitions, and reinforcements. In 1758–1759, French authorities in Canada faced dire shortages in money, men, and provisions, forcing them to withdraw their limited resources from the West to Louisburg, Quebec, and Montreal. With French material support for Indian allies flagging, and with the steady British advance in the Ohio Country, Indian zeal for the war declined sharply. In 1758, 13 Indian nations withdrew from the war, in exchange for British recognition of Indian land claims west of the Allegheny Mountains (the Treaty of Easton). Without Indian allies to assist them from that point on, French garrisons abandoned their forts in the Ohio Valley and Great Lakes one by one (including Fort Duquesne) and returned to Canada.

Anglo-American Relations After the War

The French and Indian war was a spectacular British success story. Yet it also produced the postwar friction between Britain and its colonies and sowed the seeds of American separatism. There is little evidence to support the notion that Americans had become gradually distant or alienated from Britain before the French and Indian War; certainly there is no evidence that they harbored separatist impulses before the war. Local communities and governments in America certainly resented and resisted anti-smuggling laws, the Navigation Acts, and other commercial regulations enacted by the British government in the seventeenth and eighteenth centuries, but so did communities in England itself, as well as in Britain's Caribbean colonies. At times, American settlers were critical of corruption in high places or of the imperial government's diplomatic priorities, religious policies, or military conduct. But the same was true of patriotic British subjects elsewhere, in England, Scotland, and the West Indies. White Americans – overwhelmingly English by ethnicity, culture, and identity – exhibited all the hallmarks of British patriotism. They displayed affection and reverence toward the king; displayed symbols of British authority in their public places; celebrated British political, imperial, commercial, and scientific accomplishments; volunteered for service in Britain's imperial wars; exhibited sympathy and concern for the health and welfare of British soldiers in their midst; shared other Englishmen's xenophobia and sense of cultural superiority; and were insatiable consumers of news, fashions, and goods from England.

In the eighteenth century, when the American population was growing at an extraordinary rate, the per capita consumption of British imports actually rose. Between 1750 and 1773 – the eve of the Revolution – the consumption of imported goods more than doubled. Americans consumers were flooded with a dizzying array of consumer choices, and even in the most remote and impoverished regions (such as rural North Carolina), colonists relied increasingly on imports.[1] Britons on the periphery – in Ireland, Canada, Massachusetts, Pennsylvania, Carolina, Jamaica, and Barbados – were thus drawn and woven into the material culture of the mother country. They were further integrated in the imperial culture through usage of their imported goods. Americans unfamiliar with tea etiquette, for example, studied the various rules and ceremonies of the tea table, as well as the names of the different tea utensils.

---

1 Whereas New York merchants in the 1720s listed roughly 15 different imported goods per month in their ads, by the 1770s they could list as many as 9000 different manufactured items per month. British imports carried positive associations for colonists. Colonial booksellers, for example, observed that readers preferred a London imprint over an American edition of the same title. They therefore falsely labeled local publications as English imprints

American settlers regarded themselves as British, and saw British culture and British achievements as their own. Even in the tumultuous postwar years, colonists' patriotic and sentimental attachment to the mother country persisted alongside heightened transatlantic tensions. Colonial elites – the very families that would lead the American rebellion – continued to send their sons to England to complete their education or acculturation as English gentlemen. Benjamin Franklin – who would later champion the cause of independence – famously labored to prevent a rift between colonial governments and the imperial government during the Stamp Act crisis (1765–1766). In Boston, public celebrations of George III's birthday and coronation anniversary were held annually until 1773. In New York, residents erected a statue of George III in 1770, in gratitude for his leadership in the French and Indian War, as well as his role in the 1766 repeal of the hated Stamp Act. Indeed, as late as 1773, on the eve of the Revolutionary crisis, a group of New England colonists named a new settlement in central New Hampshire in honor of General Loudoun.

Nevertheless, the French and Indian War did bring to the fore colonial fears regarding arbitrary power and administrative centralization in the empire. The postwar imperial reforms validated and exacerbated these fears in the 1760s, and the Coercive Acts transformed them into panic in 1774–1775. Colonial concern over imperial authorities overstepping their jurisdictional bounds was clearly on display during the war itself in provincial governments' cool, uncooperative, and at times obstructionist relationship with General Loudoun. But colonial alarm regarding imperial centralization manifested itself even before the war, with the unveiling of the Albany Plan of Union.

While the Albany Plan did not violate the imperial constitution as egregiously as the Dominion of New England had, it represented a similar, though subtler, challenge to the liberties of colonists and of colonial assemblies. Indeed, the argument proffered in support of the Albany Plan – illustrated in Benjamin Franklin's famous "Join, or Die" placard – was similar to the one advanced in the 1680s by the Board of Trade in favor of the Dominion. In both cases, advocates of unification pointed out that the colonies faced common threats and that their administrative fragmentation threatened their security by hindering coordination and cooperation. Their solution was to create a common government that would transcend colonial borders and rise above the parochial considerations of individual colonies. This government would be empowered to formulate regional policy (over the heads of colonial assemblies), enforce its policies on local populations, and levy taxes on colonists to finance itself. In the context of the empire's longstanding salutary-neglect constitution, the Albany Plan triggered a sense of alarm in colonial assemblies. Given the threat that such administrative centralization posed to the assemblies' own liberties and jurisdictions, and to the principle of government by consent, the Albany Plan was rejected out of hand by all the colonies.

Figure 7.3 Benjamin Franklin's call for intercolonial cooperation through the Albany Congress. Source: Wikimedia Commons, the free media repository https://commons.wikimedia.org/w/index.php?title=File:Benjamin_Franklin_-_Join_or_Die.jpg&oldid=332423636

The Albany Plan should therefore be seen not as a precursor to the Federal Union – a sign that Americans had formed a common bond and sought a common government already during the colonial era, and even before the French and Indian War. Instead, the Albany Plan should be understood as an illustration of the colonies' persistent resistance to central governance. Indeed, the suspicions, fears, and jurisdictional jealousies that impelled colonial assemblies to reject the Albany Plan in 1754 also impelled them to obstruct Loudoun during the war, resist Parliament's centralizing reforms after the war, and oppose the Federalists' centralizing reforms after the American Revolution (1787–1788). The assemblies' opposition to centralization – from the 1680s to the 1780s and beyond – testifies to Americans' consistent commitment to self-government under the salutary-neglect structure that characterized both the First British Empire and the United States under its first constitution (the Articles of Confederation).

Britain's Postwar Law-Enforcement and Bureaucratic Reforms

After the French and Indian War, the issue of imperial centralization was once again thrust into the public sphere, in both Britain and America. The war itself was a resounding success, but its impressive accomplishments came at a prohibitive cost. Financially, Britain's national debt skyrocketed from £74 million to

£132 million. Politically, the national debt led to tax increases and enhanced tax enforcement, which produced political turmoil both at home and in America. Prosecuting the war in America had led the British government to involve itself directly in colonial administration to a greater degree than ever before, through subsidies to provincial treasuries, logistical coordination with local governments, military contracting, campaigning, and the Royal Navy's blockade of French and Spanish ports in America. Administering the newly conquered territories in Canada, the American West, and Florida required the imperial government to continue its strong and active presence in North America. To protect its newly won territories, pacify the newly conquered populations, recoup its wartime financial losses, and pay the debts incurred by the war, the British government maintained 10 full regiments in North America. This entailed investing in permanent bases, roads, and bridges to connect outlying bases to supply depots, and commissioners to maintain and operate these military assets. Additionally, Britain deployed customs officers and magistrates in North American ports to collect import taxes more effectively and otherwise enforce the Navigation Acts and other commercial restrictions.

During the war, Britain's naval blockade of enemy ports placed the Royal Navy in position to enforce longstanding and long-ignored imperial restrictions on colonial trade, as articulated in the Navigation Acts. In pursuit of Britain's wartime goals, the navy acted to prevent and punish contraband trade, smuggling, and trade with the enemy. At port, Britain began to enforce writs of assistance, which empowered customs officers to randomly search public establishments and private homes for contraband or smuggled goods. (James Otis of Massachusetts lambasted these general warrants as a wanton exercise of power, asserting that "a man's house is his castle.") After the war, the British government remained committed to stamping out violations of imperial law. After all, by that point, North America represented a major investment by the British government, its creditors, and its taxpayers.

The imperial government's efforts to restructure the empire and extend its direct jurisdiction to America – enacting policies designed to improve law enforcement, economize provincial administration, and create revenues for the British treasury – reflected how important the American colonies had become for the British Empire and its economy, as well as for the government's finances. During the 1760s, Parliament and the Court enacted meaningful reforms in the structure and funding mechanisms of colonial governments to make governors and imperial magistrates more independent of colonial constituents and more accountable to Parliament and the Crown. Additionally, they beefed up the customs service in America, expanded the jurisdictions of Admiralty courts, and retained 10 regiments (roughly 8000 men) in North America.

In the immediate aftermath of the war, these troops' main mission was to pacify and control newly conquered populations. Thus, these regiments were deployed primarily in Florida, Canada, and the American West. In time, however, the high cost of maintaining remote garrisons in Indian country led imperial and provincial administrators to gradually reduce their size. By 1767–1768, these redcoats migrated in growing numbers from the American West to colonial capitals in the east, such as Boston, New York, and Philadelphia. These troops would thereafter be available to assist in law enforcement and customs enforcement in American port cities, creating increased friction between civilians and soldiers there (as manifested most violently in 1770, in the Boston Massacre and New York's infamous liberty-pole clashes). Following the Tea Act and Boston Tea Party (1773), Britain used these troops to enforce the punitive Coercive, or "Intolerable," Acts in Massachusetts, leading to the outbreak of the Revolution.

Transatlantic Opposition to Postwar Policies

The 12 years that separated the end of the French and Indian War (1763) and the outbreak of the American Revolution (1775) are, therefore, the key to understanding the causes, meaning, and purpose of the American Revolution. The Revolution was not the culmination of a long and incremental centrifugal process by which life in America gradually separated colonists in America from British culture, society, and government. Rather, the Revolution was the immediate product of the imperial policies imposed on Americans suddenly in the postwar years. What all these policies had in common was that they undermined, circumvented, and threatened colonists' institutions of self-government – namely, provincial legislatures and local courts of law. For this reason, these imperial reforms were perceived as violations of the law and of the imperial constitution.

Such concerns about arbitrary power were not uniquely American. They were not a product of a uniquely American experience, nor were they a manifestation of uniquely American political or ideological sensibilities. Indeed, these concerns were recognizably English, rooted in English experiences and reflecting English sensibilities. Just as Britain's postwar taxation and enforcement schemes drew the ire of British subjects in the colonies, so did they in Britain itself.

With roughly half the Treasury's annual revenues going to pay the interest on Britain's huge national debt, Lord Bute – the new Prime Minister who had succeeded William Pitt – won approval for several means of raising revenues in both Britain and its colonies. Prewar Britain was already a tax state, one defined by high taxes, high military spending, and a large permanent national debt. After the war, it saw further increases in import duties, sales taxes, and licensing fees. Not only were certain goods and activities subjected to new taxes, but existing rates were raised as well. And while it was the manufacturer, merchant, or vendor who paid these taxes and fees, it was the consumer who bore the cost in the form of higher retail prices for goods and services.

Consternation over taxation and tax enforcement was reminiscent of that on display under Walpole, when Britons recognized that the rising tax burden was not the product of truly representative government, in which the public consents to the laws under which it is governed, but of an unaccountable government wielding power arbitrarily. In the 1760s and 1770s, Britons increasingly felt that tax laws and government spending did not reflect the public will, but the interests of a well-connected few. Convinced that a political system designed to secure self-government had been corrupted, Britons demanded electoral reform to regain control over their government. The result was a postwar demand from below to extend voting rights to a wider segment of society, curb election fraud, clean out "rotten boroughs," and enhance public oversight of Parliament. This push for reform in Britain manifested itself in petitions, public addresses and editorials, electoral campaigns, and motions in town meetings and in Parliament. However, it also came in the form of urban riots led by populist leaders like John Wilkes, who rode this wave of public disaffection into high office.

The focus of American historians on the political tumult and violence in the colonies during the 1760s and 1770s obscures from view the fact that this was a politically tumultuous period in Britain as well. During this era, governments formed and dissolved every two or three years, Parliamentary seats changed hands between Whigs to Tories and back again from one election to the next, the public questioned and challenged the legitimacy of governmental institutions, and political violence became a more common feature of public life. Britain's war debt was a destabilizing factor in the economy, and therefore also in local, national, and imperial politics. The instability in the colonies was simply a part of this general trend. Indeed, leaders of the electoral-reform movement in England – John Wilkes in particular – picked up the cause of the Americans in the 1760s and 1770s, and were celebrated for it in America.

"No Taxation Without Representation": A Constitutional Crisis, Not a Tax Revolt

On both sides of the ocean, the theme of the opposition movement was consent, linking taxation and political representation. In America, colonists conveyed this with the slogan "no taxation without representation"; in Britain, opposition leaders expressed it with a demand for electoral reform. In both Britain and America, then, the opposition did not simply call for lowering the tax burden. It instead pointed out that the government enacted tax measures arbitrarily, without the consent of the governed. While the spark was economic, the complaint that was articulated and the proposed remedy were not economic, but constitutional – having to do with the structure and accountability of the government.

It is, therefore, misleading to characterize the American Revolution as a tax revolt. The Revolution – like the English Civil War, which was also sparked by disputes over taxation – was a constitutional crisis. This is most clearly evident when one considers advocates of the American cause in Britain. These opposition leaders opposed the new tax-enforcement measures implemented in America not because they themselves were subject to these taxes, but because they were alarmed by their own government's disregard for law, custom, and the imperial constitution. *The Crisis*, a London weekly opposing British policy in America in 1775–1776, informed its readers what was at stake concerning the government's imperial policy: "Lawless Power," "the Natural Rights of mankind," and "the Constitution of the British Empires in England and America."

What explains such fear and resentment – in the 1760s and 1770s, just as in 1642 and 1688 – is the English attachment to representative government. The English had long prided themselves on being a free people, governed by laws to which they gave their consent through their representatives. Looking across the English Channel, they saw or imagined societies in which arbitrary power was the governing principle; where the ruler's will was law, and the people mere subjects to it.

The commitment to the principle of consent reflected an English conviction that people with power will abuse it. This core belief about human nature shaped every aspect of English governance – English and Anglo-American political bodies and their arcane procedures, judicial institutions and criminal procedures, administrative structures, opposition to police forces and standing armies, and the attachment to local government. The prohibitions and principles listed in the English Bill of Rights, American state constitutions, Articles of Confederation, Federal Constitution, and American Bill of Rights were all institutional manifestations of that English conviction that people with power will abuse it. These written constitutions created institutional safeguards against arbitrary power, aiming to prevent the concentration of power in one man, one group of men, or one institution.

Indeed, the postwar opposition movement in both Britain and America highlighted the concentration of political power, not the financial burden of taxation, as the paramount threat to British subjects. It is evident therefore that the anxiety sparked by postwar taxation was first and foremost constitutional, rather than economic or financial. This is why the remedies advanced by agitators on both sides of the ocean were primarily constitutional – dealing with political representation and the structure of government – rather than economic or financial.

A Political Philosophy Learnt Practically, Through Daily Experience in Local Communities

This is not to say that American Revolutionists were moved to action by theorizing about constitutional principles and political philosophy. The English, like most people then and now, were not philosophically inclined. Rather, their fears regarding centralization and governmental power were products of practical experience. Consistent tax increases throughout the eighteenth century, especially during and after the French and Indian War, occasioned a dramatic expansion of the government's tax-enforcement agencies in both Britain and America. This is because the high taxes and fees imposed on manufacturers, importers, and retailers created a vast and profitable black market in contraband goods, from luxury items like tea, sugar, and tobacco to more basic products like liquor, paper, glass, and textiles. To combat this black market and enforce compliance with the tax laws, the excise service was expanded, with more agents available to visit factories, shops, inns, and taverns to check paperwork, impose fines, issue warrants, file lawsuits, or summon the sheriff to conduct arrests. Likewise, the customs service and coastguard were furnished with more ships, with larger crews and more cannons, to patrol British, American, and Caribbean coastlines. Additionally, the customs service itself expanded, with officers authorized to arrest smugglers and confiscate their cargos.

So Britons on both sides of the Atlantic felt violated not only on principle – on the issue of consent to the new tax laws – but in practice, in their dealings with enforcement agents of the state visiting their businesses, checking up on them, demanding licenses, charging fees, and taking them to court (increasingly without juries) for violations of these novel policies and taxes. But British taxation and regulation of manufacturing and commerce did more than merely violate English sensibilities and habits; they also made goods and services more expensive for consumers. Indeed, this is what the American Declaration of Independence complains of when noting that the king "has erected a multitude of New Offices, and sent hither swarms of Officers to harass our people, and eat out their substance" (that is, draw their salaries from the taxes and fees they forced consumers to pay).

Resentment against Britain's expanding taxation schemes explains why smugglers, contraband traders, and pirates were viewed by their neighbors in both Britain and America as public benefactors – bringing affordable goods to market, opening lucrative markets for local manufacturers, and providing good income to local laborers.[2] Smuggling and piracy were not considered criminal or disreputable acts in coastal communities, and especially in American waters, where law enforcement was both light and sporadic. These were ancient and conventional trades that were carried out in the open by respectable members of the community since the colonies' earliest days, and

---

2 Political economist John Bowring remarked that "The smuggler is in reality a public benefactor. [...] The smuggler who smuggles against a duty of 30 per cent. has 30 per cent. value in the love and affection of the inhabitants; if against 60 per cent., he has much more; if against prohibition, he has the greatest portion of friendly regard that can be shown him. Williams, N. (1961). *Contraband Cargoes*. Hamden, CT: Shoe String Press, 205.

did not carry a negative social stigma. To the contrary, smuggling, wrecking, contraband trade, and piracy were seen as economically beneficial to both the locality and the empire, whereas attempts by the central government to suppress these trades was seen as illegal, unjust, and economically injurious to local communities. Because colonial authorities shared their constituents' values, legal beliefs, and economic interests, imperial efforts to enforce trade restrictions and collect the customs duties (import taxes) were usually mild and ineffective. Local officials were skeptical of the central government's broad jurisdictional claims, and resentful of its meddlesome interference in local matters. They worked with their constituents, therefore, to resist, soften, circumvent, and otherwise undermine the enforcement of Britain's trade laws.

Until the French and Indian War, therefore, commercial activities outlawed by imperial statutory law had been legitimized in America by local custom and common law. During and especially after the war, however, American colonists suddenly faced an imperial government intent on combating these widespread commercial practices and treating them as crimes. Indeed, they were prosecuted as capital crimes, for which defendants were hauled before military tribunals to stand trial for their lives without a jury of their peers to judge them.

A Police Force for British America

This transformation was all the more distressing for Americans because British soldiers were used as law-enforcement agents from the late-1760s on, providing armed protection for customs officers and court officials as they confronted colonists who violated imperial laws regulating trade and manufacturing. For a society that had never seen a policeman and was opposed to standing armies on principle *because* they could be used as police, this was a jarring and ominous development. Britons in America saw their worst fears confirmed – soldiers left in North America to pacify conquered peoples on the western frontiers wound up policing loyal and patriotic Britons in eastern port towns.

The effectiveness of the redcoats as an urban police force can be gauged by comparing the resistance campaigns against the Stamp Act of 1765 and the Townshend duties of 1767. In 1765, when British troops were heavily deployed on the frontiers, the Sons of Liberty controlled the streets of eastern cities. In the absence of a police force, townspeople effectively policed their neighbors with both praise and punishment – gossip, public shaming, shunning, or outright violence. They thus effectively deterred would-be stamp agents and other imperial officials from doing their jobs, and dissuaded colonists from selling, buying, or displaying British imports. This resistance movement was so potent that Parliament was convinced to repeal the Stamp Act immediately. By contrast, when British redcoats began migrating from the West to eastern cities in 1767–1768, the Sons of Liberty were not as forceful or effective. American protests against the Townshend duties were less violent and more orderly than the protests of 1765; agents of imperial authority felt safe in their homes and offices, at the docks, and on the street; and colonists similarly felt safe enough to violate the revived commercial boycott on British imports. As a result, the Townshend duties remained in force for three long years before being repealed in 1770.

The use of soldiers as police spawned great resentment in the cities, as well as wild conspiracy theories about covert plans hatched in London (with sympathetic imperial officials in America) to militarily force colonists to submit to novel taxes and other imperial schemes. These conspiracy theories should be understood in the context of a historically unpoliced society which suddenly found itself saddled with a police force, and a military one at that. To British colonists in America (as for Britons across the sea), the very presence of an army in peacetime was evidence of arbitrary government, since forced compliance is required only for policies that do not enjoy the willing consent of the governed.[3]

For example, when British troops were deployed in the Ohio Valley after the French and Indian War, in conjunction with Britain's Royal Proclamation of 1763, American colonists responded with consternation. The proclamation extended the Easton Treaty of 1758, promising to reserve the trans-Appalachian West to local Indian tribes (former allies of New France), thus prohibiting English settlement beyond the Appalachians.[4] The settlers felt that Britain had taken the fruits of their victory and given them to their enemies. It denied poorer colonists, who could not afford land in the east, the opportunity to purchase cheap land on the frontier, and it denied wealthier colonists the opportunity to sell them these lands. In the minds of American provincials, therefore, the Proclamation of 1763 transformed the British Army – which colonists had seen as *their* army – into a tool of unjust and arbitrary power against them.

By the late-1760s, these same troops began migrating eastward, since their mission in the West proved both expensive and ineffective. As in the West, imperial officials in the east utilized these soldiers to enforce unpopular imperial policies. Historically, British governors were delicate in the way they handled what they considered violations of imperial law (such as smuggling, piracy,

---

3 An essay published in South Carolina following the enforcement of the Coercive Acts on Massachusetts offers insight into contemporary ideas of law, force, and the British constitution: "When an Army is sent to enforce Laws, it is always an Evidence that either the Law makers are conscious that they had no clear and indisputable right to make those Laws, or that they are bad [and] oppressive. Wherever the People themselves have had a hand in making Laws, according to the first principles of our Constitution there is no danger of Non-submission, Nor can there be need of an Army to enforce them." Kopel, D.B. (Summer 2012). How the British gun control program precipitated the American Revolution. *Charleston Law Review* 6 (2): 289–290.
4 The Proclamation also established the provinces of Quebec, East Florida, and West Florida.

and illegal trade). Experience had taught them that they could not coerce their constituents and their assemblies to comply with unpopular imperial policies, so they acquiesced to public sentiment. With the infusion of soldiers to these port towns, however, governors were emboldened to protect customs officers and other imperial officials from angry crowds, to arrest smugglers and their accomplices, and to intercept smuggling vessels, even if they happened to belong to local bigwigs like John Hancock, whose ship – *The Liberty* – was seized and confiscated in 1768. (It was commissioned into the Royal Navy and assigned to customs enforcement, only to be seized and burned by a band of Rhode Islanders soon thereafter.[5])

Deploying soldiers as law-enforcement agents in western frontiers in the early-1760s engendered resentment and fear of arbitrary, unaccountable government. Using them in the late-1760s to police eastern cities – where the settlers were more numerous, wealthy, and politically powerful – drove these fears to new heights. The unprecedented use of soldiers as police in America made manifest Parliament's new campaign to extend the central government's jurisdiction over the colonies and enforce its authority, laws, and policy preferences on the colonists. Using the king's army against the king's own subjects – first in the West, and then in the east – raised constitutional alarm bells and bolstered public support for colonial assemblies in their jurisdictional contests with Parliament in the 1760s and 1770s.

Following the Boston Massacre (1770), imperial officials in Massachusetts charged that the mob action that precipitated the shooting was preorchestrated by a band of colonists to goad the soldiers into violence. The purpose of this alleged conspiracy was to force the governor to remove the army from the city, thereby causing customs officers and other royal officials to be more fearful of retribution and thus more lenient in carrying out their duties.[6] Whether this accusation was fact or fantasy is up for debate, but the accusation itself indicates that British authorities, too, understood that using the army as a police force was a novelty. Moreover, both sides understood that aggressive enforcement of the prewar Navigation Acts and postwar Revenue Acts (including the Sugar Act and Townshend duties) was an essential component of Parliament's project to restructure the empire.

---

5 Violent resistance and vengeance against customs officers had long been a common feature of life in coastal communities in southern England (where customs enforcement was strongest). When Britain stepped up its customs enforcement in America after the war, such violence became increasingly prevalent in the colonies as well (most notoriously in the attack on the *Gaspee* in 1772).

6 Indeed, after the Boston Massacre, the governor did withdraw the soldiers from the city, under intense pressure from angry crowds and populist leaders. The result was sustained tranquility in Boston. The city and province remained at peace for three years, until the passage of the Tea Act in 1773.

Structural Reforms of the Imperial Constitution

The British government was leading a reform movement designed to stream-line the empire's constitution (that is, its governing structure). Following in the footsteps of Governor Andros, the Board of Trade, and General Loudoun, the leaders of this reform movement identified the institutional weakness of pro-vincial governors as the central problem plaguing imperial administration. They thus looked favorably on the migration of redcoats from the West to the east, seeing an opportunity to strengthen governors' ability to enforce imperial laws on a resistant populace. To that same end, these imperial reformers enacted ordinances that weakened colonial legislatures' control and supervi-sion over governors and other imperial officials in the colonies, and instead made these officials more dependent, accountable, and responsive to Parliament.

For example, imperial administrators were long frustrated by colonial assemblies' habit of funding their governments annually, rather than provid-ing permanent revenue streams for governors and courts. The postwar Revenue Acts (Sugar Act, Stamp Act, and Townshend duties) were designed to create such permanent revenues for salaries and other government expenses by funneling proceeds directly from provincial taxpayers to pro-vincial executives and judges, bypassing the appropriation process in the assemblies.

By arrogating to itself the "power of the purse" in America, Parliament undermined each assembly's influence over its executive branch (that is, the governor and his officers). Just as American legislatures had opposed such efforts in the past – the Dominion of New England, the Albany Plan, and Loudoun's administration – this feature of the Revenue Acts spurred colo-nists into active resistance in defense of their assemblies' (and their own) English liberties.

As distressing to them was the fact that Parliament also targeted the judicial system, enacting reforms that restricted American settlers' right to jury trials, limited colonial courts' jurisdictions, and expanded the legal immunities avail-able to imperial officials in America. There was a common theme to the impe-rial reforms of the 1760s and 1770s: British soldiers insulated agents of the imperial government in America from the intimidating influence of urban crowds; British funding insulated imperial officeholders from the financial control of local legislatures; legal immunities insulated imperial officials from the reach of local courts and juries; and the curtailment of jury trials insulated imperial prosecutors from hostile juries. Indeed, it was Britain's effort to undermine jury trials in America that bonded elites and common folk most effectively in joint support for the assemblies' constitutional and political resistance to Parliament.

The Right to Jury Trial as the Linchpin of Colonial Resistance

Historians have long found it easy to explain the reaction of colonial elites to Parliament's administrative reforms in 1763–1774. This is because historians could point to the ways the imperial reform movement threatened the powers, jurisdictions, interests, and liberties of colonial assemblies and of the wealthy and powerful families that led them. Historians have had a hard time, however, explaining what moved common people to join this colonial resistance, making common cause with colonial elites. The difficulty has been to explain why people on the middle and lower rungs of society – people who neither sat in the assemblies nor, in most cases, voted for representatives – cared about and felt so threatened by the policies Parliament initiated in the realm of high-politics. The answer is likely the drastic undermining of jury trials in America.

In 1700, a new "Act for the More Effectual Suppression of Piracy" transferred cases of piracy on the high seas from civilian courts (and civilian juries) to newly established Admiralty courts – military tribunals in which verdicts were pronounced by Admiralty judges, rather than juries. This was a controversial innovation at the time because it claimed royal jurisdiction at sea, limited the power of local governments and local courts, upended common-law precedents, and purposefully denied English subjects accused of piracy the hallowed right to face a jury of their peers. Indeed, these military tribunals were established in response to local magistrates and juries routinely acquitting accused pirates in civilian courts.

After the French and Indian War, in the face of similar acquittals of accused smugglers and other illegal traders in civilian courts, Britain extended the jurisdiction of Admiralty courts (through the Sugar Act of 1763) to also cover customs offenses at port – smuggling, contraband trade, and trafficking with pirates, smugglers, and illegal traders. This meant that a colonist accused of murder or rape would be tried by a jury of his peers, whereas a man accused of a customs violation could find himself on trial for his life in front of a military tribunal. In 1765, the Stamp Act gave Admiralty courts jurisdiction over violations of the Stamp Act as well.

Thus, American settlers first saw their local courts, magistrates, and juries supplanted by military tribunals of the central government in matters relating to commerce *at sea*, where the jurisdiction of local courts was indeed tenuous. Then, immediately after the war, the British extended the jurisdiction of Admiralty courts all the way to the shoreline, where local courts' jurisdiction had been undisputed beforehand. And soon after that, Admiralty courts seized jurisdiction over violations that took place hundreds of miles from the coast and had nothing to do with maritime trade.

Historically, local communities in America were able to use their courts to undermine the enforcement of imperial laws and policies that they found bad, illegal, or unconstitutional. The reforms initiated by Britain in the administration of justice made it harder for colonists to continue to do so. Moreover, while local juries were unable to shield colonial smugglers and illegal traders from prosecution, they were also denied the opportunity to punish aggressive or abusive customs officers. Previously, customs agents had been intimidated from pursuing their duties aggressively for fear of being taken to court, where they met hostile juries that were quick to convict. But in the postwar years, Britain permitted imperial officials to avoid local juries by transferring their trials from the colonies to London.

It was these kinds of daily experiences of British imperial administration – rather than philosophical abstractions on the nature and purpose of government – that shaped colonists' philosophical sensibilities and constitutional complaints in the Revolutionary era. While many Americans read and internalized the political and moral philosophy outlined in political tracts such a Cato's Letters, many more came to consider issues of consent, representation, jurisdiction, arbitrary power, and the rule of law because they, their relatives, their colleagues, or their neighbors had crossed paths with customs agents, soldiers, or officers of the court. That is, it was Britain's postwar law-enforcement campaign that focused the attention of a wide cross-section of colonial society on the imperial constitution.

Imperial law-enforcement did a great deal to educate common people on the contours of the ongoing dispute between Parliament and American assemblies regarding provincial liberties and the imperial constitution. The threat to jury trials affected sailors, dockworkers, innkeepers, and shopkeepers as it did ship owners and merchants; and it made concrete (and personal) the constitutional principles over which the assemblies and Parliament argued. It illustrated to Americans that these abstract constitutional principles were not a matter of high politics – they had real, direct, and life-threatening impact on them.[7]

Since the Middle Ages, Englishmen saw the right to be tried by a jury of their peers as their birthright. They took pride in it as a hallmark of liberty, and they saw the absence of jury trials in France as emblematic of French tyranny and arbitrary power. This devotion to juries was intimately connected to the English attachment to representative legislatures – these two were the primary forms of English self-government. Like representative legislatures, juries empower representatives who share the defendant's circumstances, interests, values, and understanding of the law. And like

---

7 It should come as no surprise that of the 10 items that comprise the American Bill of Rights, 5 (the Fourth, Fifth, Sixth, Seventh, and Eighth Amendments) protect Americans in their dealings with Federal courts of law; and 3 (the Fifth, Sixth, and Seventh) explicitly protect Americans' right to jury trials from Federal infringement.

representative legislatures, juries reflect the core English conviction that people with power will abuse it – both legislatures and juries prevent the concentration of power in the hands of one person. Indeed, for most people, the issues of liberty outlined in Magna Carta or the English Bill of Rights became palpable not on voting days, but when they or their acquaintances found themselves in court. In comparison to voting for political representatives, jury trials offered practical liberty and direct self-governance, the consequences of which were immediately visible and comprehensible in a community's daily life. Moreover, while most people in Britain and the colonies were not eligible to vote, all were eligible to face prosecution.

The British attack on the ability of local courts and local juries in America to administer justice was a huge issue in the provincial protests of the 1760s and 1770s. Modern historical accounts of these protests focus mostly on economic regulation (the economic burden of taxes, trade restrictions, stamp fees, and the like), but it was the threat to self-government – the liberties of assemblies on the high end, and of juries on the low end – that were the most visceral concern animating American resistance. Wealthy and poor folk alike (especially those who made their living at sea or on the docks) saw this constitutional issue as a real threat once customs enforcement intensified during and after the French and Indian War. Thus, when the Stamp Act Congress met in 1765 to petition the king to repeal both the Sugar and Stamp Acts as unconstitutional, it issued a list of grievances over the loss of American liberties. Chief among these was the right to a trial by jury.

Studying the American Revolution Through a Constitutional Lens

When historians examine the imperial reforms of the 1760s as a mere financial proposition – tax measures designed to produce more revenues for a government in debt – then the colonial reaction seems disproportional, hysterical, and paranoid. But there is little reason to see the taxes as primarily financial. In fact, a large portion of the tax revenues generated in America were not directed to the imperial treasury to service the national debt. They were instead used in America to provide imperial officials there with independent salaries, establish Admiralty courts, and fund other measures designed to liberate imperial officials from the influence and oversight of provincial assemblies, magistrates, and juries. When the imperial taxes are understood as a constitutional proposition purposefully designed to upend generations of constitutional and legal precedent, change the structure of government in the empire (that is, change the imperial constitution), enhance the governing role of Parliament in the localities, and limit the role of local assemblies and local courts of law, it is then easier to understand the colonists' alarm and to see their resistance as proportional. Likewise, it explains why Americans of *all* walks of life saw the assemblies' fight as their own.

When students try to understand the nature and purpose of American resistance, therefore, they must first determine the nature and purpose of the imperial reforms of the 1760s – whether they were primarily financial or constitutional measures. The evidence indicates clearly that for contemporaries – both British and American – the bone of contention between Parliament and colonial assemblies was not financial (that is, the level of taxation), but whether the British empire ought to be an empire governed from the center or one in which local communities governed themselves. Not only was this apparent in colonists' visceral outrage over the ongoing sidelining of American juries in the 1760s, but it was explicitly stated by both sides during the Stamp Act Crisis.

In 1765, when colonial assemblies and the Sons of Liberty sprang into action to resist Parliament's newly enacted Stamp Act, Benjamin Franklin happened to be in Britain, serving as Pennsylvania's agent in London. He testified before the House of Commons, explaining to members of Parliament that the financial burden – how high or low the tax was – was not the issue that animated Americans against the Stamp Act. Rather, it was being taxed by a legislature that was not their own. American colonists had their own legislatures, Franklin stressed, and they would not submit to laws legislated to them by a legislature in which they were not represented. Consequently, when Franklin offered Parliament a solution, he did not suggest a financial remedy (lowering or eliminating the tax) but a constitutional solution: allowing the American colonies actual representation in Parliament. This would give colonists a voice in Parliamentary taxation over them, thus solving the constitutional crisis.

Americans shared Franklin's analysis, but not his solution. When Pennsylvanians caught wind of Franklin's proposal, a group of Philadelphia merchants warned him "to beware of any measure that might extend to us seats in the [House of] Commons." This is yet another indication that when Americans chanted "no taxation without representation," they were not clamoring for representation in Parliament. They were instead demanding a continuation of the status quo – a salutary-neglect empire in which local communities governed (and taxed) themselves through their local legislatures. Just as protesters in Britain in the 1760s demanded greater and better representation in their own legislature – Parliament – as a solution to unaccountable government, so too did American colonists insist on being represented in *their* legislatures. Britons on both sides of the Atlantic, therefore, understood government by consent similarly. Both believed that government by consent demanded a legislature that was both representative and local; one that was responsive to constituents through elections and soft influence, and which also reflected their particular circumstances, concerns, interests, and values.

Like the colonists, members of Parliament understood that the true bone of contention regarding the Stamp Act was constitutional. This is why Parliament enacted a Declaratory Act when it repealed the Stamp Act. The Declaratory Act asserted that Parliament did have the authority to tax the colonists directly if and when it chose to do so.[8] While political considerations led the British government to withdraw the Stamp Act at that time, Parliament and the ministry clarified through the Declaratory Act that they were nevertheless committed to the governing principle behind the Stamp Act. The Declaratory Act was an explicit assertion about the imperial constitution – it explained that Parliament had supreme and direct jurisdiction throughout the empire, and thus had the authority to directly govern (and tax) British subjects in the colonies. It expressed in words what the Stamp Act had indicated in deeds.

This remained the heart of the ongoing clashes between Parliament and the assemblies over the Townshend duties (1767–1770), Tea Act (1773), Coercive Acts (1774), and Quebec Act (1774). Indeed, the Coercive Acts put into effect the twin constitutional principles outlined in the Declaratory Act – Parliament's universal jurisdiction throughout the Empire, and Parliament's supremacy over all other governing authorities in Britain and the Empire. Only during the fourth year of the War of American Independence (1778), did Britain agree to back down from these twin principles and to accept the colonists' understanding of the imperial constitution. Fearing that France would join the war on the American side after the battle of Saratoga, the British government offered the Americans terms for a peace settlement. In this offer, the British proposed returning to the constitutional status quo of 1763, before the enactment of the Sugar Act and all the imperial reforms that followed, by which Parliament had tried to shift the center of administrative power from local governments, courts, and juries to the central government in London.

This peace offer indicates that both sides understood – before the war and during the war – that the conflict was not a tax revolt or a war of national liberation, but a constitutional crisis. Both sides understood quite well what the other side wanted and why – Parliament was indeed constructing a novel and modern imperial constitution, while Americans were defending the old salutary-neglect constitution against what they saw as a lawless government. That the British government understood this is evident from both the Declaratory Act (1766) and the peace offer of 1778. Further evidence is the 1773 correspondence between Britain's colonial secretary Lord Dartmouth (William Legge) and the Massachusetts assembly, following the assembly's rejection of Parliament's authority to enact laws to regulate life within Massachusetts. The speaker of the Massachusetts House informed Dartmouth

---

8 If Parliament had such taxing powers, it had never exercised them. It is more likely that Parliament was making the case that it should have them.

that what the colonists sought was to bring matters "to the general state in which they stood at the conclusion of the late war" – that is, a return to the constitutional arrangement that existed in 1763.

Parliament had refused to reestablish salutary neglect as the constitutional framework for governing the empire during the crises that followed the Sugar Act, Stamp Act, Townshend duties, and Coercive Acts. Britain refused to do so even after the war broke out (rejecting the American Olive Branch Petition of 1775), but it relented – too late – when faced with the prospect of losing the war in 1778 against a Franco-American alliance.

The Tea Act

The immediate spark for the war – the Tea Act of 1773 – best illustrates the constitutional nature of the contest between colonies and mother country. Contrary to popular opinion, the Tea Act did not increase the tax on tea. Rather, it was a tax exemption that dramatically *lowered* the price of tea for American consumers. Parliament enacted the law as part of its effort to help the British East India Company avoid bankruptcy. The East India Company was a private company, but the government feared that its downfall would collapse financial markets and perhaps the British economy more broadly. The British Treasury therefore lent the East India Company £1.5 million to provide it with immediate financial relief, while Parliament sought to boost the Company's revenues by granting it a tax exemption on all tea imported into Britain and its colonies. This tax break, it was hoped, would allow the East India Company to corner the market on tea by underselling all other tea importers, who were still required to pay the high customs duties on imported tea.

It is easy to understand why American merchants – specifically the relatively small circle of those importing or smuggling tea – resented and opposed the Tea Act. The Tea Act enabled their main competitor, the British East India Company, to sell tea at a price that they could not match.[9] Their complaint was clearly an economic one. But the Tea Act sparked resentment among a much broader crowd than these merchants. Indeed, it was opposed by the general population of consumers who received a direct economic *benefit* from the Tea Act, in the form of cheaper tea. *Their* complaint was clearly not economic. Instead, they complained of corruption, an issue that

---

9 Unlike legal importers, smugglers did not pay the import duties. However, their operating costs were higher than that of legal importers, such as the East India Company. Their ships' hulls were smaller for added speed and maneuverability, they mounted cannons (at the expense of cargo) for self-defense, and they had to pay or bribe informants, local officials, and various associates for their services.

fit seamlessly into the decade-long debate on the imperial constitution, centralization, consent, and arbitrary power.

It was apparent to all that this was a case of a large company taking advantage of its directors' familial, social, and business ties with influential members of Parliament and the Court to receive a government bailout at taxpayers' expense. Moreover, the government loan transformed the British government into a large stakeholder in the East India Company. This made the exclusive tax break the company received from Parliament all the more egregious – by taxing the East India Company's competitors, Parliament granted its state-owned trading company a *de facto* monopoly over the entire tea trade in the Empire. Americans' anger about corruption in high places was framed by their preexisting constitutional distress regarding local liberty versus centralized power. Like the Revenue Acts, the Tea Act illustrated to colonists that Britain was using *its* local legislature (Parliament), in which the colonists were not represented, to enact laws that reshaped their local economies without their consent.

The Coercive Acts

The Tea Act thus triggered protests, a campaign to boycott East India Company tea, efforts to prevent East India Company ships from docking, and eventually an attack on a Company ship whose tea cargo was then dumped into the Boston harbor (December 16, 1773). The response to the Boston Tea Party came in the form of the Coercive Acts (1774), labeled by Americans the "Intolerable Acts." The Coercive Acts suspended the charter of Massachusetts, empowered the royal governor to replace elected officials with men appointed by himself, dissolved the Massachusetts legislature, disallowed most public meetings (including town meetings), required Massachusetts to finance the construction of barracks for troops in the city, established martial law, allowed royal officials facing trial in Massachusetts to transfer the venue to Britain, and closed the Boston harbor, which put most of Boston out of work. All these measures were to stay in force at least until the East India Company received compensation for the losses it had incurred.

These acts reprised all the perceived offenses against colonists' liberties from the previous decade – the use of soldiers as police, the curtailment of institutions of local self-government (such as legislatures, courts, and juries), insulating imperial officials from oversight by colonial authorities, enacting stifling economic regulations in the colonies, and using government force to help a well-connected company. Indeed, the Coercive Acts established in practice the constitutional principle that the Declaratory Act had stated in theory – that the British government governed the colonies directly, and that colonists governed themselves only when and to the extent Parliament permitted.

The Quebec Act

Moreover, along with the Coercive Act, Parliament also enacted the Quebec Act. It was not itself a response to the Boston Tea Party, but colonists saw it as part and parcel of the Intolerable Acts. The Quebec Act was, in essence, the first written constitution for a British colony. Crafted and enacted by Parliament, it outlined the structure of the colony's government, restored French civil law in Quebec, protected the legal privileges of the Catholic Church, afforded Catholics religious freedom, and opened political offices to them. As well, it extended Quebec's boundaries to include the Ohio Valley, thus frustrating the western territorial aspirations of both Virginia and Pennsylvania, two of the most populous and influential colonies in British America.

Historians often present Americans' outrage over the Quebec Act as reflecting paranoid, xenophobic, and anti-Catholic resentment over the various gifts the act bestowed on their former enemies in Canada. But when one examines what colonial authorities themselves had to say about the Quebec Act, their opposition emerges as more coherent and transparent. Certainly, Americans were generally wary of the French and of Catholicism, but the complaint that circulated about the Quebec Act did not focus on the French settlers there, but on Parliament and the imperial constitution. The critical component of the Quebec Act that caught the attention of American commentators was that Quebec was to be governed without a legislature, by a governor and an unelected council. In this respect, it resembled the Dominion of New England.

Those already concerned and agitated by the imperial reforms of the previous decade saw Quebec, as constituted by Parliament in the Quebec Act, as Britain's model colony. They understood the Quebec constitution as a blueprint for what Parliament was hoping to accomplish in colonial administration more generally. Indeed, the act gave credence to the Sons of Liberty's accusations that Parliament had long conspired to emasculate and sideline American assemblies, extend Parliament's jurisdiction over the colonies, and strengthen direct royal governance within them. At a time when the ideological trend on both sides of the British Atlantic was toward greater transparency and accountability in government, Parliament initiated multiple reforms that made colonial governments and courts more opaque and unaccountable to colonial constituents, and more transparent and accountable to Parliament.

The Quebec Act was received with great alarm and a grave sense of urgency because of its timing, in conjunction with the Coercive Acts in Massachusetts. It seemed that after a decade of tinkering with half measures that curtailed local governance and oversight over imperial officials, Parliament was finally acting on its decade-long conspiracy to fundamentally transform America – by legislation in Quebec, and by brute force in Massachusetts. The events in Massachusetts and Quebec seemed to indicate that Parliament had tired of debating the colonists over jurisdiction, law, and the imperial constitution; it was instead pressing ahead and forcing its will on them. It was that fear, and that urgency, that led sober men of property and standing into a rebellion that was extremely dangerous to their and their families' wealth, position, and lives.

Deconstructing the Timing of the Imperial Reform Movement

As suggested in the section "Studying the American Revolution Through a Constitutional Lens," when historians analyze the imperial reforms of the 1760s as mere financial schemes to generate more revenues for the British treasury, colonial resistance appears paranoid and excessive. Similarly, when the Quebec Act is examined merely as an internal reform in Canada (or a territorial land grab in the Ohio Valley), the vehement response from the 13 colonies to the south is perplexing, and thus often attributed to irrational factors such as xenophobia and religious bigotry. But when these imperial reforms are understood as they were understood by contemporaries – both imperial reformers and colonists – then the resistance becomes intelligible. It was an effort to preserve the old constitutional order (salutary neglect) against a purposeful effort to transform the empire from a loose confederation of self-governing polities under a common king to an imperial state governed by the British government.

As to why Britain launched this reform movement after the Seven Years War, opinions differ. Some observe that the war directed the attention of frustrated imperial administrators to the consequences of the empire's salutary-neglect governing principles. Specifically, they were frustrated by the weakness of colonial governors vis-à-vis local assemblies, local courts, local juries, and local crowds. The result of this weakness was that naval blockades were less effective, mobilization for campaigns was slow and inefficient, and the army's operating costs were exceptionally high. In time, they got higher still as the British treasury subsidzed a growing share of the colonies' military expenditures. Victory thus came at a cost of a ballooning national debt.

Other scholars point out that the impulse to centralize imperial bureaucracies actually preceded the French and Indian War. They identify this impulse, for example, in the 1733 Molasses Act and the 1729 White Pines Act, which gave the king direct monopoly over the logging of all white pines in British America, even on private land. Both acts met with colonial resistance and went unheeded and mostly unenforced, but they reveal an emerging managerial mindset in Whitehall (the site of Britain's government offices in London) and in Parliament. They suggest that the postwar imperial reforms had their origins in prewar ideas about imperial governance, rather than in the war debt; they were managerial, rather than strictly financial.

The British Empire was unconventional – it did not look or operate like the Spanish and French empires, nor like the historical empires of the classical era. Like Charles I and James II before them, British imperial administrators in the eighteenth century were envious of French governance, believing that the French administered their empire more effectively than the British. Fears of French encirclement in America during the 1750s only intensified concern over the strength of French imperial governance. Increasingly, members of both Parliament and the Court saw their quirky salutary-neglect empire as clumsy, archaic, and inefficient by comparison. Consequently, a new, more modern, professional, and centralized bureaucratic culture took form in Whitehall in the mid-eighteenth century, before the French and Indian War. When this new managerial mentality was finally coupled with enforcement, thanks to the naval and military manpower brought to America during the war, it started producing actual results, triggering vehement and violent resistance.[10]

A third factor that scholars use to explain the timing of the imperial reform movement is that after the war, Britain found itself as sovereign of not only the older settler colonies, but also of conquered peoples in Canada, the trans-Appalachian West, Florida, the West Indies, the African coast, and India. This was a novel challenge for Britons and their government, who quickly recognized that retaining control of these territories and peoples required a different kind of governing system for the empire. Salutary neglect and local self-government was a workable approach to governing an empire populated by patriotic and willing subjects in the settler colonies; it was a foolhardy approach to governing conquered populations who shared with their new rulers neither mutual affection nor common language, culture, religion, and interests. Britain therefore governed its newly conquered peoples through a more conventional imperial model. This new model simultaneously enhanced Parliament's role in the British state and allowed Britain to hold and govern its new imperial possessions. However, it also addressed longstanding frustrations of the Board of Trade and other imperial administrators regarding the old settler colonies. Indeed, the settlers in the original colonies immediately felt the effect of this shift toward a new imperial model. In the Royal Proclamation of 1763, the

---

10 This explanation acknowledges that the national debt placed financial pressures on Parliament after the French and Indian War to shore up the debt with new tax revenues. But this solution to the debt problem was possible only because the ideological and constitutional framework for such taxing authority had been constructed in imperial circles in the 1740s and 1750s. For example, in the 1740s Parliament debated bills aiming to make royal instructions law in the colonies. While these measures failed to gain a majority in the House of Commons, they enjoyed support elsewhere in the government. Colonial assemblies vehemently opposed them, charging that they violated the constitutions of both Britain and the empire, and clashed with the ancient right of Englishmen to be governed by laws that they themselves – through representative assemblies – enacted.

Crown positioned itself not as the ally and champion of British settlers in the American colonies, but as a neutral arbitrator between two sets of subjects of equal standing vis-à-vis Britain. From that point on, it became increasingly apparent to settlers that imperial administrators started to perceive Anglo-Americans as one of the many populations that they ruled abroad.

The Constitutional Trajectories of England, the British Empire, and the United States

While scholars differ on the roots of the imperial reform movement, its contours are clear. The jurisdictional claims made by Parliament in the 1766 Declaratory Act and the 1774 Coercive Acts were breathtakingly broad. When James II had claimed such powers and jurisdictions in America, during the era of the Dominion of New England (1686–1688), he triggered ideological, constitutional, and political resentment, which eventually led to the overthrow of Governor Andros's regime and the restoration of salutary neglect as the empire's structural constitution and governing philosophy. When Parliament did so in the 1760s and 1770s, it produced a resistance movement that was similar to that of 1688 in both sensibilities and ends. These two peaks of imperial centralization reveal the transformation in Parliament's role in the empire during the intervening 80 years. Whereas James II centralized imperial administration through royal prerogative (the king's ancient authority as sovereign in the provinces), Parliament did so through ordinary legislation. The notion that Parliament had jurisdiction beyond Britain, wielding power over and above provincial legislatures, was a novelty. Indeed, it charts the gains Parliament had made against the Crown in the realms of sovereignty and jurisdiction since the Glorious Revolution. The colonists' constitutional claim that they were beyond Parliament's reach threatened this impressive and hard-won Parliamentary achievement. This explains Parliament's tenacity in the face of American resistance.

After the American Revolution, both sides carried forth with their constitutional projects. Parliament continued its centralizing reforms, and the Second British Empire (following the loss of the American colonies) functioned like a modern imperial state, one governed from the center, with provinces organized along the principles outlined in the Quebec Act. The American Revolutionists, meanwhile, carried out their backward-looking mission to restore the old salutary-neglect structure of the First British Empire. Following their victory in the war, they created a republic whose structure, or constitution, mirrored that of the British Empire before 1763 – a loose confederation of self-governing states under a weak central government. Moreover, to prevent their own central government from expanding its powers and jurisdictions as Parliament had done, Americans produced a written document that clearly articulated the constitution, or governing structure, of the new republic. Ratified by the Continental Congress and all 13 states, the Articles of Confederation had the force of law, thus cementing the primary accomplishment of military victory – self-government in each of the 13 states.

Questions for Discussion

1 What was the imperial constitution?
2 What explains Britain's increased interest and involvement in American affairs over the course of the eighteenth century?
3 The large national debt following the French and Indian War is often presented as the explanation for Britain's attempt to tighten and centralize imperial administration. What are the strengths and weaknesses of this assessment?
4 What explains intercolonial unity in 1774 and 1775, in the context of intercolonial discord during the imperial wars of the late-seventeenth and early-eighteenth centuries?
5 What did American elites in the assemblies want from Britain in 1774–1775? What, if anything, did "rank and file Americans" want from Britain? Why did common people in America support the elites? What made them care about high politics?
6 Were Americans paranoid or perceptive with regard to the Quebec Act?
7 Was there a difference in the attachment of Britons and Americans to the concept of government by consent? Did the two British populations have different ideas by the 1770s regarding the importance of consent, representation, accountability, and the like?

Further Readings

Anderson, F. (2005). *The War That Made America: A Short History of the French and Indian War*. Old Saybrook, Conn: Tantor Media.

Beattie, D.J. (1986). The adaptation of the British Army to Wilderness Warfare, 1755–1763. In: *Adapting to Conditions: War and Society in the Eighteenth Century* (ed. M. Ultee), 56–83. Alabama: University of Alabama Press.

Bilder, M. (2004). *The Transatlantic Constitution: Colonial Legal Culture and the Empire*. Cambridge: Harvard University Press.

Black, B. (1976). The constitution of empire: the case for the colonists. *University of Pennsylvania Law Review* 124: 1157–1211.

Breen, T.H. (May 1988). 'Baubles of Britain': the American and consumer revolutions of the eighteenth century. *Past and Present* 119: 73–104.

Bushman, R. (1984). *King and People in Provincial Massachusetts*. Chapel Hill: University of North Carolina Press.

Marshall, P.J. (2005). *The Making and Unmaking of Empires: Britain, India, and America c.1750–1783*. Oxford: Oxford University Press.

Pargellis, S.M.C. (1936). Braddock's defeat. *American Historical Review* 41: 253–269.

Pargellis, S.M.C. (1933). *Lord Loudoun in North America*. New Haven: Yale University Press.

Reid, J.P. (2004). *Rule of Law: The Jurisprudence of Liberty in the Seventeenth and Eighteenth Centuries*. DeKalb: Northern Illinois University Press.

Reid, J.P. (2005). *The Ancient Constitution and the Origins of Anglo-American Liberty*. DeKalb: Northern Illinois University Press.

Shy, J. (1965). *Toward Lexington: The Role of the British Army in the Coming of the American Revolution*. Princeton: Princeton University Press.

Truxes, T. (2008). *Defying Empire: Trading with the Enemy in Colonial New York*. New Haven: Yale University Press.

8

The War

Once the imperial government implemented the Coercive Acts, the Virginia assembly immediately declared its support for Massachusetts, other colonial legislatures followed suit, George Washington declared that the cause of Boston was the cause of America, and a variety of civic associations throughout the colonies (correspondence societies, public safety committees, fraternal lodges, and the like) began exchanging letters and issuing public condemnations of the "Intolerable Acts." Recalling the resistance they mounted to the Stamp Act, colonial legislatures sent delegates to Philadelphia to form a Continental Congress (September 1774). The First Continental Congress drew a list of grievances against Parliament and petitioned the king for relief. Early in 1775, Patriots in Massachusetts formed an ostensibly illegal provisional government (the Massachusetts Provincial Congress) and the British declared the colony to be in a state of rebellion. Accordingly, British authorities in Boston attempted to confiscate a cache of firearms and munitions in Concord, prompting "the shot heard round the world" on the Lexington Green (April 19, 1775).[1] Following the battles of Lexington and Concord, the 13 colonial assemblies formed the Second Continental Congress, which served them as a war council throughout the war.

Even after armed hostilities began in earnest – at Ticonderoga and Bunker Hill – the Continental Congress appealed to the king (in the Olive Branch

---

1 A similar gun-control measure was carried out in Virginia the following day (April 20, 1775), well before news of Lexington and Concord could reach Virginia. As in New England, Virginians responded with fear and outrage, prompting local militias to muster throughout the colony. The confiscation of colonists' munitions was already recommended by the British secretary of state for American affairs in October of 1774. The British government followed this up immediately by ordering an embargo on imports of guns and powder to America. Coming on the heels of the Sugar Act, Declaratory Act, Townshend Duties, Coercive Acts, and Quebec Act, these gun-control measures reconfirmed American fears that they were interpreting Parliament's imperial intentions correctly.

The Colonists' American Revolution: Preserving English Liberty, 1607–1783, First Edition. Guy Chet.
© 2020 John Wiley & Sons, Inc. Published 2020 by John Wiley & Sons, Inc.
Companion website: www.wiley.com/go/Chet/ColonistsAmericanRevolution

Petition) to avert a war by reining in Parliament's intrusive policies. Congress issued its Declaration of Independence a year later, once most Americans (and therefore also their delegates) came to understand that the king would not intercede on their behalf against Parliament. Thomas Paine's *Common Sense* (published January 1776) had a measurable effect in shaping public opinion in this regard, by explicitly tying the king to Parliament's policies and presenting him not as the protector of his American subjects, but as an accomplice to an abusive and predatory Parliament.

A Predictable, Rather than Miraculous, Victory

There are two conflicting views of the War of American Independence. Americans of the Revolutionary era believed they had won on the strength of overwhelming public support for the Patriot cause throughout the 13 rebellious colonies. By contrast, most historians in the twentieth century held that only 20–30% of Americans supported the Revolution. They thus painted the Revolutionists' victory as surprising, if not actually miraculous; a product of tremendous grit, guile, and social organization and control by a dedicated minority. Yet more recent scholarship is rehabilitating the original assessment of the war, presenting military victory as foreseeable and conventional; a product of the rebels' decisive manpower advantage. These findings are crucial for understanding the war militarily, but they also shed light on the nature of the Revolution itself. Indeed, the Revolution's military history offers critical insights into its social and political history. The fact that Patriot support ran so deep and wide – over 50% in every state, and as high as 70% in some – indicates that Revolutionists' ideology and constitutional beliefs were not radical, but well within the mainstream of Anglo-American thought.

Even before France entered the war, forcing the British to deploy forces in Europe and the West Indies, Patriots enjoyed a clear manpower advantage – well above two to one – in the American theater of operations. This represented a manpower crisis for the British because their military plans in each and every region hinged on their expectation to recruit provincial troops to support British regulars, as they had done in the French and Indian War. Whereas the rebels regularly replenished their forces after costly battles and campaigns, British manpower losses – even in uneventful or successful campaigns – had lasting detrimental effects.

British commanders have been criticized by generations of mystified military historians for being overly cautious during the American War. Yet this cautious demeanor becomes understandable in the context of broad public support for the Revolution, weak Loyalist support, and the crippling manpower deficiencies the British encountered. Britain's inability to draw on American military manpower repeatedly hampered its logistical and tactical operations from the very beginning of the war. Tactical defeats such as Saratoga (1777), Kings Mountain (1780), and Yorktown (1781), and the expansion of the war to Europe and the Caribbean (1778–1783), merely exacerbated this manpower crunch; they did not create it.

By the same token, the Americans' overwhelming advantage in manpower reserves explains why they chose to fight a conventional war against Britain, rather than adopt guerrilla tactics, which are widely understood as the weapon of the weak. The war thus started and ended as a conventional eighteenth-century war of attrition, which favored the side with greater manpower resources. The British lost this contest because of logistical, financial, and political exhaustion, rather than by losing major battles.

Early Engagements

Following the battles of Lexington and Concord, many Patriots had great faith that colonial militia could stand up to British regulars as they had done on the Lexington road. Following the English tradition, Patriot pamphleteers, editorialists, and recruiters called on Americans to organize and dedicate themselves for military service, since a militia of free men was the natural weapon and true protector of a free society. The Massachusetts provisional government asked many of the militiamen that rose up in rebellion on April 19 to stay armed and ready. By the end of April, a rebel camp of over 10 000 men from Massachusetts, Connecticut, and New Hampshire encamped outside Boston, holding General Thomas Gage and his army captive in the city. The commander of the New England army, Artemas Ward, did not insist on military formalities and camp protocols. Discipline was lax, with citizen-soldiers coming and going from camp at will, and taking orders casually, if at all.

Many Patriots, and especially the troops themselves, did not find this disorderly conduct troubling. Indeed, they reveled in the contrast between themselves and British regulars, stressing that the joyous freedom that Patriot troops were living in their camps was emblematic of the liberty they were fighting to preserve in their civic lives. Moreover, they held that even militarily, liberty was more energetic than disciplined force. The successful Patriot attack on Fort Ticonderoga (May 10, 1775) – an attempt to capture artillery pieces for the New England army besieging Boston – reinforced this belief. Undermanned and caught by surprise, the fort's defenders offered no resistance whatsoever.

This optimism faded quickly after the Battle of Bunker Hill (June 17, 1775), one of the bloodiest battles of the entire war. By launching frontal assaults on the fortified Patriot positions, rather than flanking them, the British lost 1054 men (40% of the force). The Patriots lost 411 men (30% of their force). Both sides were stung by the fierce action that day, recognizing the need for a better approach in future engagements.

Building the Continental Army

On the British side, William Howe replaced Gage as commander in chief of British forces in America in the fall of 1775. He decided that if a war was to be fought in earnest, Boston – the heart of the rebellion – was the wrong location for it. Instead, he targeted New York City. Taking New York would allow him to capture the Hudson River Valley, thus cutting off the rebellious New England colonies from the remaining colonies, which he and most British policymakers assumed were loyal, and would provide his army with both men and provisions. Howe thus evacuated Boston, relocating his army to Halifax, Nova Scotia (March 17, 1776). By August, he transported his army of 10 000 to Staten Island, where he rendezvoused with 20 000 more troops arriving from Britain. Howe's large army was supported by a naval fleet of 70 vessels and 13 000 sailors, commanded by Howe's brother, Admiral Richard Howe.

On the rebel side, the Second Continental Congress adopted the citizens' army around Boston as its own in June 1775, voting to raise additional companies from New York, Pennsylvania, Maryland, and Virginia. This transformed the New England army into the Continental Army, which was placed under the command of George Washington. Washington owed his post to the support of influential New Englanders in Congress, who wanted a southern commander in chief (preferably a Virginian) in order to generate interregional support for what had started out as a local rebellion. Congress also created a central officer corps for the new army – four major generals and eight brigadier generals.[2]

Washington's first order of business was to transform the citizen soldiers encamped around Boston into a professional army that could contend with the soldiery of the British Army. Patriot troops' morale was already flagging after their defeat at Bunker Hill, and as morale declined, desertions rose. Washington was certain that if he had to rely on the type of army that fought at Lexington, Concord, Ticonderoga, and Bunker Hill – an army of farmers and artisans – he would eventually find himself alone on the battlefield. Such an army, he feared, would not be able to absorb more blows like the one it took at the Battle of Bunker Hill. Washington understood from the start that the rebellion would last only as long as the army would last. And if the army was to survive, it would have to be placed on a professional footing, since, in Washington's words, "to place any dependence upon militia is assuredly resting upon a broken staff."

Washington was dismayed by what he found when he arrived in Massachusetts to take command of his army (July 1775). The camp was "exceedingly dirty and nasty," officers mingled with their troops, and the men came and went as they

---

2 Because most of the troops were from New England, most of these 12 top officers were New Englanders and New Yorkers, but there were also 2 Virginians (Charles Lee and Horatio Gates), in addition to Washington.

pleased and did not take kindly to orders, discipline, and punishment. Washington began his command by cleaning the camp and ending the fraternization and informalities between the officers and the men. Whereas sleeping on watch, public drunkenness, stealing food, and the like were treated with mild rebukes beforehand, under Washington they were treated with courts martial and floggings.

This was a precarious and delicate undertaking, since Washington and his officers could not prevent the men from simply leaving if they felt oppressed by their officers. Moreover, Washington was sensitive to the wariness of New Englanders regarding their army being taken over by a general who was not one of their own. He therefore had to be circumspect and delicate about punishments, rewards, demotions, and promotions in order to avoid a mutiny, led by Massachusetts officers, against the Virginian commander that the Continental Congress imposed on New England.

American and British Strategies for Victory

Washington's strategy for the war took into account the poor soldiery of his men, the complete absence of an American navy, and the logistical difficulties the British faced when fighting in America. He doubted his men's ability to defeat the British on the battlefield, but hoped that they could do well enough to remain in the field and draw the war out. As a student of early-modern warfare, he understood that wars are primarily contests of administration and attrition, and that in a long war, the rebels could exhaust British logistics, finances, diplomacy, and political will.

General Howe likewise understood from the start that although Britain was much stronger and richer, many of its advantages were diminished in the American theater. In fact, already in 1774, when Parliament enacted the Coercive Acts, Howe warned Lord George Germain, the secretary for American affairs in London, that Britain would need to send 14 000 regular troops to saturate New England in order to prevent a general uprising. Otherwise, he cautioned, a rebellion might break out that would necessitate many more than 14 000 men to suppress. In the summer of 1776, when he landed in New York with 30 000 men, Howe was hoping and planning for a short war; one in which decisive early victories in the field might convince Americans to come to their senses, lay down their arms, and enjoy peace and prosperity as a part of the British Empire.

Howe had clear plans to capture the Hudson Valley and thus isolate New England to the east. He did not have a clear determination, however, regarding the level of military intensity he would utilize in his campaign. Germain advocated a scorched-earth policy with the paramount goal being a quick entrapment or destruction of Washington's army by forcing Washington to try to stop this ongoing violence against American towns, farms, and civilians. Germain held that because there was no center to the rebellion, it would persist as long as the main rebel force remained in the field. Thus, he advocated winning the war militarily first, and worrying about rebuilding the bonds of friendship and loyalty later on.

The Howe brothers, by contrast, felt that a scorched-earth policy, even if successful militarily, would only feed anti-British sentiment in America, and would thus necessitate stationing an army of occupation there to prevent future unrest. Moreover, like many in England, they were convinced that the rebellion was carried forth by a vocal minority and that there was a silent Loyalist majority forced to remain silent due to Patriot violence and intimidation. Thus, the Howes wanted to use their army and fleet gently, to impress and intimidate the Americans, rather than to terrorize them, burn their farms, seize their crops and livestock, and destroy their infrastructure. They considered the American War to be a war over the hearts and minds of Americans, and did not want to lend credence to Patriot propaganda about British tyranny. Indeed, the Howes were appointed by the Crown to act as peace commissioners once the rebels surrendered. So they were not simply concerned, as was Germain, with winning the war; they were thinking also about the war's impact on postwar relations.

The New York Campaign (1776)

By the time the Howe brothers arrived in New York (August 1776), the Declaration of Independence had already been signed, published, and disseminated, leading to a swell in the number of volunteers filling the ranks from the middle and northern states, excited about the prospect of recreating victories like Concord and Ticonderoga. At this point, the American army in New York numbered 28 000. Virtually all were untrained militiamen or half-trained Continentals. The army had no core of trained, experienced soldiers. Additionally, the army had no naval support whatsoever, allowing Howe to land his army wherever he chose.

In the battle that followed (the Battle of Brooklyn Heights, or Battle of Long Island), Howe's army attacked the American line both frontally and on its flank. The Americans were routed (losing over 1500 casualties) and pinned with their backs to the East River. At this desperate point, Admiral Richard Howe failed to sail into the East River to trap Washington's army between his fleet and his brother's army. And instead of assailing this battered and wounded army, General William Howe started preparations for a siege.

Why the Howes did not take this opportunity – the best chance Britain had during the war to do irreparable damage to rebel forces – is still a subject of speculation. Some argue that unfavorable winds prevented Admiral Howe from entering the East River, while others suggest it was a simple lapse of

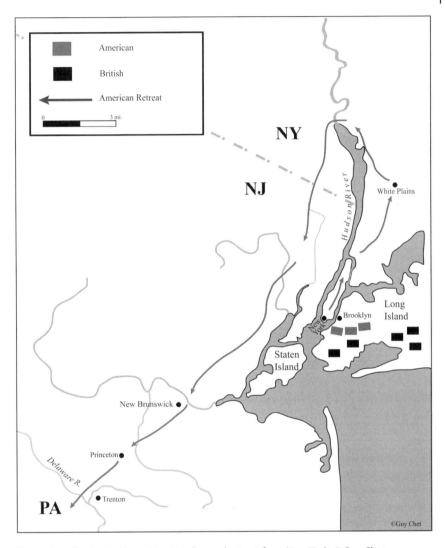

Figure 8.1 The Battle of Brooklyn Heights and retreat from New York. © Guy Chet.

judgment. Some claim that General Howe was cautious by nature and constantly feared that he did not have sufficient manpower to accomplish his mission. Others defend Howe, pointing out that he followed the accepted European practice, as well as the lesson he himself learned as an officer at the Battle of Bunker Hill. Considering his limited manpower, he chose not to risk a frontal assault against entrenched forces. After all, as peace commissioner, Howe was interested in de-escalating the war by persuading the colonists that his army was unstoppable, that resistance was futile, and that surrender was the only responsible solution. A single tactical defeat at the hands of Washington would make this scenario impossible, forcing the British to wage multiple campaigns in America. Moreover, even a successful assault on Washington's army spelled danger for Howe – a massacre of Washington's men in Brooklyn threatened to inflame Americans further, converting Loyalists in the middle and southern colonies into Patriots. Howe therefore chose to besiege the Americans and force a surrender over time, without losing British troops, without risking defeat, and without annihilating the rebel army.

After quickly considering his dire position, Washington used the cover of night to spirit his army out of Long Island, crossing the East River to Manhattan, taking advantage of Richard Howe's failure to take command of the river. In the following weeks and months, Howe slowly and cautiously pursued Washington north through Manhattan and the Hudson River Valley, and then southward through New Jersey, inflicting casualties and taking captives throughout.

As he was chased through New Jersey, Washington (through Congress) called on New Jersey militia to turn out in force to support the army's retreat by slowing down Howe's columns, but the numbers that materialized were inconsequential and could not impede Howe. Washington eventually managed to escape Howe by crossing the Delaware River into Pennsylvania (December 1776). His army confiscated all the boats in the area, preventing Howe's army from crossing the river in pursuit.

Washington's Crossing of the Delaware: Salvaging the 1776 Campaign

The Battle of Brooklyn Heights and the long dismal retreat that followed were important in shaping Washington as a general. They instilled in him fear and caution; he never again allowed himself to be drawn into such a strategically risky situation. By the same token, the New York campaign signaled to Americans that the war would not feature a reprise of Lexington and Concord. The assumption that armed citizens could outfight professional troops evaporated quickly during the summer and fall of 1776. Also evaporating was Washington's army. The rate of desertion spiked in the winter of 1776–1777, with enlistments for 1777 slowing to a trickle.

When the chase ended at the banks of the Delaware River, Howe set up winter quarters for his army, concluding that the rebellion, like the Continental Army itself, was in an advanced state of disintegration. What was left to do the following campaigning season was to mop up remaining enemy concentrations and negotiate peace. Washington shared that assessment. His troops were leaving him, and if December 31 – the end of his troops' enlistment contracts – arrived before the army claimed a victory of sorts to show that it was still active and viable, no Continentals would renew their contracts, no new recruits would volunteer for service, the army would be gone, and the rebellion over. And Washington himself would be captured, hanged, and his family's property confiscated.

Washington had already burned his bridges behind him, as did the leaders of the rebellion in Congress and in the states. He was thus forced into an aggressive act, now that the rebellion seemed fated for failure. Desperate for some show of strength, even a small tactical victory, Washington planned a three-pronged Christmas-night attack across the Delaware against the British forces in Trenton, New Jersey. The British camp was left unfortified on the assumption that the year's hostilities had ended, with both armies in winter quarters.

Washington's elaborate plan did not come to pass, as only one of his three forces (2400 men, under Washington himself) managed to cross the river. The American attack surprised the 1500 defenders, who offered a brief resistance before surrendering to Washington. On December 30, Washington again crossed into New Jersey, skirmishing inconclusively with General Charles Cornwallis near Trenton. On January 3, 1777, he surprised the British garrison at Princeton, notching another small tactical victory to halt or reverse the public-relations effect of his long retreat from New York.

This burst of military activity at the turn of the new year was of limited operational significance, but it was crucial for troop morale and for enlistments for the 1777 campaigning season. During the winter, his army dwindled to roughly 3000 men, but by May, it expanded to roughly 10000. As important, Washington's winter skirmishes near Trenton and Princeton restored public faith in the war effort after a dispiriting summer and fall. They therefore put an end to discussions in the army and in Congress about replacing Washington with another general. Throughout the rest of the war, Washington repeated this course of action. Avoiding large battles with the British, he and his generals struck occasionally, when numbers or conditions were in their favor. In doing so, they not only inflicted material and manpower losses on the British – convincing the British government and public that the war would last years longer and require additional sacrifices from them – but also demonstrated the army's vitality and reach to Americans, both Patriots and Loyalists.

Howe's New Strategy: The Philadelphia Campaign (1777)

The British plan for the war – taking control of the Hudson River Valley and cutting off New England – was designed to prevent a long war. Lord George Germain's plan for the 1777 campaign called for General John Burgoyne to descend from Canada along the Hudson, linking up with Howe, who would ascend from New York City. But Howe lost faith that this strategy could prevent a long war at that stage; he no longer believed that the rebellion was localized primarily in New England. He therefore abandoned the original strategy and made one last attempt to win the war quickly. What he hoped to do was to recreate the Battle of Brooklyn Heights, setting up a large-scale battle that would (this time around) destroy the American Army and thus win the war. To draw Washington into such a battle for a second time, Howe moved 15 000 men (by sea, to avoid having to deal with Washington's skirmishers on land) from New York City to Philadelphia, the seat of the rebel government. His hope was to compel Washington to defend his capital city and the Continental Congress itself.

Washington was reluctant to take the bait this time, but he had reason to try to impress Congress by responding to Howe's challenge. Earlier that summer, Congress replaced General Philip Schuyler with Horatio Gates as commander of the Northern Department (that is, the New England theater of operations). Gates, a commoner who had risen to the rank of major in the British army before settling in America, was a rising star among Patriots. Washington doubtless knew that some in Congress were critical of his own generalship and open to the idea of replacing him. Moreover, when Howe advanced toward Philadelphia, leaving Burgoyne unsupported along the Hudson, Washington predicted that New Englanders would turn out in force against Burgoyne. Knowing the logistical difficulties Burgoyne faced, Washington expected Gates to do well on that front. He did not want Congressmen to see him allowing the British to occupy the capital unopposed, while Gates was fending them off in New York.

Washington therefore dutifully arrived at Philadelphia with 11 000 troops to block Howe's access to the city. However, when Howe flanked his line – as he had done at Brooklyn Heights the year before – Washington withdrew his army to avoid being routed or trapped. The American defeat at the Battle of Brandywine Creek (September 11, 1777) allowed Howe to take Philadelphia later that month. The fall of Philadelphia and Congress's flight from the city were troubling developments. They put in jeopardy strenuous American efforts to secure a military alliance with France. And given Gates's success and impending victory in Saratoga, the fall of Philadelphia reignited the murmuring campaign against Washington in both the army and Congress. Indeed, at the height of Gates's popularity, following his victories in Saratoga, he started corresponding directly with Congress, rather than reporting to Washington, his commanding officer. For both these reasons – the diplomatic efforts with France and his own standing in the army – Washington felt compelled to respond to the occupation of Philadelphia. Instead of risking another major confrontation with the strength of Howe's army, however, Washington nibbled at its edges, attacking a British force in Germantown, just north of Philadelphia (October 4, 1777). Although the Americans surprised the British, the defenders organized themselves and were able to drive the Americans off, claiming 650 casualties and 400 captives (British casualties came to 520).

After the embarrassments of Brandywine and Germantown, Washington faced tremendous pressure to act. Facing growing criticism in Congress and in occupied Philadelphia for mismanaging the army and the campaign, he ordered Nathanael Greene – against the advice of his generals, in a council of war – to attack a large British force under Cornwallis. Greene's response convinced Washington to rescind the order:

> [The] Enemy so situated as to be very difficult to approach, and [...] superior to us in Numbers. Under these Disadvantages – Your Excellency has the choice of but two things, to fight the Enemy without the least Prospect of Success [...] or remain inactive & be subject to the Censure of an ignorant & impatient populace. In [pursuing an attack] you may make a bad matter worse and [...] stand condemned [...] by all military Gentlemen of Experience; in [inaction] you [...] give your Country an opportunity to [build up its army for future campaigns] & also act upon such military Principles as will justify you to the best Judges in the present day, & to all future Generations. [...] The Cause is too important to [...] sport away upon unmilitary Principles.[3]

Washington was disappointed by his two failures outside Philadelphia, but he saved his army from destruction, and with the attack on Germantown, he demonstrated – to Howe and the British government, to American audiences, and to French observers – that the defeat at Brandywine Creek did not disperse or cripple his army. Indeed, his action in Germantown was instrumental to Gates's Saratoga victory, which is largely credited for drawing France into the war. The reason Gates and Benedict Arnold could operate freely to the south of Burgoyne's army in Saratoga was that were no British forces advancing northward up the Hudson, as Germain had originally planned. In early October, a force of 4000 British troops headed north from New York to relieve Burgoyne, but following the Battle of Germantown, it was diverted to Philadelphia to assist Howe instead.

American operations in New York and Philadelphia convinced the French royal government that the war offered France an opportunity to exacerbate and take advantage of Britain's military distress. The Franco-American alliance (1778–1783) broke the British blockade of North America and provided the United States government with an infusion of cash, supplies, and troops. Moreover, it was the French navy that was responsible for the British surrender at Yorktown in 1781.

Recognizing the strategic importance of the French alliance, Lord North's government enacted the Taxation of Colonies Act, by which Parliament

---

3 Letter to George Washington from Major General Nathanael Greene, November 24, 1777.

committed to refrain from raising revenues from the colonies through taxes, duties, or assessments. With this promise in hand, Britain approached Congress with a peace plan, offering a return to the constitutional condition of 1763 – that is, to turn back the clock and undo the constitutional innovations in the Sugar Act, Stamp Act, Declaratory Act, Townshend duties, Tea Act, and Coercive Acts. But given the expanding circle of violence and anger during the previous three years, and armed with the French alliance, Congress declined to negotiate before all British forces withdrew from the rebellious states. The war thus continued unabated.

When Howe failed to end the war in Philadelphia, he felt that the war could not be won and resigned his command. He was succeeded as commander in chief by General Henry Clinton. Having failed to muster sufficient local support in New England in 1775–1776, and in New Jersey and Pennsylvania in 1777, Clinton launched a southern campaign, believing that Loyalist support was stronger in the South. Instead of trying to capture or destroy the American army, as Howe had tried to do, Clinton's plan was to conquer and hold territory, thus consolidating British control of the South and bolstering Loyalist local governments there, which could in turn provide the British Army with logistical support.

Clinton's New Strategy: The Southern Campaign (1778–1780)

The British put together a string of victories in the South in 1778–1780. Even in victory, however, their campaigns drained their manpower, provisions, and finances. This logistical predicament was exacerbated by their newly won territorial commitments; that is, by the need to leave garrisons behind, to defend strategic locations they had captured. By this point, the Dutch and Spanish had joined the war, and French forces challenged British control of New York by both land and sea, thus preventing the dispatch of reinforcements to bolster British operations in the South. The war had become a global conflict for Britain, forcing it to increase domestic taxation, expand military recruitment at home, spread its resources thin, and nearly double its national debt.

The fighting in America effectively ended in 1781, when General Cornwallis invaded Virginia, having despaired of the prospects of controlling the Carolinas, and seeking to change the direction of the war by successful campaigning in eastern Virginia. Encamped on the Virginia Peninsula, Cornwallis's army was trapped by George Washington's army and a French fleet. Cut off by sea and outnumbered two to one by land, Cornwallis surrendered on October 19, 1781, six and a half years to the day after the battles of Lexington and Concord.

British and American Manpower

From 1775 to 1781, the British Army's operations in America show the British high command grabbing at straws strategically – formulating a plan for victory in Massachusetts in 1775 only to change it in 1776 with the New York campaign; abandoning the 1776 plan in 1777 to target Philadelphia; changing course again in 1778 with Clinton's southern campaign; and forsaking the southern scheme in 1781 for operations in Virginia. These shifts in geographic focus represented a conceptual shift in strategy, from trying to pacify the Americans through economic asphyxiation, to targeting their army, to conquering territory and shoring up Loyalist local governments, to again seeking a decisive battle.

At each stage and in every location, British strategy expected and depended on what was believed to be strong Loyalist support in a given region – the middle colonies, southern colonies, and trans-Appalachian West. The British Army traveled from colony to colony in search of Loyalist manpower that could make its war plans feasible, but the Loyalist groundswell never materialized. It remains for historians to determine whether Loyalist support was effectively intimidated and suppressed by effective Patriot control of local town governments and militias, or whether it was never there to begin with. What is apparent is that British policymakers were trapped in a misunderstanding of the conflict. They believed that the Patriot opposition was a radical and fringe element, when in fact, the Revolutionists' understanding of English law, the imperial constitution, and Parliament's lawlessness was conventional and widespread. Only in 1781 did the British government finally comprehend that it would not find Loyalist support in America, and that winning the war without the colonists was beyond its financial capabilities.

Manpower represented an acute, though different, challenge for Patriots as well. After the disastrous campaign of 1776, the ranks of the Continental Army shank dramatically. As the circle of violence expanded in the following years, American men of military age defended their families, homes, and communities primarily by serving in their local militias, rather than enlisting in the Continental Army, engaged as it was in distant campaigns. That said, when the Continentals operated in a given region, local militia were usually called out to either support the army's operations or actually join the Continentals on the battlefield.

Studies of the Continental Army and of the militia indicate that as the war wore on, the army became increasingly populated by socially marginal Americans – men at the bottom rungs of the socioeconomic ladder and at the outskirts of society. This was partly because men of property, who were more anchored in their families and communities, felt that they could serve in the Continental Army for only one campaigning season before returning home to tend to their various responsibilities and commitments. Staying in the service longer meant letting one's affairs go. Indeed, some longer-serving Continentals were in such dire straits economically, that states enacted laws prohibiting creditors from pulling soldiers from the ranks and having them thrown into jail for their debts.

As middle-class Americans came in and out of the service, the Continental Army convinced poorer folks to sign long-term contracts for multiple campaigning seasons by offering things that they struggled to find in civilian life – food, shelter, pay, and social bonds. Nevertheless, the army struggled to fill its ranks year after year. To help mitigate Congress's recruiting woes, many states offered exemptions from militia service to Americans who hired substitutes or enrolled their servants or slaves for service in the Continental Army.[4] Moreover, states occasionally permitted the impressment (involuntary conscription) of vagrants, Loyalists, and British deserters, and some jurisdictions gave convicted felons the option of joining the Continental Army.

The sociological composition of the Continental Army thus stands in stark contrast to that of local militias, which featured a more representative cross-section of the male citizenry in each state. The fact that most Americans stayed home, rather than joining the national army's far-flung campaigns, is not evidence of tepid support on their part for the Revolutionary cause. Not only did these militiamen serve as combatants alongside the Continental Army at times, they also did combat in their localities against enemy forces – Loyalist militias, Britain's Indian allies, and British redcoats themselves. Moreover, the ubiquitous presence of Patriot militias in the countryside forced the British Army to approach foraging expeditions as foraging campaigns. The fact that British foraging parties required heavy military protection limited their range, speed, and effectiveness, while also straining British manpower allocation.

And as essential as militias were in the field militarily, they were the key to Patriot civic control in countless American towns. This local administrative control in communities throughout the country enabled Patriots to sustain the Continental Army with provisions and recruits over the course of eight long years. As important, it helped them deny the British Army these invaluable resources.

Who Won the War?

Ever since the Revolution, historians have debated the relative roles of the army and militia in securing American victory and independence. During the Revolution and in the decades that followed – when Americans believed

---

4 For many slaves, military service represented a promise of freedom – they served with the understanding that their states or their masters would reward their loyalty and service with liberty. Thousands of slaves indeed won their freedom this way, through military service to both Britain and the United States.

the war was won thanks to Patriot majorities in the colonies – it was widely understood that it was the militia that had won the war. In the twentieth century, when scholars came to believe that America owed its independence to a relatively small and supremely dedicated Patriot minority, Americans naturally transferred the laurels of victory from the militia to the Continental Army. Thus, when twentieth-century historians and laypeople considered the Revolutionary War, they focused primarily on the national army's operations and were generally dismissive of the militias. This is reflected in both academic and popular histories, as well as in museum exhibits, documentaries, literature, and film. The fact that the weight of scholarship is once again swinging in favor of Patriot majorities throughout the 13 colonies will doubtless lead scholars to reassess, highlight, and give due credit to Patriot militias as indispensable to American victory in the war.

This question – whether it was the militia or the army that won the war – has never been purely academic. Rather, this historical question has been intimately related to the way Americans organized their political lives in any given era since the Revolution. The militia and the army are emblems of administrative systems – state governments and national government – that have competed with one another since the birth of the republic. In the centuries that followed the Revolution, Americans engaged in fierce contests over the proper roles, jurisdictions, and powers of the Federal and state governments. The competing narratives about the Continental Army and Revolutionary militias illustrated the political and administrative principles that Americans championed in their various contemporary debates over Federal power and states' rights.

Thus, an effective militia that was the backbone of the war effort served Americans in the early-republic as a testament to the efficacy of democratic civic institutions. It taught that the states had led the war effort and won the war, and should therefore take the lead in administering public life in the young republic. By contrast, the twentieth-century narrative of a feckless militia and strong army was a testament to the need for professional expertise to run important executive bodies. It taught that the national government had won the war, and that it should therefore direct public policy.

Federal power and states' rights were intensely contested issues in the early-republic, with the advocates of states' rights largely winning the ideological, political, and public-relations battle. It should come as no surprise, then, that Americans in Revolutionary America and the early-republic – living as they did in a states'-rights republic – largely judged the militias favorably, as the bulwark of American independence. By contrast, during the Progressive Era (1890–1930) and increasingly ever since, the United States has transformed into a modern nation-state, in which states' rights have receded in the face of Federal power. It makes sense, therefore, that during this time, Americans have shifted their historical understanding of the Revolutionary War, determining that the Continental Army, rather than the militias, had won the war.

Questions for Discussion

1 Britain changed its war strategy repeatedly during the war. Why?
2 Was Britain fated to lose the war when the war broke out or when the French entered the war? Or was its fate sealed only at Yorktown (1781)?
3 What does the military history of the Revolution reveal about its political and social history?
4 Who won the war – the Continental Army or the militia?

Further Readings

Bowler, A. (1875). *Logistics and the Failure of the British Army in America, 1775–1783*. Princeton: Princeton University Press.
Buel, R. (1998). *In Irons: Britain's Naval Supremacy and the American Revolutionary Economy*. New Haven: Yale University Press.
Mackesy, P. (1964). *The War for America*. London: Longmans.
Martin, J.K. and Lender, M. *A Respectable Army: The Military Origins of the Republic, 1763–1789*, 1982. Arlington Heights, Illinois: Harlan Davidson.
Shy, J. (April 1963). A new look at Colonial Militia. *William and Mary Quarterly* 20 (2): 175–185.
Spring, M. (2008). *With Zeal and With Bayonets Only: The British Army on Campaign in North America, 1775–1783*. Norman: University of Oklahoma Press.

Conclusion

Articles of Confederation

The natural progress of things is for liberty to yield and government to gain ground.

—Thomas Jefferson (1788).

The Origins and the Ends of the Revolution

When studying the past, one must decide who is the more reliable guide to the minds of people long dead – their ideas, beliefs, values, fears, motivations, intentions, and goals. Is it modern historians, who have insights about the past that contemporaries did not have – hindsight, integrated data, and analytical tools such as political science, cultural anthropology, psychoanalytical theory, textual deconstruction, and the concepts of nationalism, class, race, gender, and postcolonialism? Or are people in the past the most credible witnesses about themselves and their culture? Both approaches to the past have their merits and drawbacks, and both have respectable pedigrees. The American Revolution brings this question to the fore, as it is clear that the modern understanding of the Revolution clashes with the colonists' own understanding of their Revolution. These two views clash even on the most basic question – when did the Revolution begin and end?

To identify when the Revolution began – whether it was generations in the making or only a decade – is to determine what caused it. The modern narrative of the Revolution holds that over the course of the colonial era, English colonists had undergone a transformation – a long and persistent process of Americanization. They gradually became less English and more American in their culture, habits, ideas, and values. This is a story of a constant and growing cultural divide between colonists and mother country. According to this narrative, the Revolution of 1776 simply gave political form, after the fact, to the real revolution that had taken place in the hearts and minds of Americans over the previous century and a half.[1] This story of gradual Americanization thus began in 1607, with its final chapter ending in *1789*, with the establishment of a new nation-state, a new form of government, and a new philosophy of government (articulated in the 1787 Constitution).

This is the story most Americans absorb in school, college, and from popular culture. When teachers, professors, textbook authors, documentarians, and moviemakers end the story of American independence in 1789, it is virtually impossible for audiences *not* to see the Revolution as a story of change; as a revolt designed to create a new system of government for a new nation. The Federal Constitution certainly was that – it drew up a novel system of government, and in doing so, it created a new and sovereign country in North America. This storyline, however, obscures the *first* constitution of the United States – the Articles of Confederation – which did not create a new form of government, did not articulate a new philosophy of government, and certainly did not create a sovereign state for Americans.

The first American constitution is habitually given fleeting coverage, as a faulty wartime stopgap that was soon fixed. Indeed, the Articles are utilized as a narrative bridge from the conclusion of the war (1783) to the convening of the Constitutional Convention in Philadelphia (1787). By racing ahead to study the second constitution, modern Americans pay little attention to the constitution that the Revolutionists created for themselves when they won the war. This is because modern Americans are understandably more interested in their *own* country – the country in which they live today, and the constitution that shapes it – than in the country that eighteenth-century Americans established for themselves with *their* Revolution.

Yet it is crucial to remember that the Revolutionists saw the Articles of Confederation and the 1783 peace treaty as the end point of the Revolution. When the story of the Revolution is told with 1783 as its conclusion, the Revolution emerges as most Revolutionists understood it at the time – a backward-looking movement to preserve old English liberties; a movement that looked to past precedent to preserve the old order, rather than a movement to create a new system of government for a new nation. American settlers saw themselves as British, and they rebelled *because* they were British. What produced the Revolution was not slow gradual change in Americans themselves – in their culture and identity – but a sudden change in imperial policy in the decade immediately preceding the war. The significant change was sudden, not gradual; it took place in London, not America; and American rebels – like English rebels in 1642 and 1688 – saw themselves not as advocates for change, but as reversing the clock to resist change and restore the old

---

1 See Wood, G. (1991). *The Radicalism of the American Revolution*. New York: Knopf.

imperial constitution. The Revolutionists approved of salutary neglect, they complained and resisted when Parliament threatened salutary neglect, they went to war to safeguard salutary neglect, and when they won, they recreated salutary neglect – a loose confederation of self-governing states under a weak central government, as outlined in the Articles of Confederation.

The Articles were drafted in 1777, but were ratified as the constitution of the United States only in 1781. They reflected the structure, authorities, and jurisdictions of the United States government during war, when the Continental Congress functioned as a war council of the 13 rebellious states. This constitution did not set up a centralized executive branch or a judicial branch. The United States government instead comprised only a legislature and five executive offices to coordinate the war effort – a war office, navy, postal service, foreign office, and treasury. Under the Articles of Confederation, the United States government wielded no coercive governing powers over its member states or their citizens. Crucially, the United States did not have the authority to tax either the states or the states' citizens. The 13 member states of the Confederation retained their full independence and sovereignty, agreeing merely to cooperate voluntarily through this forum on matters of security. Indeed, state governments retained control over their finances, security, and diplomacy, paralleling the Confederation's authorities. Naturally, each state had its own military establishment.

Everything that the Revolutionists wanted to deny the British government before the war, under the imperial constitution, they denied the United States government after the war, under the first American constitution. This is further indication that American rebels wanted to preserve the existing system of government, rather than change it. It was the British government that actively tried to change imperial governance, reversing its long-held habit of salutary neglect. In this context, it makes perfect sense that the leaders of the rebellion were the rich and powerful in their communities – families that had prospered by the existing order and wanted to preserve it. Indeed, in the decade preceding the Revolution, advocates of the American cause indicated by their words (official remonstrances and petitions, alongside unofficial complaints in the popular press) that their aim was to preserve Britain's old imperial constitution. The constitution they instituted upon victory lived up to that claim.

The Articles of Confederation also further clarify that the complaint that led Americans into revolt was constitutional, rather than economic. The Revolution was not a tax revolt, or a war to promote the rebels' economic self-interest. Waging war against the world's greatest military, naval, and economic power was hardly a promising proposition for any rebel's economic wellbeing. Moreover, the Revolutionists explained their actions in constitutional, rather than economic, terms – they decried the imperial government's transgressions against English law, the imperial constitution, and the ancient right of Englishmen to govern themselves and to be tried by a jury of their peers.

Indeed, they denounced both the Stamp Act, which imposed a tax, and the Tea Act, which lifted a tax. The constitution they drafted in 1777 and ratified in 1781 was consistent with these prewar constitutional complaints regarding arbitrary power unchecked by law. The Articles of Confederation recreated the salutary-neglect constitution of the First British Empire, confirming that what the Revolutionists feared most – before, during, and after the war – was the concentration of power in the central government. This is why they rejected the Albany Plan, denounced British reforms that expanded Parliament's jurisdiction in the colonies at the expense of local legislatures, protested the displacement of local courts and juries by British courts and tribunals, and then held the newly formed United States government to the same standard.

An Anglo-American Political Mentality

The American Declaration of Independence lists "a long train of abuses and usurpations [revealing] a design to reduce [the colonists] under absolute Despotism." In summation, the authors of the Declaration explain the nature of these various abuses and usurpations as "attempts by [Parliament] to extend an unwarrantable jurisdiction over us." This was always the heart of the American complaint against Britain during the Revolutionary era. It clarifies that the Revolution was an effort by local governments to resist and reverse a decade of centralization, thus restoring and enshrining the principle of government by consent.

It is difficult for modern readers – even those living in democracies, and even those living in the United States of America – to understand what made government by consent so viscerally important to American settlers that they risked so much for it in the face of such great odds; what made them fear and oppose arbitrary power *on principle* to a degree that most modern readers would not oppose even when it is actually practiced on them.

American settlers' attachment to government by consent is best understood as commonly English (or British), rather than uniquely American. The intense fear of centralized governance that sparked American resistance in the 1760s had already produced two major rebellions in England in the 1640s and 1680s, and two more in Scotland in the 1710s and 1740s. What was common to all these British rebellions was a conviction that centralized power invites abuse of power because it is arbitrary by its very nature. This British political mentality rested on the widespread assumption that people with power will abuse it. The insistence on government by consent was simply the practical remedy to this very human problem.

Everything that is associated with Anglo-American political culture flowed from this understanding of human nature – the political institutions, legislative protocols, procedures in British and American legislatures, the attachment to local government and to jury trials, procedures in courts of law, and the fear of concentrating power in one person or in one institution. The provisions articulated in the English Bill of Rights, American state constitutions, Articles of Confederation, Federal Constitution, and American Bill of Rights were simply institutional solutions to the basic expectation that people with power will abuse it.

As to why the British held this view of human nature, opinions differ. There is certainly evidence that this assumption regarding humanity was uniquely British. Constituting roughly 90% of the white population in the 13 colonies in 1775, Anglo-Americans overwhelmingly saw Parliament's centralizing reforms as a threat to their own liberties. By contrast, German, Dutch, and Scandinavian settlers in British America had little zeal for the Patriot cause. By the same token, when American Revolutionists tried to foment a rebellion in Canada in 1775, they expected the 70 000 French Canadians there to be most responsive to Revolutionary propaganda regarding arbitrary power wielded by the imperial government. Yet the French were mostly unresponsive. Instead, the ones most receptive to Revolutionary propaganda were the few thousands of British settlers in Quebec.

It is doubtless true that history repeatedly taught the British powerful lessons about the dangers posed by rulers who were able to concentrate political power in their hands (Henry VIII, Bloody Mary, Charles I, Cromwell, and James II), but the British were not unique in having such historical exemplars of arbitrary power. It is also true that Britons absorbed certain beliefs regarding human nature and human governments from histories of ancient Greece and Rome, and from Enlightenment political theorists whose ideas trickled down to common folk through various means. But again, this Western heritage was not unique to the British.

The strongest intellectual force in the lives of Britons and Anglo-Americans was Protestantism. The Bible and religious sermons were much more prominent than historical, philosophical, and political tracts in shaping the ideas, beliefs, and sentiments of Britons and Americans. Protestantism emphasized innate and immutable human sinfulness, and Biblical history confirmed and reconfirmed this theological message. The Old Testament, which offered a particularly rich and vivid chronicle of human wickedness and abuse of power, held an elevated position in the religious lives and imaginations of Britons in the early-modern era. This was partly because it was central to Protestant theological scholarship and the Protestant project of accurately translating the Bible into vernacular languages. But the Hebrew Bible resonated with English readers in particular because they identified in this chronicle of Jewish national history many cultural, spiritual, and political parallels with their own national life. The Bible was by far the most widely owned and read book in both Britain and America, and the Great Awakening made this Bible-centered civilization all the more so. It is evident, for example, that almanacs (which were widely sold in colonial America) assumed a high degree of Biblical literacy among their readers.

The Bible provided settlers with reading lessons, moral and religious instruction, entertainment, bedtime stories, and general education about the world. Biblical history offered its readers a guide to both human psychology and constitutional theory. The Book of Samuel, for example, taught readers that King Saul was a bad king not because he was a bad man. In fact, Saul was a uniquely good, humble, and admirable man, but kingly power transformed him into a despot. A long line of Israelite kings followed, who likewise were wicked. Each of them confirmed Samuel's blistering exhortation to the Israelites against instituting a monarchy. As Samuel had warned, these kings used the Israelites' sons and daughters as soldiers and servants, they increased the tax burden to finance their palaces, ruled harshly, took property arbitrarily, and instigated wars. Yet readers understood that Samuel's prediction proved correct not because he knew the future – he did not – but because he had a Biblical (that is, distrustful) understanding of human nature. He opposed monarchy because he believed that people with power will abuse it.

As a civilization that shared this philosophical and theological belief about human nature, Anglo-Americans were fearful of government officials, since political power naturally and predictably produced abuse of power. It is in this philosophical context that Thomas Jefferson made his stoic observation that "the natural progress of things is for liberty to yield and government to gain ground." James Monroe similarly noted mankind's difficulties, "in all ages and countries, to preserve their dearest rights and best privileges, impelled as it were by an irresistible fate of despotism." It is this bleak view of human history that explains Americans' vigilance and fearfulness regarding the imperial reforms of the 1760s. Ever on the lookout for creeping advances of arbitrary power over the consent of the governed, they viewed with alarm Parliamentary policies that strengthened the central government and weakened local communities' control over their governments and courts of law.

Once independent, Americans approached the United States government with the same suspicion and vigilance. Educated by Biblical, classical, and English history, many of the Revolutionary generation feared that American citizens would follow the same natural impulses that transformed all historical republics into monarchies or dictatorships. With salutary neglect as their constitutional guide, they therefore crafted a constitution that created an emasculated central government unable to impose its will on local communities. When confronted (in the 1780s) by Federalist efforts to replace the Articles of Confederation with a new constitution that promised to strengthen the central government and curtail local communities' ability to govern themselves, American resistance forced Madison, Hamilton, and their allies to moderate and introduce various protections for self-government in the states.

Epilogue

The Natural Progress of Things

G.K. Chesterton noted that the natural progress of things, when left alone, is change – a white fencepost will not remain white unless one keeps repainting it white periodically. Chesterton's point was that preserving the status quo requires an act of restoration; a revolution, in the eighteenth-century sense of the word. The old American Revolutionists would have appreciated this observation. They believed that tyranny, not liberty, is the natural condition of humankind. They were grateful for the English liberties that they inherited as their birthright, and they were convinced that these liberties would wither away unless actively preserved against the natural progress of despotism. With the Revolution, they disrupted this "natural progress of things" to artificially restore the liberties they had lost under British rule. They were certain that independence, republicanism, representative government, and a written constitution could not guarantee the preservation of these liberties. Future generations of Americans would have to repeatedly intervene – politically or even militarily – to halt or reverse the natural progress of things.

Following the Revolution, the British Empire continued on the path it took after the French and Indian War. The "Second British Empire" (the Empire as it was constituted in the nineteenth and twentieth centuries) operated like the kind of Empire that imperial administrators had envisioned and tried to create in the 1760s and 1770s. The First British Empire was a *settler* empire, in which British settlers governed themselves. By contrast, the Second British Empire was populated predominantly by non-British subjects; it was therefore an empire governed from the center, rather than the decentralized salutary-neglect empire it had been in the seventeenth and eighteenth centuries.

As a country that was established to halt centralization and preserve the jurisdictions and liberties of local governments, the United States took a much slower and moderate path toward centralized governance. Replacing the Articles of Confederation with the more centralized Federal Constitution required Federalists to moderate their positions (for example, by adopting the

The Colonists' American Revolution: Preserving English Liberty, 1607–1783, First Edition. Guy Chet.
© 2020 John Wiley & Sons, Inc. Published 2020 by John Wiley & Sons, Inc.
Companion website: www.wiley.com/go/Chet/ColonistsAmericanRevolution

Connecticut Compromise) and accede to Anti-Federalists demands (most famously by agreeing to add a Bill of Rights to the Constitution). These concessions gave American advocates of limited government the tools to impede and delay Federal centralization over the decades and centuries that followed.

The Federalist Solution to the Problem of Human Nature

The postwar debates and contests between Federalists and Anti-Federalists resuscitated old prewar fears about centralized and arbitrary power. Usually disagreements on policy preferences reflect philosophical or ideological differences, but the ratification debates were odd in that they pitted two sides who did not disagree philosophically. Federalists and Anti-Federalists shared a negative view of human nature. Both sides were convinced that governments are necessary (to preserve law, order, and justice), but also extremely dangerous – given that the powers of government are wielded by humans, governments virtually guarantee abuses of power, arbitrary government, lawlessness, and tyranny.[1]

Anti-Federalists saw this as a problem that cannot be solved. Thus, since corruption and abuse in high places cannot be prevented, the most any society can do is to do away with high places. Like the Revolutionists of 1776, the Anti-Federalists accepted that governmental abuse was an inescapable fact of life, and therefore preferred to endure small local abuses from small local governments than great abuses from a powerful central government.

By contrast, Federalists tried to find a clever solution to the problem of human nature. Madison's formulation of a central government splintered into separate branches, and limited strictly to a set of enumerated powers, was a plan to cheat history. Federalists believed that the Federal Government's internal divisions would pit competing interest groups against one another within the structure of the Federal Government, thus counteracting the gradual and natural concentration of power that had characterized all previous governments in human history, both monarchical and republican. This "separation of powers" within the government itself (between the legislative, executive, and judicial branches of the Federal Government, and between the two houses of Congress) was to act as an internal structural guardrail against the consolidation of power in the

---

1 James Madison explained that "the essence of Government is power; and power, lodged as it must be in human hands, will ever be liable to abuse." Similarly, when George Washington, in his farewell address, warned that occupants of public offices love power and are prone to abuse it, he was not suggesting that the people that are drawn to government service are power-hungry knaves. Rather, he expressed the widely held Anglo-American understanding that all people, when empowered with political authority, gravitate toward abuse.

central government. It was buttressed by an external and theoretical guardrail – the insistence that the central government would be limited; restricted by law, courts, local governments, and public opinion to exercising only certain enumerated powers *and no others.*

The ratification contest revealed that the American people were more skeptical than Madison. To draw support away from the Anti-Federalists, Federalists agreed to add to the Constitution explicit prohibitions (in the form of a Bill of Rights) as a third guardrail. These 10 amendments to the Constitution overtly barred the Federal Government from taking certain actions. The Bill of Rights thus reflects the fears of eighteenth-century Americans that future Federal legislators, executives, and judges might not be mindful of Madison's safeguards, and that the separation of powers and the doctrine of enumerated powers were insufficient to interrupt "the natural progress of things."[2]

In this respect, the Bill of Rights is an Anti-Federalist document – if the Articles of Confederation reflected the fears and complaints Americans had before 1776, the Federal Constitution reflected the anxieties Federalists had in 1780s, and the Bill of Rights reflected the anxieties Anti-Federalists expressed in 1787–1788. Anti-Federalists warned that the new powerful central government could, in time, threaten self-government in the states and wield arbitrary power, just as Parliament had done in the 1760s and 1770s. The Bill of Rights addressed these fears one by one – to those who feared the central government might establish a national Church, regulate speech, or break up public gatherings, it offered the First Amendment; to

---

2 Any discussion of Madison's role in framing the Federal Constitution requires at least a brief mention of "The Madison Problem." At the Constitutional Convention in Philadelphia, and during the ratification contest, Madison was a leader and ally of the most strident Federalists – those Hamiltonians that historians refer to as "the nationalists." But during Washington's presidency, Madison took a 180° turn, becoming the leading figure in the Jeffersonian camp that opposed Hamilton, championed states' rights, railed against the aggrandizement of Federal power, and warned against the concentration of power in the central government. Historians have tried to solve this puzzle ever since. Some point to Madison's personal relationship with Jefferson; others explain that as Virginia's representative in Congress, Madison came to better understand and appreciate the interests, concerns, and fears of his Virginian constituents – and by extension, southern farmers in general – vis-à-vis the central government. A simpler explanation is that when the Federal Government was only a theoretical construct of Madison's imagination (in 1787–1788), he had faith that his safeguards would prevent this government from being a source of danger to American citizens; it would represent the citizens' interests, rather than threaten them. But after Washington's inauguration, when Hamiltonians started to actually use the machinery of government created by the Constitution, perhaps Madison's eyes were opened to the logic of those Anti-Federalist skeptics who had insisted on a Bill of Rights and warned that centralization is a slippery slope that gets more slippery and more sloped with time. He might have discovered, as young people sometimes do, that their elders might actually know a thing or two.

those who feared the new government might restrict Americans' ability to possess firearms, it offered the Second Amendment; to those who feared the central government might do away with jury trials, it offered the Fifth, Sixth, and Seventh Amendments; and so forth.

Federalists did not have serious reservations about the prohibitions against Federal activism listed in the Bill of Rights. This is because the framers of the Constitution, like their Anti-Federalist opponents, were also afraid of centralized power. They never envisioned a central government that would reach into the states to govern them directly. What they imagined was a large country characterized by regional pluralism, in which localities with different circumstances, interests, and cultures produced different governmental systems and arrangements. Indeed, Federalists feared – in the 1780s as in the 1760s – a consolidated government over such diverse regions and communities. Seeing government coercion as a necessary evil, they wished to adopt centralized power only as a last resort. Believing that local governments are more consensual, more accountable, and less powerful than central governments, they wanted governance to be primarily local.

The Federal Constitution therefore preserved tremendous autonomy for states and localities to govern themselves and shape different policies on religious establishment, religious worship, slavery, freedom of speech and assembly, guns, criminal procedures, and the like. The Bill of Rights simply reinforced this pluralism through explicit and absolute prohibitions against certain Federal actions. Even a casual reading of the Bill of Rights reveals that it does *not* guarantee to Americans the various rights and freedoms it discusses; it merely denies the newly established Federal Government powers that were widely understood to belong to local governments.

The language of the Bill of Rights is absolutist on religion, speech, and guns not because eighteenth-century Americans were absolutists on these issues; they were not. The authors of the Constitution and of the Bill of Rights believed that people's various liberties (such as speech, assembly, religious worship, and gun ownership) can and should be curtailed by their governments in various ways. They insisted, however, that the central government have no role in such curtailments. It was universally understood that the prohibitions in the Bill of Rights applied exclusively to the Federal Government. The citizens of the various states thus remained as free as they had been under the Articles of Confederation (and under Britain's old imperial constitution) to restrict speech, establish an official Church, outlaw certain religious practices, enact gun control measures, and determine their own criminal court procedures. Indeed, some states had an established state Church well into the nineteenth century; it was not unconstitutional, and when these state Churches were eventually dismantled, it was done not by the authority of the Bill of Rights, but by the citizens of those states, voluntarily and democratically.

The absolutist prohibitions in the Bill of Rights are not evidence that Americans were absolutists on those issues. They are evidence that Americans were absolutists about barring the Federal Government – and the Federal Government alone – from acting on those matters.[3]

The Transformation of the Federal Constitution

The notion that the Bill of Rights instructs local governments on what they can and cannot do with regard to speech, religion, guns, juries, and other criminal court procedures is a twentieth-century novelty. This innovation in Constitutional jurisprudence has been pivotal in the transformation of the United States from a federated republic in which local communities governed themselves into a modern nation-state governed from the center.

The key to this transformation was the Fourteenth Amendment, enacted in the aftermath of the U.S. Civil War. A product of unique postwar circumstances, the Fourteenth Amendment was ratified with the purpose of empowering the Federal Government to "reconstruct" the defeated South; that is, to reshape political institutions, practices, and culture in the southern states, as they prepared to reenter the Union. Thus, unlike the 10 amendments that comprise the Bill of Rights, the Fourteenth Amendment did not contain prohibitions against the Federal Government, but prohibitions against state governments. In the context of the multitude of liberated slaves in the South, the Fourteenth Amendment established the Federal Government as the arbiter of citizenship in the United States, conferred citizenship on the freed slaves, and prohibited states from curtailing the rights and privileges (liberties) of U.S. citizens without due process of law, or denying any of their residents "the equal protection of the laws."

There is, therefore, an inherent clash between the pre-Civil War Constitution and the Fourteenth Amendment. The Constitution provides the structure for limited government by constraining Federal authority and power. To buttress these constraints, the Bill of Rights provides explicit limitations on Federal power. The Fourteenth Amendment, by contrast, provides the structure for the opposite type of government – it empowers the central government to act within local jurisdictions on a vast spectrum of issues, ranging from the most public (elections, policing, criminal law, public education) to the most private (commerce, religion, housing, medicine, home defense, marriage, family life, nutrition, sports, civic associations).

---

3 This is why citizens and non-citizens enjoyed the same protections under the Bill of Rights. The Bill of Rights does not list the people, or categories of people, who have the right to speak freely, bear arms, assemble freely, or worship freely. It only lists the one government – the Federal Government – that was prohibited from restricting these activities.

Whereas the pre-Civil War Constitutional Amendments envisioned the states as the defenders of the people against Federal encroachment and abuse, the Fourteenth Amendment did the opposite. Not only did it identify state governments as potential threats to the citizenry, it empowered the Federal government to monitor, curtail, and correct abusive or predatory conduct by local governments. It is no surprise, therefore, that when one traces the process by which the Federal Government has extended its authority and reach into the localities, one finds that most of the centralizing reforms have been accomplished through reference to, reliance on, and application of the Fourteenth Amendment.

The post-Civil War Constitution was thus a house divided against itself. As Abraham Lincoln pointed out on another matter altogether, a house divided against itself cannot stand; it must "become all one thing, or all the other." Indeed, in the century and a half that followed the Civil War, the Fourteenth Amendment established itself at the heart of the Constitution and remade it in its own image. This transformation took place in the early-twentieth century, when Federal courts began citing the Fourteenth Amendment (specifically, the due-process clause), alongside legal precedents established during Reconstruction, to "incorporate" – that is, apply – the Bill of Rights to states and municipalities. Whereas until then, it was universally understood that the Bill of Rights restricted the Federal Government alone, the courts used the "incorporation doctrine" to apply the prohibitions of the Bill of Rights also to state and local governments. By the late-twentieth century, the incorporation doctrine had become a firmly entrenched orthodoxy in American legal and political culture. It placed the Federal Government (Federal courts first and foremost) as a guarantor of civil rights in local jurisdictions, inviting it to supervise, police, and correct local governments in matters that had long been understood as purely local and beyond the jurisdiction of the central government.

"Incorporation" thus allowed the Fourteenth Amendment to create the kind of strong central government that Madison's Constitution had aimed to prevent, one empowered to govern the states and towns of America. The incorporation doctrine has even turned the Bill of Rights on its head, transforming it from a document that plainly and explicitly prohibited the Federal Government from acting in any way in many realms of American life, into a document that not only allows the Federal Government to act in these realms, but indeed *compels* it to act.

Yet the incorporation doctrine was merely the boldest method Americans have devised over the centuries to liberate their national government from the straitjacket imposed on it by the framers of the U.S. Constitution. Madison's Constitution featured two "parchment barriers" (that is, mere words scribbled on parchment) against the growth of Federal power. The first was the doctrine of enumerated powers, articulated explicitly in the Constitution's Article 1, Section 8, and again in the Ninth and Tenth Amendments of the Bill of Rights. It stated that the Federal Government was authorized to perform only a limited set of tasks that were plainly listed (enumerated) in the pages of the Federal

Constitution. The second parchment barrier was the remainder of the Bill of Rights – Amendments One through Eight. Even before the ink on the Bill of Rights was dry, however, both these obstacles were overcome by creative reading of the Constitution.

When Thomas Jefferson and James Madison cited the doctrine of enumerated powers and the Ninth and Tenth Amendments to oppose Alexander Hamilton's Bank Bill (1791), Hamilton countered that the Constitution's "necessary and proper" clause actually granted Congress implied powers beyond the explicit powers enumerated in the Constitution. Both Congress and President Washington affirmed Hamilton's expansive reading of the Constitution, as did the Supreme Court years later (*McCulloch vs. Maryland*, 1819).

The story of the Bank Bill thus offers a guide to the future course of American constitutional history. It reveals to historians, as it did to Jefferson and Madison at the time, that the parchment barriers and backstops in the Constitution and Bill of Rights were too weak to counteract "the natural progress of things." In the decades that followed, Federal officials and judges continued to find additional *implied* powers not only in the Constitution's "necessary and proper" clause, but also in its "commerce clause" and "general welfare clause." The Federal Government's field of jurisdiction thus expanded progressively well before the Fourteenth Amendment and the invention of the incorporation doctrine transformed the national government into one of innumerable powers and responsibilities.

Madison's most effective and lasting barrier against Federal activism in American life, therefore, has always been the structure of the Federal Government itself. Future generations of Americans could choose their own path when confronting the Constitution's parchment barriers – they could apply those prohibitions selectively or universally, interpret them loosely or strictly, understand them figuratively or literally, ignore them altogether, or revise them with new Constitutional Amendments. But these future generations had no choice but to occupy the Federal institutions of government bequeathed to them by the framers. By creating wholly separate branches of government – Congress, president, and judiciary – and by splitting the Congress into two separate legislatures, the Founders hoped to compel future generations to observe their strictures against the concentration of power. These built-in fractures within the central government were to create competing powers within it, with different institutions checking and obstructing others. The byproduct of such a divided and internally conflicted government was liberty for the citizenry.

Yet, even on this front, Americans have proved too ingenious for the Founders. While the Federal Government still features the same internal structural divisions it did in 1789, Americans have coalesced around political parties whose function it is to paper over and mitigate these institutional divisions between House, Senate, White House, and Federal Court.

The purpose of a written constitution is to compel future generations to live by rules set for them by a previous generation. Given that Americans have the world's oldest written constitution still in use, it is understandable that they have chafed under the restrictions imposed on them by a generation of Americans long dead.

The country's founding generation was animated by a conviction that people with power will abuse it. This was the underlying belief at the heart of English political culture in the early-modern era. It manifested itself in the great events of that era – the English Civil War, Glorious Revolution, Jacobite rebellions, and American Revolution – and in the way English communities governed themselves daily in their localities. This conviction about human nature thus shaped the rules and procedures Anglo-Americans instituted in their courts of law, churches, and local and central governments. Following Edmund Burke's formulation that "the greater the power, the more dangerous the abuse," the framers of the U.S. Constitution did their best to combat the concentration of governmental power. They were not seeking to remove roadblocks and impediments from the path of the national government they created; quite the contrary. Like the framers of the English Bill of Rights, they designed a system in which local communities governed themselves and were shielded from the central government. And when Anti-Federalists warned that the new Federal Government would stretch and break the constitutional boundaries created for it 1787, the framers added to the Constitution a Bill of Rights as a bulwark against such Federal aggrandizement.

But just as America's founding generation gave political form to its convictions about human nature in the Constitution and Bill of Rights, modern Americans have given political form to their own political and philosophical beliefs in the Fourteenth Amendment, the incorporation doctrine, and the doctrine of a "living Constitution." These reflect a sea change in the way Americans view their national government. Americans have learned over the course of the nineteenth and twentieth centuries to trust the Federal Government, identify with it, bond with it emotionally, look to it for moral and political leadership, and to expect numerous services and protections from it. This explains Americans' frustration with life under an eighteenth-century Constitution animated by distrust and fear of central governance, and their ongoing efforts to liberate their central government from the Constitutional constraints placed on it by Madison and his colleagues.

The Founders would likely have been pleasantly surprised that their construction of limited government survived the citizens' impulses for as long as it did – roughly a full century. After all, the failure of the Constitution to prevent the concentration of power in the central government was not only predictable; it was predicted as the natural progress of things.

Questions for Further Discussion

1   What fueled anti-British sentiment in the colonies from the mid-1760s to the War of Independence? Was it a natural outcome of decades of colonial life, or was it a response to specific British policies during and after the French and Indian War?

2   Opposition to concentrated governmental power was a constant feature of colonial politics. Yet this American preoccupation persisted after the transition from monarchy to republicanism. Was the Revolution waged against monarchy? Is there evidence that American colonists were ideologically uncomfortable with or opposed to monarchy before the outbreak of the War of American Independence? If not, why not, and why did they direct their ire against the king (and against monarchy itself) from 1776 on?

3   Was the Great Awakening an important factor in the coming of the American Revolution?

4   When did the American Revolution end? When were its goals and ends accomplished – in 1783 (the end of the War of Independence) or 1788–1789 (the ratification of the Federal Constitution and inauguration of Washington's first administration)?

5   Did a sense of American nationhood exist before the War of Independence, or was it a product of the war?

6   The two U.S. constitutions focused on limiting the powers and jurisdictions of the central government. What can they tell us about Revolutionary Americans' beliefs about the proper powers and jurisdictions of state and local governments?

7   Why were Americans more amenable to centralized governance in the nineteenth century than in the seventeenth and eighteenth centuries? Why were they even more amenable to it in the twentieth century than the nineteenth?

The Colonists' American Revolution: Preserving English Liberty, 1607–1783, First Edition. Guy Chet.
© 2020 John Wiley & Sons, Inc. Published 2020 by John Wiley & Sons, Inc.
Companion website: www.wiley.com/go/Chet/ColonistsAmericanRevolution

Bibliography

Abbot, E. (2006). *Our Company Increases Apace: History, Language, and Social Identity in Early Colonial Andover, Massachusetts.* Dallas: SIL International.

Alden, J.R. (1961). *The First South.* Baton Rouge: Louisiana State University Press.

Anderson, F. (1984). *A People's Army: Massachusetts Soldiers and Society in the Seven Years' War.* Chapel Hill: University of North Carolina Press.

Anderson, F. (2000). *Crucible of War: The Seven Years' War and the Fate of Empire in British North America, 1754–1766.* New York: Knopf.

Anderson, F. (2005). *The War that Made America: A Short History of the French and Indian War.* Old Saybrook, Conn: Tantor Media.

Anderson, V. (1991). *New England's Generation: The Great Migration and the Formation of Society and Culture in the Seventeenth Century.* Cambridge [England]; New York: Cambridge University Press.

Anderson, V. (2004). *Creatures of Empire: How Domestic Animals Transformed Early America.* Oxford: Oxford University Press.

Andrews, C.M.L. (1968). *The Colonial Background of the American Revolution.* New Haven: Yale University Press.

Andrews, K.R., Canny, N., and Hair, P.E.H. (eds.) (1978). *The Westward Enterprise: English Activities in Ireland, the Atlantic, and America, 1480–1650.* Liverpool: Liverpool University Press.

Andrews, K. (1984). *Trade, Plunder, and Settlement.* Cambridge: Cambridge University Press.

Archer, R. (2001). *Fissures in the Rock: New England in the Seventeenth Century.* Hanover, NH: University Press of New England.

Armitage, D. (2000). *The Ideological Origins of the British Empire.* Cambridge: Cambridge University Press.

Ash, E. (2004). *Power, Knowledge, and Expertise in Elizabethan England.* Baltimore: Johns Hopkins University Press.

Ashworth, W. (2003). *Customs and Excise: Trade Production and Consumption in England, 1640–1845.* New York: Oxford University Press.

The Colonists' American Revolution: Preserving English Liberty, 1607–1783, First Edition. Guy Chet.
Companion website: www.wiley.com/go/Chet/ColonistsAmericanRevolution

Atton, H. and Holland, H. (1967). *The King's Customs*, 2 vols. New York: Augustus M. Kelley.

Axtell, J. (1981). *The European and the Indian: Essays in the Ethnohistory of Colonial North America*. Oxford: Oxford University Press.

Axtell, J. (1985). *The Invasion Within: The Contest of Cultures in Colonial North America*. New York: Oxford University Press.

Bailyn, B. (1962). Political experience and enlightenment ideas in eighteenth-century America. *The American Historical Review* 67 (2): 339–351.

Bailyn, B. (1970). *The Origins of American Politics*. New York: Vintage.

Bailyn, B. (1976). *The Ordeal of Thomas Huntchinson*. Cambridge: Harvard University Press.

Bailyn, B. (1979). *The New England Merchants in the Seventeenth Century*. Cambridge: Harvard University Press.

Bailyn, B. and Morgan, P.D. (1991). *Strangers Within the Realm: Cultural Margins of the First British Empire*. Chapel Hill: University of North Carolina Press.

Baker, H.M. (1909). *The First Siege of Louisburg, 1745*. Concord: The Rumford Press.

Balmer, R. (1989). *A Perfect Babel of Confusion: Dutch Religion and English Culture in the Middle Colonies*. New York: Oxford University Press.

Banks, C. (1931). *The History of York, Maine, Successively Known as Bristol (1632), Agamenticus (1641), Gorgeana (1642), and York (1652), 1931–1935*. Boston: The Calkins press.

Bannerman, G. (2008). *Merchants and the Military in Eighteenth-Century Britain: British Army Contracts and Domestic Supply, 1739–1763*. London: Pickering & Chatto.

Barbour, V. (1929). Marine risks and insurance in the seventeenth century. *Journal of Economic and Business History* 1 (4): 561–596.

Barker, E. (1941). *The Ideas and Ideals of the British Empire*. Cambridge: Cambridge University press.

Barrow, T. (1967). *Trade and Empire: The British Customs Service in Colonial America, 1660–1775*. Cambridge: Harvard University Press.

Beattie, D.J. (1986). The adaptation of the British Army to wilderness warfare, 1755–1763. In: *Adapting to Conditions: War and Society in the Eighteenth Century* (ed. M. Ultee), 56–83. Alabama: University of Alabama Press.

Becker, C. (1915). *Beginnings of the American People*. New York: Houghton Mifflin.

Beer, G.L. (1893). *The Commercial Policy of England Toward the American Colonies*. New York: Columbia College.

Ben Atar, D. and Oberg, B. (eds.) (1998). *Federalists Reconsidered*. Charlottesville: University Press of Virginia.

Benton, L. (1999). Colonial law and cultural difference: jurisdictional politics and the formation of the colonial state. *Comparative Studies in Society and History* 41 (3): 563–588.

Benton, L. (2002). *Law and Colonial Cultures: Legal Regimes in World History, 1400–1900*. New York: Cambridge University Press.

Benton, L. (2005). Legal spaces of empire: piracy and the origins of ocean regionalism. *Comparative Studies in Society and History* 47 (4): 700–724.

Benton, L. (2010). *A Search for Sovereignty: Law and Geography in European Empires, 1400–1900*. New York: Cambridge University Press.

Berkin, C. (1996). *First Generations: Women in Colonial America*. New York: Hill and Wang.

Berlin, I. (1998). *Many Thousands Gone: The First Two Centuries of Slavery in North America*. Cambridge: Harvard University Press.

Berlin, I. (2003). *Generations of Captivity: A History of African-American Slaves*. Cambridge: Harvard University Press.

Best, J. (1980). Licensed to steal: toward a sociology of English piracy, 1550–1750. In: *Changing Interpretations and New Sources in Naval History* (ed. R.W. Love), 96–109. New York: Garland.

Bilder, M. (2004). *The Transatlantic Constitution: Colonial Legal Culture and the Empire*. Cambridge: Harvard University Press.

Bitterli, U. (1989). *Cultures in Conflict: Encounters Between European and Non-European Cultures, 1492–1800*. Cambridge: Polity.

Black, B. (1976). The constitution of empire: the case for the colonists. *University of Pennsylvania Law Review* 124: 1157–1211.

Black, J. (2004). *The British Seaborne Empire*. New Haven: Yale University Press.

Black, J. (2006). *George III: America's Last King*. New Haven: Yale University Press.

Black, J. (2008). *Crisis of Empire: Britain and America in the Eighteenth Century*. New York: Continuum.

Bloch, R. (2003). *Gender and Morality in Anglo-American Culture, 1650–1800*. Berkeley: University of California Press.

Bonomi, P. (1971). *A Factious People: Politics and Society in Colonial New York*. New York: Columbia University Press.

Bonomi, P. (1986). *Under the Cope of Heaven: Religion, Society, and Politics in Colonial America*. New York: Oxford University Press.

Boorstin, D. (1958). *The Americans: The Colonial Experience*. New York: Random House.

Boot, H.M. (November 1999). Real incomes of the British middle class, 1760–1850: the experience of clerks at the East India Company. *The Economic History Review* 52 (4): 638–668.

Bourne, R. (1990). *The Red King's Rebellion: Racial Politics in New England, 1675–1678*. New York: Atheneum.

Bowler, A. (1875). *Logistics and the Failure of the British Army in America, 1775–1783*. Princeton: Princeton University Press.

Boyd, S.R. (ed.) (1985). *The Whiskey Rebellion: Past and Present Perspectives*. Westport, Conn: Greenwood Press.

Boyer, P. and Nissenbaum, S. (1974). *Salem Possessed: The Social Origins of Witchcraft*. Cambridge: Harvard University Press.

Bozeman, T.D. (1977). *To Live Ancient Lives: The Primitivist Dimension in Puritanism*. Chapel Hill: University of North Carolina Press.

Braddick, M. (1996). *The Nerves of State: Taxation and the Financing of the English State, 1558–1714*. Manchester: Manchester University Press.

Braddick, M. (2000). *State Formation in Early Modern England, 1550–1700*. New York: Cambridge University Press.

Breen, T.H. (1970). *The Character of the Good Ruler: A Study of Puritan Political Ideas in New England, 1630–1730*. New Haven: Yale University Press.

Breen, T.H. (1980). *Puritans and Adventurers: Change and Persistence in Early America*. New York: Oxford University Press.

Breen, T.H. (1985). *Tobacco Culture: The Mentality of the Great Tidewater Planters on the Eve of Revolution*. Princeton: Princeton University Press.

Breen, T.H. (May 1988). 'Baubles of Britain': the American and consumer revolutions of the eighteenth century. *Past and Present* 119: 73–104.

Breen, T.H. (2005). *The Marketplace of Revolution: How Consumer Politics Shaped American Independence*. New York: Oxford University Press.

Breen, T.H. (2010). *American Insurgents, American Patriots: The Revolution of the People*. New York: Hill and Wang.

Brewer, J. (1990). *The Sinews of Power: War, Money and the English State, 1688–1783*. Cambridge: Harvard University Press.

Brooks, J. (2002). *Captives and Cousins: Slavery, Kinship, and Community in the Southwest Borderlands*. Chapel Hill: The University of North Carolina Press.

Brown, M.L. (1980). *Firearms in Colonial America: The Impact on History and Technology, 1492–1792*. Washington: Smithsonian Institution Press.

Buel, J. and Buel, R. (1984). *The Way of Duty: A Woman and Her Family in Revolutionary America*. New York: Norton.

Buel, R. (1998). *In Irons: Britain's Naval Supremacy and the American Revolutionary Economy*. New Haven: Yale University Press.

Buffington, A. (1935). The puritan view of war. *Publications of the Colonial Society of Massachusetts* 28: 67–86.

Burnard, T. (2002). *Creole Gentlemen: The Maryland Elite, 1691–1776*. New York: Routledge.

Burnard, T. (2015). *Planters, Merchants, and Slaves: Plantation Societies in British America, 1650–1820*. Chicago: University of Chicago Press.

Bushman, R. (1967). *From Puritan to Yankee: Character and the Social Order in Connecticut, 1690–1765*. Cambridge: Harvard University Press.

Bushman, R. (1984). *King and People in Provincial Massachusetts*. Chapel Hill: University of North Carolina Press.

Butler, J. (September 1982). Enthusiasm described and decried: the great awakening as interpretative fiction. *The Journal of American History* 69 (2): 305–325.

Butler, J. (1990). *Awash in a Sea of Faith: Christianizing the American People*. Cambridge: Harvard University Press.

Byrd, J.P. (2013). *Sacred Scripture, Sacred War: The Bible and the American Revolution*. Oxford: Oxford University Press.

Cable, J. (1998). *The Political Influence of Naval Force in History*. New York: Macmillan.

Calhoon, R.M. (1989). *The Loyalist Perception and Other Essays*. Columbia: University of South Carolina Press.

Calloway, C.G. (1990). *The Western Abenakis of Vermont, 1600–1800: War, Migration, and the Survival of an Indian People*. Norman: University of Oklahoma Press.

Canny, N.P. (1976). *The Elizabethan Conquest of Ireland: A Pattern Established, 1565–76*. Sussex: Harvester Press.

Canny, N.P. (1988). *Kingdom and Colony: Ireland in the Atlantic World, 1560–1800*. Baltimore: Johns Hopkins University Press.

Canny, N. and Pagden, A. (eds.) (1987). *Colonial Identity in the Atlantic World, 1500–1800*. Princeton: Princeton University Press.

Canup, J. (1990). *Out of the Wilderness: The Emergence of an American Identity in Colonial New England*. Middletown, Conn: Wesleyan University Press.

Carp, W. (1984). *To Starve the Army at Pleasure: Continental Army Administration and American Political Culture, 1775–1783*. Chapel Hill: University of North Carolina Press.

Carroll, P.N. (1969). *Puritanism and the Wilderness: The Intellectual Significance of the New England Frontier, 1629–1700*. New York: Columbia University Press.

Chaplin, J. (1993). *An Anxious Pursuit: Agricultural Innovation and Modernity in the Lower South, 1730–1815*. Chapel Hill: University of North Carolina Press.

Chapman, L.B. (1895). Block and Garrison Houses of Ancient Falmouth. In: *Collections and Proceedings of the Maine Historical Society*, second series, vol. VI, 37–53. Portland: The Society.

Charters, E. (2014). *Disease, War and the Imperial State: The Welfare of the British Armed Forces During the Seven Years' War*. Chicago: University of Chicago Press.

Chet, G. (2003). *Conquering the American Wilderness: The Triumph of European Warfare in the Colonial Northeast*. Amherst: University of Massachusetts Press.

Chet, G. (Summer 2007). The literary and military career of Benjamin Church: change or continuity in early American warfare. *Historical Journal of Massachusetts* 35 (2): 105–112.

Chet, G. (2010). Colonial failures, imperial triumphs and the loss of the American colonies. In: *The American Experience of War* (ed. G. Schild), 21–31. Paderborn: Schoeningh.

Chet, G. (2014). *The Ocean Is a Wilderness: Atlantic Piracy and the Limits of State Authority, 1688–1856*. Amherst: University of Massachusetts Press.

Cheyney, E.P. (1905). International law under Queen Elizabeth. *English Historical Review* 20 (80): 659–672.

Christie, I.R. (1966). *Crisis of Empire: Great Britain and the American Colonies 1754–1783*. London: E. Arnold.

Clark, G. (April 2004). Insurance as an instrument of war in the 18th century. *The Geneva Papers on Risk and Insurance* 29 (2): 247–257.

Cohen, C.L. (1986). *God's Caress: The Psychology of Puritan Religious Experience*. New York: Oxford University Press.

Colas, A. and Mabee, B. (eds.) (2010). *Mercenaries, Pirates, Bandits and Empires: Private Violence in Historical Context*. London: Hurst.

Cole, W.A. (1958). Trends in eighteenth-century smuggling. *The Economic History Review* 10 (3): 395–410.

Coleman, R.V. (1948). *First Frontier*. New York: C. Scribner's Sons.

Colley, L. (2009). *Britons: Forging the Nation, 1707–1837*. New Haven: Yale University Press.

Conway, S. (2002). *The British Isles and the War of American Independence*. Oxford: Oxford University Press.

Conway, S. (January 2002). From fellow-nationals to foreigners. *William and Mary Quarterly* 59 (1): 65–100.

Conway, S. (2007). *War, State, and Society in Mid-Eighteenth-Century Britain and Ireland*. New York: Oxford University Press.

Conway, S. (2011). *Britain, Ireland, and Continental Europe in the Eighteenth Century: Similarities, Connections, Identities*. New York: Oxford University Press.

Cookson, J.E. (1997). *The British Armed Nation, 1793–1815*. New York: Oxford University Press.

Coombs, J. (July 2011). The phases of conversion: a new chronology for the rise of slavery in early Virginia. *William and Mary Quarterly* 68 (3): 332–360.

Cornell, S. (1999). *The Other Founders: Anti-Federalism and the Dissenting Tradition in America, 1788–1828*. Chapel Hill: University of North Carolina Press.

Cort, C. (1883). *Col. Henry Bouquet and his Campaigns of 1763 and 1764*. Lancaster: Steinman and Hensel.

Cott, N. (1977). *The Bonds of Womanhood: "Women's Sphere" in New England, 1780–1835*. New Haven: Yale University Press.

Countryman, E. (1981). *A People in Revolution: The American Revolution and Political Society in New York, 1760–1790*. Baltimore: Johns Hopkins University Press.

Countryman, E. (1985). *The American Revolution*. New York: Hill and Wang.

Cowing, C. (1971). *The Great Awakening and the American Revolution*. Chicago: Rand McNally.

Cressy, D. (1987). *Coming Over: Migration and Communication Between England and New England in the Seventeenth Century*. New York: Cambridge University Press.

Crothers, G. (2004). Commercial risk and capital formation in early America: Virginia merchants and the rise of American marine insurance, 1750–1815. *The Business History Review* 78 (4): 607–633.

Crowhurst, P. (1977). *The Defence of British Trade, 1689–1815.* Folkestone: Dawson.

Cunningham, W. (1968). *The Growth of English Industry and Commerce in Modern Times*, 2 vols. New York: Augustus M. Kelly.

Daniels, B. (1995). *Puritans at Play: Leisure and Recreation in Colonial New England.* New York: St. Martin's Press.

Darlington, M.C. (ed.) (1920). *History of Colonel Henry Bouquet and the Western Frontiers of Pennsylvania, 1747–1764.* Pittsburgh: Privately Printed.

Daunton, M. (2002). Trusting Leviathan: the politics of taxation, 1815–1914. In: *The Political Economy of British Historical Experience, 1688–1914* (ed. D. Winch and P. O'Brien), 319–350. Oxford University Press/British Academy.

Davis, D.B. (1975). *The Problem of Slavery in Western Culture.* Ithaca: Cornell University Press.

Davis, D.B. (1984). *Slavery and Human Progress.* New York: Oxford University Press.

Davis, D. (2000). *Religion and the Continental Congress, 1774–1789.* New York: Oxford University Press.

Davis, R. (1962). *The Rise of the English Shipping Industry in the Seventeenth and Eighteenth Centuries.* London: Macmillan.

Dederer, J.M. (1990). *War in America to 1775: Before Yankee Doodle.* New York: New York University Press.

Demos, J. (1970). *A Little Commonwealth: Family Life in Plymouth Colony.* Oxford: Oxford University Press.

Demos, J. (ed.) (1972). *Remarkable Providence: Readings on Early American History.* New York: G. Braziller.

Demos, J. (1993). The Deerfield massacre. *American Heritage* 44 (1): 82–89.

Demos, J. (1995). *The Unredeemed Captive: A Family Story from Early America.* New York: Vintage Books.

Demos, J. (2004). *Circles and Lines: The Shape of Life in Early America.* Cambridge: Harvard University Press.

Drake, J.D. (1999). *King Philip's War: Civil War in New England, 1675–1676.* Amherst: University of Massachusetts Press.

Drake, S.A. (1897). *The Border Wars of New England.* New York: Scribner.

Du Rivage, J. (2018). *Revolution against Empire: Taxes, Politics, and the Origins of American Independence.* New Haven: Yale University Press.

Dunn, R.S. (1972). *Sugar and Slaves: The Rise of the Planter Class in the English West Indies, 1624–1713.* Chapel Hill: University of North Carolina Press.

Eames, S.C. (2011). *Rustic Warriors: Warfare and the Provincial Soldier on the New England Frontier, 1689–1748.* New York: New York University Press.

Earle, P. (2005). *The Pirate Wars.* New York: St. Martin's.

Ebert, C. (November 2011). Early modern Atlantic trade and the development of maritime insurance to 1630. *Past and Present* 213: 88–114.

Eckert, E.K. (ed.) (1990). *In War and Peace: An American Military History Anthology.* Belmont, California: Wadsworth.

Eid, L.V. (1981). The neglected side of American Indian War in the northeast. *Military Review* 61: 9–21.

Ekirch, A.R. (1987). *Bound for America: The Transportation of British Convicts to the Colonies, 1718–1775*. Oxford: Clarendon Press.

Elkins, S. and McKittrick, E. (1993). *The Age of Federalism*. New York: Oxford University Press.

Ellis, G. (1855). Life of John Mason. In: *Library of American Biography*, 2 series III (ed. J. Sparks), 207–428.

Ellis, G.W. and Morris, J.E. (1906). *King Philip's War: Based on the Archives and Records of Massachusetts, Plymouth, Rhode Island and Connecticut, and Contemporary Letters and Accounts*. New York: The Grafton Press.

Ellis, J. (1993). *Passionate Sage: The Character and Legacy of John Adams*. New York: Norton.

Ellis, J. (1996). *American Sphinx: The Character of Thomas Jefferson*. New York: Knopf.

Ellis, J. (2004). *His Excellency, George Washington*. New York: Knopf.

Eltis, D. (1989). Fluctuations in mortality in the last half century of the transatlantic slave trade. *Social Science History* 13 (3): 315–340.

Erwin, J.S. (1985). Captain Myles Standish's military role at Plymouth. *Historical Journal of Massachusetts* 13: 1–13.

Ferguson, E.J. (1961). *The Power of the Purse: A History of American Public Finance, 1776–1790*. Chapel Hill: Univ. of North Carolina Press.

Ferling, J.E. (1977). *The Loyalist Mind: Joseph Galloway and the American Revolution*. University Park: Pennsylvania State University Press.

Ferling, J.E. (1980). *A Wilderness of Miseries: War and Warriors in Early America*. Westport, CT: Greenwood Press.

Ferling, J.E. (1981). The New England soldier: a study in changing perceptions. *American Quarterly* 33: 26–45.

Fischer, D.H. (1994). *Paul Revere's Ride*. New York: Oxford University Press.

Forbes, A. (1934). *Some Indian Events of New England: A Collection of Interesting Incidents in the Lives of the Early Settlers of this Country and the Indians*. Boston: State street Trust Company.

Forbes, A. (1941). *Other Indian Events of New England: A Collection of Interesting Incidents in the Lives of the Early Settlers and the Indians of this Country*. Boston: State Street Trust Company.

Forster, C. (1978). *The Uncontrolled Chancellor: Charles Townshend and His American Policy*. Providence: Rhode Island Bicentennial Foundation.

Fox, E.T. (2010). Jacobitism and the 'Golden Age' of piracy, 1715–1725. *International Journal of Maritime History* 22 (2): 277–303.

Frazer, G. (2012). *The Religious Beliefs of America's Founders: Reason, Revelation, and Revolution*. Lawrence: University Press of Kansas.

Frazier, P. (1992). *The Mohicans of Stockbridge*. Lincoln: University of Nebraska Press.

French, A. (1941–1944). The arms and military of our colonizing ancestors. *Proceedings of the Massachusetts Historical Society* 68: 3–21.

Frey, S. (1981). *The British Soldier in America: A Social History of Military Life in the Revolutionary Period*. Austin: University of Texas Press.

Fuller, J.F.C. (1926). *British Light Infantry in the Eighteenth Century*. London: Hutchinson.

Fuller, J.F.C. (1946). *Armament and History: A Study of the Influence of Armament on History from the Dawn of Classical Warfare to the Second World War*. London: Eyre & Spottiswoode.

Galenson, D. (1981). *White Servitude in Colonial America*. Cambridge: Cambridge University Press.

Galenson, D. (1985). *Traders, Planters and Slaves: Market Behavior in Early English America*. Cambridge: Cambridge University Press.

Gallay, A. (2002). *The Indian Slave Trade: The Rise of the English Empire in the American South, 1670–1717*. New Haven: Yale University Press.

Gallup-Diaz, I., Shankman, A., and Silverman, D.J. (2014). *Anglicizing America: Empire, Revolution, Republic*. Philadelphia: University of Pennsylvania Press.

Galvin, P. (1999). *Patterns of Pillage: A Geography of Caribbean-Based Piracy in Spanish America, 1536–1718*. New York: Peter Lang.

Garitee, J.R. (1977). *The Republic's Private Navy: The American Privateering Business as Practiced by Baltimore during the War of 1812*. Middletown, Conn: Wesleyan University Press.

Garvan, A.N.B. (1951). *Architecture and Town Planning in Colonial Connecticut*. New Haven: Yale University Press.

Gildrie, R.P. (April 1988). Defiance, diversion, and the exercise of arms: the several meanings of colonial training days in colonial Massachusetts. *Military Affairs* 52: 53–55.

Gilje, P.A. (2004). *Liberty on the Waterfront: American Maritime Culture in the Age of Revolution*. Philadelphia: University of Pennsylvania Press.

Gilje, P.A. (2005). *The Making of the American Republic*. Pearson.

Gillingham, H. (1933). *Marine Insurance in Philadelphia, 1721–1800*. Philadelphia: Patterson & White.

Gipson, L.H. (1939). *The Coming of the American Revolution*. New York: Knopf.

Gipson, L.H. (1960). *The British Empire Before the American Revolution*. New York: Knopf.

Glete, J. (1993). *Navies and Nations: Warships, Navies and State Building in Europe and America, 1500–1860*, 2 vols. Stockholm: Almqvist & Wiskell International.

Gould, E. (2000). *The Persistence of Empire: British Political Culture in the Age of the American Revolution*. Chapel Hill: University of North Carolina Press.

Gould, E. (July 2003). Zones of law, zones of violence: the legal geography of the British Atlantic, circa 1772. *William and Mary Quarterly* 60 (3): 471–510.

Gould, E. (2010). Liberty and modernity: the American revolution and the making of Parliament's imperial history. In: *Exclusionary Empire: English Liberty*

Overseas, 1600–1900 (ed. J. Greene), 112–131. New York: Cambridge University Press.

Gragg, L. (2003). *Englishmen Transplanted: The English Colonization of Barbados, 1627–1660*. New York: Oxford University Press.

Grassby, R. (1995). *The Business Community of Seventeenth-Century England*. New York: Cambridge University Press.

Greene, J.P. (November 1961). The role of the lower houses of assembly in eighteenth-century politics. *The Journal of Southern History* 27 (4): 451–474.

Greene, J.P. (1963). *The Quest for Power: The Lower Houses of Assembly in the Southern Royal Colonies, 1689–1776*. Chapel Hill: University of North Carolina Press.

Greene, J.P. (1974). Society and economy in the British Caribbean during the seventeenth and eighteenth centuries. *American Historical Review* 79: 1500–1517.

Greene, J.P. (1986). *Peripheries and Center: Constitutional Development in the Extended Polities of the British Empire and the United States, 1607–1788*. Athens: University of Georgia Press.

Greene, J.P. (1988). *Pursuits of Happiness: The Social Development of Early Modern British Colonies and the Formation of American Culture*. Chapel Hill: University of North Carolina Press.

Greene, J.P. (1992). The glorious revolution and the British Empire, 1688–1783. In: *The Revolution of 1688–1689* (ed. L. Schwoerer), 260–271. Cambridge: Cambridge University Press.

Greene, J.P. (1995). *Understanding the American Revolution: Issues and Actors*. Charlottesville: University Press of Virginia.

Greene, J.P. (2000). The American revolution. *The American Historical Review* 105 (1): 93–102.

Grenier, J. (2005). *The First Way of War: American War Making on the Frontier, 1607–1814*. Cambridge: Cambridge University Press.

Greven, P. (1970). *Four Generations: Population, Land, and Family in Colonial Andover, Massachusetts*. Ithaca: Cornell University Press.

Greven, P. (1977). *The Protestant Temperament: Patterns of Child-Rearing, Religious Experience, and the Self in Early America*. New York: Knopf.

Gross, R. (1976). *The Minutemen and Their World*. New York: Hill and Wang.

Gundersen, J.R. (1996). *To Be Useful to the World: Women in Revolutionary America*. New York: Twayne.

Gwyn, J. (2003). *Frigates and Foremasts: The North American Squadron in Nova Scotia Waters, 1745–1815*. Vancouver: UBC Press.

Hall, D.D. (1989). *Worlds of Wonder, Days of Judgment: Popular Religious Belief in Early New England*. Cambridge: Harvard University Press.

Hall, L. (2001). *Land and Allegiance in Revolutionary Georgia*. Athens: University of Georgia Press.

Hamilton, E.P. (1962). *The French and Indian Wars: The Story of Battles and Forts in the Wilderness The French and Indian Wars.* Garden City, NY: Boubleday.

Hamilton, E.P. (1968). Colonial warfare in North America. *Proceedings of the Massachusetts Historical Society* 80: 3–15.

Hancock, D. (1997). *Citizens of the World: London Merchants and the Integration of the British Atlantic Community, 1735–1785.* Cambridge: Cambridge University Press.

Hanna, M.G. (2015). *Pirate Nests and the Rise of the British Empire, 1570–1740.* Chapel Hill: University of North Carolina Press.

Harding, C. (2007). 'Hostis Humani Generis'—the pirate as outlaw in the early modern law of the sea. In: *Pirates? The Politics of Plunder, 1550–1650* (ed. C. Jowitt), 20–38. New York: Palgrave Macmillan.

Harding, R. (1999). *Seapower and Naval Warfare, 1650–1830.* Annapolis, MD: Naval Institute Press.

Hargreaves, R. (1968). *The Bloodybacks: The British Servicemen in North America and the Caribbean, 1655–1783.* New York: Walker.

Haring, C.H. (1910). *The Buccaneers in the West Indies in the XVII Century.* London: Methuen.

Harling, P. (1996). *The Waning of 'Old Corruption': The Politics of Economical Reform in Britain, 1779–1846.* Oxford: Clarendon.

Harman, J.E. (1969). *Trade and Privateering in Spanish Florida, 1732–1763.* St. Augustine, FL: St. Augustine Historical Society.

Hatch, N. (1977). *The Sacred Cause of Liberty: Republican Thought and the Millennium in Revolutionary New England.* New Haven: Yale Univerity Press.

Hattendorf, J.B. (1980). The machinery for the planning and execution of English grand strategy in the war of Spanish succession, 1703–1713. In: *Changing Interpretations and New Sources in Naval History* (ed. R.W. Love), 80–95. New York: Garland.

Hauptman, L.M. (1992). John Underhill: a psychological portrait of an Indian fighter, 1597–1672. *Hudson Valley Regional Review* 9: 101–111.

Hay, D. (1975). Property, authority and the criminal law. In: *Albion's Fatal Tree* (ed. D. Hay, P. Linebaugh, J.G. Rule, et al.), 17–63. New York: Pantheon.

Hay, D. et al. (eds.) (1975). *Albion's Fatal Tree: Crime and Society in Eighteenth-Century England.* New York: Pantheon.

Hays, S.H. (ed.) (1967). *Taking Command: The Art and Science of Military Leadership.* Harrisburg, PA: Stackpole Books.

Heimert, A. (1966). *Religion and the American Mind from the Great Awakening to the Revolution.* Cambridge: Harvard University Press.

Henretta, J.A. (1972). *"Salutary Neglect": Colonial Administration Under the Duke of Newcastle.* Princeton: Princeton University Press.

Higman, B.W. (2010). *A Concise History of the Caribbean.* Cambridge: Cambridge University Press.

Hill, C. (1996). *Liberty Against the Law: Some Seventeenth-Century Controversies.* New York: Penguin.

Hillman, H. and Gathmann, C. (September 2011). Overseas trade and the decline of privateering. *Journal of Economic History* 71 (3): 730–761.

Hinderaker, E. and Mancall, P.C. (2013). *At the Edge of Empire: The Backcountry in British North America.* Baltimore: Johns Hopkins University Press.

Hobsbawm, E.J. (1959). *Primitive Rebels: Studies in Archaic Forms of Social Movement in the 19th and 20th Centuries.* Manchester: Manchester University Press.

Hobsbawm, E.J. (1969). *Bandits.* London: Weidenfeld & Nicolson.

Hoffer, P. (2013). *Prelude to Revolution: The Salem Gunpowder Raid of 1775.* Baltimore: Johns Hopkins University Press.

Holton, W. (1999). *Forced Founders: Indians, Debtors, Slaves, and the Making of the American Revolution in Virginia.* Chapel Hill: University of North Carolina Press.

Hoon, E. (1968). *The Organization of the English Customs System, 1696–1786.* New York: Augustus Kelley.

Horn, J. (1994). *Adapting to a New World: English Society in the Seventeenth Century Chesapeake.* Chapel Hill: University of North Carolina Press.

Hornstein, S. (1991). *The Restoration Navy and English Foreign Trade, 1674–1688: A Study in the Peacetime Use of Sea Power.* Aldershot: Scolar.

Horowitz, D. (1978). *The First Frontier: The Indian Wars and America's Origins 1607–1776.* New York: Simon and Schuster.

Howard, M., Andreopoulos, G., and Shulman, M. (1994). *The Laws of War: Constraints on Warfare in the Western World.* New Haven: Yale University Press.

Howarth, D. (2003). *British Seapower: How Britain Became Sovereign of the Seas.* New York: Carroll & Graff.

Huddleston, L.E. (1967). *Origins of the American Indians; European Concepts, 1492–1729.* Austin: University of Texas Press.

Hughson, S.C. (1894). *The Carolina Pirates and Colonial Commerce, 1640–1740.* Baltimore: Johns Hopkins University Press.

Hulsebosch, D. (2005). *Constituting Empire: New York and the Transformation of Constitutionalism in the Atlantic World, 1664–1830.* Chapel Hill: University of North Carolina Press.

Huntington, E.B. *History of Stamford, Connecticut, from its Settlement in 1641, to the Present Time, Including Darien, Which Was One of its Parishes Until 1820,* vol. 1979. Harrison, N.Y: Harbor Hill Books.

Innes, J. and Styles, J. (October 1986). The crime wave: recent writing on crime and criminal justice in eighteenth-century England. *Journal of British Studies* 25 (4): 380–435.

Innes, S. (1995). *Creating the Commonwealth: The Economic Culture of Puritan New England.* New York: Norton.

Isaac, R. (July 1976). Dramatizing the ideology of the revolution: popular mobilization in Virginia, 1774 to 1776. *William and Mary Quarterly* 33: 357–385.

Isaac, R. (1982). *The Transformation of Virginia, 1740–1790.* Chapel Hill: University of North Carolina Press.

Isham, E.S. (1889). *Frontenac and Miles Standish in the Northwest.* New York: Printed for the New York Historical Society.

Israel, J. (1991). *The Anglo Dutch Moment: Essays on the Glorious Revolution and its World Impact.* New York: Cambridge University Press.

Jackson, H. M. *Rogers' Rangers.* 1953.

Jarvis, M.J. (2010). *In the Eye of All Trade: Bermuda, Bermudians, and the Maritime Atlantic World, 1680–1783.* Chapel Hill: University of North Carolina Press.

Jasanoff, M. (2011). *Liberty's Exiles: American Loyalists in the Revolutionary World.* New York: Knopf.

Jenkin, A. and Hamilton, K. (1934). *Cornish Seafarers: The Smuggling, Wrecking and Fishing Life of Cornwall.* Toronto: J. M. Dent.

Jennings, F. (1976). *The Invasion of America: Indians, Colonialism, and the Cant of Conquest.* New York: Norton.

John, A.H. (May 1958). The London assurance company and the marine insurance market of the eighteenth century. *Economica* 25 (98): 126–141.

Johnson, R.R. (1977). The search for a usable Indian: an aspect of the defense of colonial New England. *Journal of American History* 64: 623–651.

Jordan, W.D. (1968). *White Over Black: American Attitudes Toward the Negro, 1550–1812.* Chapel Hill: University of North Carolina Press.

Joyce, L. (1966). *Church and Clergy in the American Revolution: A Study in Group Behavior.* New York: Exposition Press.

Kammen, M. (1970). *Empire and Interest: The American Colonies and the Politics of Mercantilism.* New York: Lippincott.

Karlsen, C.F. (1987). *The Devil in the Shape of a Woman: Witchcraft in Colonial New England.* New York: Norton.

Karraker, C.H. (1953). *Piracy Was a Business.* Rindge: Smith.

Karras, A. (2009). *Smuggling: Contraband and Corruption in World History.* Lanham: Rowman & Littlefield.

Katz, S. (1968). *Newcastle's New York: Anglo-American Politics, 1732–1753.* Cambridge: Harvard University Press.

Keegan, J. (1995). *Warpaths: Travels of a Military Historian in North America.* London: Hodder & Stoughton.

Keeley, L. (1996). *War Before Civilization.* New York: Oxford University Press.

Keener, C.S. (Fall 1999). An ethnohistorical analysis of Iroquois assault tactics used against fortified settlements of the northeast in the seventeenth century. *Ethnohistory* 46 (4): 777–807.

Kenny, R.W. (1940). The beginnings of the Rhode Island train bands. *Collections of the Rhode Island Historical Society* 33: 25–38.

Kerber, L. (1980). *Women of the Republic: Intellect and Ideology in Revolutionary America*. Chapel Hill: University of North Carolina Press.

Kert, F. (2005). *Trimming Yankee Sails: Pirates and Privateers of New Brunswick*. Fredericton, NB: Goose Lane.

Kidd, T. (2009). *The Great Awakening: The Roots of Evangelical Christianity in Colonial America*. New Haven: Yale University Press.

Kidd, T. (2010). *God of Liberty: A Religious History of the American Revolution*. New York: Basic Books.

Kingston, C. (June 2007). Marine insurance in Britain and America, 1720–1844: a comparative institutional analysis. *Journal of Economic History* 67 (2): 379–409.

Kinkel, S. (2014). The King's pirates? Naval enforcement of imperial authority, 1740–76. *William and Mary Quarterly* 71 (1): 3–34.

Klooster, W. (1998). *Illicit Riches: Dutch Trade in the Caribbean, 1648–1795*. Leiden: KITLV Press.

Knight, R. and Wilcox, M. (2010). *Sustaining the Fleet, 1793–1815: War, the British Navy, and the Contractor State*. Rochester, NY: Boydell.

Knouff, G. (2003). *The Soldiers' Revolution: Pennsylvanians in Arms and the Forging of Early American Identity*. University Park: Pennsylvania State University Press.

Kolchin, P. (1993). *American Slavery, 1619–1877*. New York: Hill and Wang.

Konig, T. (October 1982). Dale's laws' and the non-common law origins of criminal justice in Virginia. *The American Journal of Legal History* 26 (4): 354–375.

Koot, C.J. (2011). *Empire at the Periphery: British Colonists, Anglo-Dutch Trade, and the Development of the British Atlantic, 1621–1713*. New York: New York University Press.

Kopel, D.B. (Summer 2012). How the British gun control program precipitated the American revolution. *Charleston Law Review* 6 (2): 289–290.

Kopperman, P.E. (1977). *Braddock at the Monongahela*. Pittsburgh: University of Pittsburgh Press.

Kulikoff, A. (2000). *From British Peasants to Colonial American Farmers*. Chapel Hill: University of North Carolina Press.

Kupperman, K. (1980). *Settling with the Indians: The Meeting of English and Indian Cultures in America, 1580–1640*. Totowa, N.J: Rowman and Littlefield.

Kupperman, K. (1992). *North America and the Beginnings of European Colonization*. Washington: American Historical Association.

Kupperman, K.O. (ed.) (1995). *America in European Consciousness, 1493–1750*. Chapel Hill: The University of North Carolina Press.

Kurtz, S.G. and Hutson, J.H. (eds.) (1973). *Essays on the American Revolution*. University of North Carolina Press.

Labaree, B. (1975). *Patriots and Partisans: The Merchants of Newburyport, 1764–1815*. New York: Norton.

Lane, K. (1998). *Pillaging the Empire: Piracy in the Americas, 1500–1750*. Armonk, NY: M. E. Sharpe.

Langewiesche, W. (2004). *The Outlaw Sea: A World of Freedom, Chaos, and Crime*. New York: North Point Press.

Langford, P. (1991). *Public Life and the Propertied Englishman, 1689–1798*. New York: Oxford University Press.

Langston, P. (2006a). *Pursuit of Happiness: Struggling to Preserve Status Quo in Revolutionary Era Nova Scotia*. Master's thesis: University of North Texas.

Langston, P. (Winter 2006b). "Tyrant and Oppressor!": colonial press reaction to the Quebec act. *Historical Journal of Massachusetts* 34 (1): 1–17.

Lazaro, F.L. (June 2011). Predation's place within profit: pirates and capitalists within the seventeenth-century rise of Lockean liberalism. *International Journal of Maritime History* 23 (1): 241–276.

Leach, D.E. (1958). *Flintlock and Tomahawk: New England in King Philip's War*. New York: The Macmillan Company.

Leach, D.E. (1973). *Arms for Empire: A Military History of the British Colonies in North America, 1607–1763*. New York: The Macmillan Company.

Leach, D.E. (1974). *The Northern Colonial Frontier 1607–1763*. Albuquerque: University of New Mexico Press.

Leach, D.E. (1986). *Roots of Conflict: British Armed Forces and Colonial Americans, 1677–1763*. Chapel Hill University of North Carolina Press.

Lee, W.E. (2001). *Crowds and Soldiers in Revolutionary North Carolina: The Culture of Violence in Riot and War*. Gainesville: University Press of Florida.

Lee, W.E. (2004). Fortify, fight, or flee: Tuscarora and Cherokee defensive warfare and military culture adaptation. *The Journal of Military History* 68 (3): 713–770.

Leeson, P. and Nowrasteh, A. (2011). Was privateering plunder efficient? *Journal of Economic Behavior and Organization* 79 (3): 303–317.

Lengel, E.G. (2005). *General George Washington: A Military Life*. New York: Random House.

Lepore, J.M. (1998). *The Name of War: King Philip's War and the Origins of American Identity*. New York: Knopf.

Levitt, J.H. (1981). *For Want of Trade: Shipping and the New Jersey Ports, 1680–1783*. Newark: New Jersey Historical Society.

Levy, B. (1988). *Quakers and the American Family: British Quakers in the Delaware Valley, 1650–1765*. New York: Oxford University Press.

Lincoln, M. (2002). *Representing the Royal Navy: British Sea Power, 1750–1815*. Burlington, VT: Ashgate.

Lipson, E. (1961–1962). *The Economic History of England*, 3 vols. London: Adam & Charles Black.

Little, T.J. (2013). *The Origins of Southern Evangelicalism: Religious Revivalism in the South Carolina Lowcountry, 1670–1760*. University of South Carolina Press.

Loades, D. (1995). From the King's ships to the Royal Navy, 1500–1642. In: *The Oxford Illustrated History of the Royal Navy* (ed. J.R. Hill), 24–55. New York: Oxford University Press.

Lockridge, K.A. (1970). *A New England Town: The First Hundred Years: Dedham, Massachusetts, 1636–1736*. New York: Norton.

Lockridge, K.A. (1981). *Settlement and Unsettlement in Early America*. Cambridge: Cambridge University Press.

Long, J.C. (1933). *Lord Jeffrey Amherst: A Soldier of the King*. New York: The Macmillan Company.

Lovejoy, D.S. (1985). *Religious Enthusiasm in the New World: Heresy to Revolution*. Cambridge: Harvard University Press.

Lowe, R.G. (July 1966). American seizure of Amelia Island. *Florida Historical Quarterly* 45: 18–30.

Lunsford, V. (2005). *Piracy and Privateering in the Golden Age Netherlands*. New York: Palgrave.

Lydon, J.G. (1970). *Pirates, Privateers, and Profits*. Upper Saddle River, NJ: Gregg.

Mabee, B. (June 2009). Pirates, privateers and the political economy of private violence. *Global Change, Peace & Security* 21 (2): 139–152.

Mackesy, P. (1964). *The War for America*. London: Longmans.

Mahon, J.K. (1958). Anglo-American methods of Indian warfare, 1676–1794. *Mississippi Valley Historical Review* 45: 254–275.

Mahon, R.H. (1921). *Life of General James the Hon. Murray: A Builder of Canada*. London: John Murray.

Maier, P. (1972). *From Resistance to Revolution: Colonial Radicals and the Development of American Opposition to Britain, 1765–1776*. New York: Knopf.

Maier, P. (1980). *The Old Revolutionaries*. New York: Norton.

Main, J.T. (1961). *The Anti-Federalists: Critics of the Constitution, 1781–1788*. Chapel Hill: University of North Carolina Press.

Malone, Patrick M. English and Indian/Indian and English military systems. Doctoral dissertation.Bro wn University, 1971.

Malone, P.M. (1991). *The Skulking Way of War: Technology and Tactics Among the New England Indians*. New York: Madison Books.

Mancall, P. (1991). *Valley of Opportunity: Economic Culture along the Upper Susquehanna, 1700–1800*. Ithaca: Cornell University Press.

Mancall, P.C. and Merrell, J.H. (eds.) (2000). *American Encounters: Natives and Newcomers from European Contact to Indian Removal, 1500–1850*. New York: Routledge.

Marcus, R.H. (1969). The Connecticut Valley: a problem in inter-colonial defense. *Military Affairs* 33: 230–242.

Markham, R. (1883). *A Narrative History of King Philip's War and the Indian Troubles in New England*. New York: Dodd, Meade & Company.

Marshall, P.J. (2005). *The Making and Unmaking of Empires: Britain, India, and America c.1750–1783*. Oxford: Oxford University Press.

Martin, A. (2008). *Buying into the World of Goods: Early Consumers in Backcountry Virginia*. Baltimore: Johns Hopkins University Press.

Martin, J.K. and Lender, M. (1982). *A Respectable Army: The Military Origins of the Republic, 1763–1789*. Arlington Heights, Illinois: Harlan Davidson.

Martin, J.F. (1991). *Profits in the Wilderness: Entrepreneurship and the Founding of New England Towns in the Seventeenth Century.* Chapel Hill: University of North Carolina Press.

Marx, J. (1992). *Pirates and Privateers of the Caribbean.* Malabar, FL: Krieger.

Mason, L.B. (1935). *The Life and Times of Major John Mason of Connecticut, 1600–1672.* New York: G. P. Putnam.

Mathews, L.K. (1909). *The Expansion of New England: The Spread of New England Settlement and Institutions to the Mississippi River 1620–1865.* Boston: Houghton Mifflin Company.

Matson, C. (1998). *Merchants and Empire: Trading in Colonial New York.* Baltimore: Johns Hopkins University Press.

May, V.A. (1976). *A Plantation Called Petapawag: Some Notes on the History of Groton, Massachusetts.* Groton: Groton Historical Society.

Mayer, H. (1996). *Belonging to the Army: Camp Followers and Community During the American Revolution.* Columbia: University of South Carolina Press.

McCardell, L. (1958). *Ill-Starred General: Braddock of the Coldstream Guards.* Pittsburgh: University of Pittsburgh Press.

McCarthy, M. (2013). *Privateering, Piracy and British Policy in Spanish America, 1810–1830.* Woodbridge: Boydell Press.

McCulloch, I. (1993). Buckskin soldier: the rise and fall of major Robert Rogers. *Beaver* 73: 17–26.

McCusker, J. and Menard, R. (1999). *The Economy of British America, 1607–1789.* Chapel Hill: University of North Carolina Press.

McDonald, F. (1965). *E Pluribus Unum: The Formation of the American Republic, 1776–1790.* Boston: Houghton Miflin.

McDonald, F. (1985). *Novus Ordo Seclorum: The Intellectual Origins of the Constitution.* Lawrence: University Press of Kansas.

McIlwain, C.H. (1923). *The American Revolution: A Constitutional Interpretation.* Ithaca: Great Seal Books.

McKnight, E. (1901). *Myles Standish, Captain of Plymouth.* Chorley: Sandiford.

McLachlan, J.O. (1938). The uneasy neutrality: a study of Anglo-Spanish disputes over Spanish ships prized, 1756–1759. *Cambridge Historical Journal* 6 (1): 55–77.

McLoughlin (1977). 'Enthusiasm for liberty': the great awakening as the key to the revolution. In: *Preachers and Politicians: Two Essays on the Origins of the American Revolution* (ed. P. Greene and W.G. McLoughlin), 47–73. Worcester.

McNeill, J.R. (1985). *Atlantic Empires of France and Spain: Louisbourg and Havana, 1700–1763.* Chapel Hill: University of North Carolina Press.

Melvoin, R.I. (1989). *New England Outpost: War and Society in Colonial Deerfield.* New York: Norton.

Merrell, J.H. (1989). *The Indians' New World: Catawbas and Their Neighbors from European Contact Through the Era of Removal.* Chapel Hill; London: University of North Carolina Press.

Merrell, J.H. (1999). *Into the American Woods: Negotiators on the Pennsylvania Frontier.* New York; London: Norton.

Miles, H.H. (1872). *The History of Under French Regime. 1535–1763.* Montreal: Dawson Brothers.

Miller, J. (1960). *The Federalist Era, 1789–1801.* New York: Harper.

Mitchell, B.R. (1962). *Abstract of British Historical Statistics.* Cambridge: Cambridge University Press.

Mitchell, R. (1976). *Commercialism and Frontier: Perspectives on the Early Shenandoah Valley.* Charlottesville: University Press of Virginia.

Monod, P. (April 1991). Dangerous merchandise: smuggling, Jacobitism, and commercial culture in Southeast England, 1690–1760. *Journal of British Studies* 30 (2): 150–182.

Monod, P. (1993). *Jacobitism and the English People, 1688–1788.* Cambridge: Cambridge University Press.

Morgan, E. (1975). *American Slavery, American Freedom: The Ordeal of Colonial Virginia.* New York: Norton.

Morgan, E. (1988). *Inventing the People: The Rise of Popular Sovereignty in England and America.* New York: Norton.

Morgan, E. and Morgan, H. (1953). *The Stamp Act Crisis: Prologue to Revolution.* Chapel Hill: University of North Carolina Press.

Morgan, K. (1993). *Bristol and the Atlantic Trade in the Eighteenth Century.* New York: Cambridge University Press.

Morgan, P. (1998). *Slave Counterpoint: Black Culture in the Eighteenth-Century Chesapeake and Lowcountry.* Chapel Hill: University of North Carolina Press.

Morieux, R. (February 2009). Diplomacy from below and belonging: fishermen and cross-channel relations in the eighteenth century." (trans. S. Kane). *Past and Present* 202: 83–125.

Morrison, K.M. (1984). *The Embattled Northeast: The Elusive Ideal of Alliance in Abenaki-Euroamerican Relations.* Berkeley: University of California Press.

Morton, L. (1948). The origins of American military policy. *Military Affairs* 22: 75–82.

Morton, L. (1955). The end of formalized warfare. *American Heritage* 6: 12–19.

Mui, H.-c. and Mui, L.H. (July 1961). William Pitt and the enforcement of the commutation act, 1784–1788. *English Historical Review* 76 (300): 447–465.

Mui, H.-c. and Mui, L.H. (1975). 'Trends in eighteenth-century smuggling' reconsidered. *The Economic History Review* 28: 28–43.

Murrin, John M. Anglicizing an American colony: The transformation of provincial Massachusetts. Doctoral dissertation. Yale University, 1966.

Murrin, J.M. (2018). *Rethinking America: From Empire to Republic.* New York, NY: Oxford University Press.

Myatt, F. (1983). *The British Infantry, 1660–1945: The Evolution of a Fighting Force,* vol. I. Poole: Blandford Press.

Nash, G. (1970). *Red, White, and Black: The Peoples of Early America.* Englewood Cliffs N.J: Prentice-Hall.

Nash, G. (1979). *The Urban Crucible: Social Change, Political Consciousness, and the Origins of the American Revolution.* Cambridge: Harvard University Press.

Norton, M.B. (1996). *Founding Mothers and Fathers: Gendered Power and the Formation of American Society*. New York: Knopf.

Nosworthy, B. (1990). *The Anatomy of Victory: Battle Tactics 1689–1763*. New York: Hippocrene Books.

Novak, M. (2001). *On Two Wings: Humble Faith and Common Sense at the American Founding*. San Francisco: Encounter Books.

OBrien, P. (1988). The political economy of British taxation, 1660–1815. *The Economic History Review* 41: 1–32.

O'Brien, P. (2002). Fiscal exceptionalism: Great Britain and its European rivals from civil war to triumph at Trafalgar and Waterloo. In: *The Political Economy of British Historical Experience, 1688–1914* (ed. D. Winch and P. O'Brien), 245–265. New York: Oxford University Press.

Olson, A. (June 1982). The London mercantile lobby and the coming of the American revolution. *Journal of American History* 69 (1): 21–41.

Olson, A. (September 1992a). Eighteenth-century colonial legislatures and their constituents. *Journal of American History* 79 (2): 543–567.

Olson, A. (1992b). *Making the Empire Work: London and American Interest Groups, 1690–1790*. Cambridge: Harvard University Press.

Osgood, H.L. (1907). *American Colonies in the Seventeenth Century*. New York: Macmillan.

Osgood, H.L. (1924). *The American Colonies in the Eighteenth Century*. New York: Columbia University Press.

O'Shaughnessy, A.J. (2000). *An Empire Divided: The American Revolution and the British Caribbean*. Philadelphia: University of Pennsylvania Press.

Pagden, A. (1982). *The Fall of Natural Man: The American Indian and the Origins of Comparative Ethnology*. New York: Cambridge University Press.

Pares, R. (1936). *War and Trade in the West Indies, 1739–1763*. Oxford: Oxford University Press.

Pares, R. (1938). *Colonial Blockade and Neutral Rights, 1739–1763*. Oxford: Oxford University Press.

Pares, R. (1968). *Yankees and Creoles: The Trade Between North America and the West Indies Before the American Revolution*. Hamden, CT: Archon.

Paret, P. (1997). Colonial experience and European military reform at the end of the eighteenth century. In: *Warfare and Empire: Contact and Conflict Between European and Non-European Military and Maritime Forces and Cultures* (ed. D.M. Peers), 357–370. Brookfield: Ashgate.

Pargellis, S.M.C. (1933). *Lord Loudoun in North America*. New Haven: Yale University Press.

Pargellis, S.M.C. (1936). Braddock's defeat. *American Historical Review* 41: 253–269.

Parker, H.F. (1860). *Discoverers and Pioneers of America*. New York: Derby and Jackson.

Parker, King Lawrence. Anglo-American Wilderness campaigning, logistical and tactical developments. Doctoral dissertation. Columbia University, 1970.

Parkman, F. (1924). *The Conspiracy of Pontiac and the Indian War After the Conquest of Canada*. Boston: Little, Brown and Company.

Parkman, F. (1927). *A Half-Century of Conflict*. Boston: Little, Brown and Company.

Parkman, F. (1984). *Montcalm and Wolfe*. New York: Atheneum.

Payne, B.J. (2010). *Fishing a Borderless Sea: Environmental Territorialism in the North Atlantic, 1818–1910*. East Lansing: Michigan State University Press.

Pearce, C. (2010). *Cornish Wrecking, 1700–1860: Reality and Popular Myth*. Woodbridge, Suffolk: Boydell.

Pearce, R.H. (1953). *Savagism and Civilization*. Baltimore: Johns Hopkins Press.

Peckham, H.H. (1964). *The Colonial Wars 1689–1762*. Chicago: University of Chicago Press.

Pennell, C.R. (ed.) (2001). *Bandits of the Sea: A Pirate Reader*. New York: New York University Press.

Perl-Rosenthal, N.R. (July 2009). The 'divine right of republics': Hebraic republicanism and the debate over kingless government in revolutionary America. *William and Mary Quarterly* 66 (3): 535–564.

Pérotin-Dumon, A. (2001). The pirate and the emperor: power and the law on the seas, 1450–1850. In: *Bandits of the Sea: A Pirate Reader* (ed. C.R. Pennell), 25–54. New York: New York University Press.

Perry, J.H. (1905). *The Great Swamp Fight in Fairfield*. New York.

Peterson, H. (June 1947). The military equipment of the Plymouth and bay colonies, 1620–1690. *New England Quarterly* 20: 197–208.

Peterson, H. (1956). *Arms and Armor in Colonial America, 1526–1783*. Harrisburg: The Stackpole Company.

Phillips, C.R. (1990). The growth and composition of trade in the Iberian Empires, 1450–1750. In: *The Rise of Merchant Empires: Long-Distance Trade in the Early Modern World, 1350–1750* (ed. J. Tracy), 34–101. New York: Cambridge University Press.

Phillips, J.D. (1933). *Salem in the Seventeenth Century*. Boston: Houghton Mifflin Company.

Phillips, J.D. (1937). *Salem in the Eighteenth Century*. Boston: Houghton Mifflin Company.

Pierce, A. (1984). *Tobacco Coast: A Maritime History of Chesapeake Bay in the Colonial Era*. Baltimore: Johns Hopkins University Press.

Piggott, F. (1919). *The Declaration of Paris: A Study—Documented*. London: University of London Press.

Pike, L.O. (1968). *A History of Crime in England*, 2 vols. Montclair, NJ: Patterson Smith.

Pincus, S. (2009). *1688: The First Modern Revolution*. New Haven: Yale University Press.

Pole, J.R. (1962). Historians and the problem of early American democracy. *The American Historical Review* 67: 626–646.

Pole, J.R. (1966). *Political Representation in England and the Origins of the America Republic*. London: Macmillan.

Pole, J.R. (1975). *Decision for American Independence*. Philadelphia: Lippincott.

Pole, J.R. (1979). *Paths to the American Past*. New York: Oxford University Press.

Pole, J.R. (1983). *The Gift of Government: Political Responsibility from the English Restoration to American Independence*. Athens University of Georgia Press.

Pole, J.R. (1986). *Equality, Status, and Power in Thomas Jefferson's Virginia*. Williamsburg: Colonial Williamsburg Foundation.

Pole, J.R. (2010). *Contract and Consent: Representation and the Jury in Anglo-American Legal History*. Charlottesville: University of Virginia Press.

Porter, H.C. (1979). *The Inconstant Savage: England and the North American Indian, 1500–1660*. London: Duckworth.

Posthumus, N.W. (1946). *Inquiry into the History of Prices in Holland*. Leiden: Brill.

Powell, J.W. (1930). *Bristol Privateers and Ships of War*. Bristol: J. W. Arrowsmith.

Price, R. (1999). *British Society, 1680–1880: Dynamism, Containment and Change*. New York: Cambridge University Press.

Pritchard, J. (2004). *In Search of Empire: The French in the Americas, 1670–1730*. New York: Cambridge University Press.

Quinn, D.B. (1945). Sir Thomas Smith (1513–1577) and the beginnings of English colonial theory. *Proceedings of the American Philosophical Society* 89 (4): 543–560.

Radabaugh, J.S. (Spring 1954). The militia of colonial Massachusetts. *Military Affairs* 18: 1–18.

Raddall, T. (1971). *Halifax: Warden of the North*. Toronto: McClelland & Stewart.

Rahe, P.A. (1992). *Republics Ancient and Modern: Classical Republicanism and the American Revolution*. Chapel Hill: University of North Carolina Press.

Rakove, J. (1996). *Original Meanings: Politics and Ideas in the Making of the Constitution*. New York: Knopf.

Ramsay, G.D. (1957). *English Overseas Trade During the Centuries of Emergence*. London: Macmillan.

Raphael, R. (2002). *The First American Revolution Before Lexington and Concord*. New York: New Press.

Rediker, M. (1987). *Between the Devil and the Deep Blue Sea: Merchant Seamen, Pirates, and the Anglo-American Maritime World, 1700–1750*. New York: Cambridge University Press.

Rediker, M. (2004). *Villains of All Nations: Atlantic Pirates in the Golden Age*. Boston: Beacon.

Reid, J.G. (1992). Unorthodox warfare in the northeast, 1703. *The Canadian Historical Review* 73: 211–220.

Reid, J.P. (1986). *Constitutional History of the American Revolution*. Madison: University of Wisconsin Press.

Reid, J.P. (1988). *The Concept of Liberty in the Age of the American Revolution*. Chicago: University of Chicago Press.

Reid, J.P. (1989). *The Concept of Representation in the Age of the American Revolution*. Chicago: University of Chicago Press.

Reid, J.P. (2004). *Rule of Law: The Jurisprudence of Liberty in the Seventeenth and Eighteenth Centuries.* DeKalb: Northern Illinois University Press.

Reid, J.P. (2005). *The Ancient Constitution and the Origins of Anglo-American Liberty.* DeKalb: Northern Illinois University Press.

Reps, J.W. (1969). *Town Planning in Frontier America.* Princeton: Princeton University Press.

Richter, D. (2001). *Facing East from Indian Country: A Native History of Early America.* Cambridge: Harvard University Press.

Richter, D. (2011). *The Ordeal of the Longhouse: The Peoples of the Iroquois League in the Era of European Colonization.* Chapel Hill: The University of North Carolina Press.

Ritchie, R. (1986). *Captain Kidd and the War Against the Pirates.* Cambridge: Harvard University Press.

Ritchie, R. (1986). Government measures against piracy and privateering in the Atlantic area, 1750–1850. In: (ed. D.J. Starkey, E.S. van Eyck van Heslinga and J.A. de Moor), 10–28. Pirates and Privateers.

Robbins, C. (1959). *The Eighteenth Century Commonwealthman: Studies in the Transmission, Development, and Circumstance of English Liberal Thought from the Restoration of Charles II Until the War with the Thirteen Colonies.* Cambridge: Harvard University Press.

Robertson, E.A. (1959). *The Spanish Town Papers.* New York: Macmillan.

Robinson, W.B. (1977). *American Forts: Architectural Form and Function.* Chicago: University of Illinois Press.

Robson, E. (1952). British light infantry in the eighteenth century: the effect of American conditions. *Army and Defense Quarterly* 61: 209–222.

Rodger, N.A.M. (1996). *The Wooden World: An Anatomy of the Georgian Navy.* New York: Norton.

Rodger, N.A.M. (1998). *The Safeguard of the Sea: A Naval History of Britain, 660–1649.* New York: Norton.

Rodger, N.A.M. (2005). *The Command of the Ocean: A Naval History of Britain, 1649–1815.* New York: Norton.

Roeber, A.G. (1993). *Palatines, Liberty, and Property: German Lutherans in Colonial British North America.* Baltimore: Johns Hopkins University Press.

Rogers, A. (1974). *Empire and Liberty: American Resistance to British Authority, 1755–1763.* Berkeley: University of California Press.

Rogers, H.C.B. (1977). *The British Army of the Eighteenth Century.* London: George Allen & Unwin.

Rogers, N. (2012). *Mayhem: Post-War Crime and Violence in Britain, 1748–53.* New Haven: Yale University Press.

Rouse, P. (April 1970). Early shipping between England and Chesapeake Bay. *The American Neptune: A Quarterly Journal of Maritime History* 30 (2): 133–138.

Rowe, W.H. (July 1948). The Maine West India trade. *The American Neptune: A Quarterly Journal of Maritime History* 8 (3): 165–178.

Rozbicki, M.J. (2011). *Culture and Liberty in the Age of the American Revolution.* Charlottesville: University of Virginia Press.

Rubin, A.P. (1986–87). The law of piracy. *Denver Journal of International Law and Policy* 15: 173–233.

Rule, J. (1975). Wrecking and coastal plunder. In: *Albion's Fatal Tree* (ed. Hay et al.), 167–188. New York: Pantheon.

Rugemer, E.B. (July 2013). The Development of Mastery and Race in the Comprehensive Slave Codes of the Greater Caribbean during the Seventeenth Century. *William and Mary Quarterly* 70 (3): 429–458.

Russell, P.E. (October 1978). Redcoats in the wilderness: British officers and irregular warfare in Europe and America, 1740 to 1760. *William and Mary Quarterly* 35: 629–652.

Ruwell, M.E. (1993). *Eighteenth-Century Capitalism: The Formation of American Marine Insurance Companies.* New York: Garland.

Salinger, S. (1987). *To Serve Well and Faithfully: Labor and Indentured Servants in Pennsylvania, 1682–1800.* Cambridge: Cambridge University Press.

Salisbury, N. (1982). *Manitou and Providence: Indians, Europeans, and the Making of New England, 1500–1643.* New York: Oxford University Press.

Sargent, L.T. (Winter 1983). Utopianism in colonial America. *History of Political Thought* 4 (3): 483–522.

Schultz, E. and Tougias, M. (1999). *King Philip's War: The History and Legacy of America's Forgotten Conflict.* Woodstock: Countryman Press.

Segal, C. and Stineback, D. (1977). *Puritans, Indians, and Manifest Destiny.* New York: G.P. Putnam's Sons.

Selesky, Harold E. Military leadership in an American colonial society: Connecticut, 1635–1785. Doctoral dissertation. Yale University, 1984.

Selesky, H.E. (1990). *War and Society in Colonial Connecticut.* New Haven: Yale University Press.

Shammas, C. (1982). How self sufficient was early America? *Journal of Interdisciplinary History* 13 (2): 247–272.

Shammas, C. (1990). *The Pre-Industrial Consumer in England and America.* Oxford: Clarendon.

Sharp, Morrison. The New England trainbands in the seventeenth century. Doctoral dissertation, Harvard University. 1938.

Sheldon, G. (1972). *A History of Deerfield, Massachusetts.* Somersworth: New Hampshire Publishing Company.

Shelley, H.C. (1932). *John Underhill: Captain of Connecticut and New Netherland.* New York: D. Appleton.

Shepard, J. (1913). *Connecticut Soldiers in the Pequot War of 1637.* Meriden, CT: Journal Publication Company.

Shepherd, J.F. and Walton, G.M. (1972). *Shipping, Maritime Trade, and the Economic Development of Colonial North America.* New York: Cambridge University Press.

Shy, J. (April 1963). A new look at colonial militia. *William and Mary Quarterly* 20 (2): 175–185.

Shy, J. (1965). *Toward Lexington: The Role of the British Army in the Coming of the American Revolution*. Princeton: Princeton University Press.

Shy, J. (1976). *A People Numerous and Armed: Reflections on the Military Struggle for American Independence U*. New York: Oxford University Press.

Simms, B. (2007). *Three Victories and a Defeat: The Rise and Fall of the First British Empire*. New York: Allen Lane.

Slaughter, T.P. (1986). *The Whiskey Rebellion: Frontier Epilogue to the American Revolution*. New York: Oxford University Press.

Slotkin, R. (1973). *Regeneration Through Violence; the Mythology of the American Frontier, 1600–1860*. Middletown, Conn: Wesleyan University Press.

Smith, A.E. (1947). *Colonists in Bondage: White Servitude and Convict Labor in America, 1607–1776*. Chapel Hill: University of North Carolina Press.

Smith, D.S. (1972). The demographic history of colonial New England. *The Journal of Economic History* 32 (1): 165–183.

Smith, David R. Nathanael Greene and the myth of the valiant few. Doctoral dissertation. University of North Texas, 2017.

Smith, J. (2006). *Borderland Smuggling: Patriots, Loyalists, and Illicit Trade in the Northeast, 1783–1820*. Gainesville: University Press of Florida.

Sobel, M. (1987). *The World They Made Together: Black and White Values in Eighteenth-Century Virginia*. Princeton: Princeton University Press.

Sosin, J. (1961). *Whitehall and the Wilderness: The Middle West in British Colonial Policy, 1760–1775*. Lincoln, University of Nebraska Press.

Sosin, J. (1980). *English America and the Restoration Monarchy of Charles II*. Lincoln: University of Nebraska Press.

Sosin, J. (1982). *English America and the Revolution of 1688: Royal Administration and the Structure of Provincial Government*. Lincoln: University of Nebraska Press.

Sosin, J. (1985). *English America and Imperial Inconstancy: The Rise of Provincial Autonomy, 1696–1715*. Lincoln: University of Nebraska Press.

Spooner, F.C. (1983). *Risks at Sea: Amsterdam Insurance and Maritime Europe, 1766–1780*. New York: Cambridge University Press.

Spring, M. (2008). *With Zeal and with Bayonets Only: The British Army on Campaign in North America, 1775–1783*. Norman: University of Oklahoma Press.

Spruill, J. (1938). *Women's Life and Work in the Southern Colonies*. Chapel Hill: University of North Carolina Press.

Stanley, John Henry. A Preliminary Investigation of Military Manuals of American Imprint Prior to 1800. Unpublished Master's Thesis. Brown University, 1964.

Starkey, A. (January 1994). Paoli to Stony Point: military ethics and weaponry during the American Revolution. *The Journal of Military History* 58: 7–27.

Starkey, A. (1998). *European and Native American Warfare, 1675–1815*. Norman: University of Oklahoma Press.

Starkey, D. (1990). *British Privateering Enterprise in the Eighteenth Century*. Exeter: University of Exeter Press.

Starkey, D. (2001). The origins and regulation of eighteenth-century British privateering. In: *Bandits of the Sea: A Pirate Reader* (ed. C.R. Pennell), 69–81. New York: New York University Press.

Starkey, D., van Eyck van Heslinga, E.S., and de Moor, J.A. (eds.) (1997). *Pirates and Privateers: New Perspectives on the War on Trade in the Eighteenth and Nineteenth Centuries*. Exeter: University of Exeter Press.

Starkey, M. (1955). *A Little Rebellion*. New York: Knopf.

Steele, I.K. (1969). *Guerrillas and Grenadiers: The Struggle for Canada, 1689–1760*. Toronto: The Ryerson Press.

Steele, I.K. (1986). *The English Atlantic, 1675–1740: An Exploration of Communication and Community*. New York: Oxford University Press.

Steele, I.K. (1990). *Betrayals: Fort William Henry and the "Massacre"*. New York: Oxford University Press.

Steele, I.K. (1994). *Warpaths: Invasions of North America*. Oxford: Oxford University Press.

Steele, I.K. (2010). Review of Cornish Wrecking, 1700–1860: reality and popular myth by Cathryn Pearce. *International Journal of Maritime History* 22 (2): 378–379.

Steffen, C. (1993). *From Gentlemen to Townsmen: The Gentry of Baltimore County, Maryland, 1660–1776*. Lexington: University Press of Kentucky.

Storing, H.J. (1981). *What the Anti-Federalists Were for: The Political Thought of the Opponents of the Constitution*. Chicago: The University of Chicago Press.

Stout, H.S. (October 1977). Religion, communications, and the ideological origins of the American revolution. *William and Mary Quarterly* 34: 519–541.

Stout, N. (1973). *The Royal Navy in America, 1760–1775*. Annapolis, MD: Naval Institute Press.

Sullivan, Timothy Lee. The Devil's Brethren: Origins and nature of pirate counterculture, 1600–1730. Doctoral dissertation. University of Texas at Arlington. (2003)

Swanson, C.E. (July 1985). American privateering and imperial warfare, 1739–1748. *William and Mary Quarterly* 42 (3): 357–382.

Swanson, C.E. (1989). Privateering in early America. *International Journal of Maritime History* 1 (2): 253–278.

Swanson, C.E. (1991). *Predators and Prizes: American Privateering and Imperial Warfare, 1739–1748*. Columbia: University of South Carolina Press.

Sweet, W.W. (1973). *The Story of Religion in America*. Grand Rapids: Baker Book House.

Sylvester, H.M. (1910). *Indian Wars of New England*. Boston: W.B. Clarke Company.

Tagliacozzo, E. (2005). *Secret Trades, Porous Borders: Smuggling and States Along a Southeast Asian Frontier, 1865–1915*. New Haven: Yale University Press.

Tagliacozzo, E. (2010). Violent undertows: smuggling as dissent in nineteenth-century Southeast Asia. In: *Mercenaries, Pirates, Bandits and Empires: Private Violence in Historical Context* (ed. A. Colas and B. Mabee), 107–132. New York: Columbia University Press.

Taylor, A. (1995). *William Cooper's Town: Power and Persuasion on the Frontier of the Early American Republic*. New York: Knopf.

Taylor, A. (2001). *American Colonies: The Settling of North America*. New York: Viking.

Taylor, A. (2005). *Writing Early American History*. Philadelphia: University of Pennsylvania Press.

Taylor, G.R. (ed.) (1949). *The Turner Thesis: Concerning the Role of the Frontier in American History*. Boston: Heath.

Tebbel, J. and Jennison, K. (1960). *The American Indian Wars*. New York: Harper and Brothers Publishing.

Thompson, E.P. (1971). The moral economy of the English crowd in the eighteenth century. *Past and Present* 50 (1): 76–136.

Thomson, J.E.M. (1994). *Pirates, and Sovereigns: State-Building and Extraterritorial Violence in Early Modern Europe*. Princeton: Princeton University Press.

Tillson, A. (1991). *Gentry and Common Folk: Political Culture on a Virginia Frontier, 1740–1789*. Lexington: University Press of Kentucky.

Tolles, F. (1948). *Meeting House and Counting House: The Quaker Merchants of Colonial Philadelphia, 1682–1763*. Chapel Hill: University of North Carolina Press.

Tonso, W.R. (1982). *Gun and Society: The Social and Existential Roots of the American Attachment to Firearms*. Lanham: University Press of America.

Trelease, A.W. (1960). *Indian Affairs in Colonial New York: The Seventeenth Century*. Ithaca: Cornell University Press.

Truxes, T. (2008). *Defying Empire: Trading with the Enemy in Colonial New York*. New Haven: Yale University Press.

Turner, M. (1984). *Enclosures in Britain 1750–1830*. London: Macmillan.

Turney-High, H.H. (1942). *The Practice of Primitve War*. Missoula, Mont: Montana State University.

Uhlig, F. (1994). *How Navies Fight: The U.S. Navy and Its Allies*. Annapolis, MD: Naval Institute Press.

Ulrich, L. (1982). *Good Wives: Image and Reality in the Lives of Women in Northern New England, 1650–1750*. New York: Knopf.

Ultee, M. (ed.) (1986). *Adapting to Conditions: War and Society in the Eighteenth Century*. Alabama: University of Alabama Press.

Usner, D. (1992). *Indians, Settlers, and Slaves in a Frontier Exchange Economy: The Lower Mississippi Valley before 1783*. Chapel Hill: University of North Carolina Press.

Utley, R.M. (1973). *Frontier Regulars: The United States Army and the Indian, 1866–1891*. New York: Macmillan Publishing.

Van Cleve, G. (2017). *We Have Not a Government: The Articles of Confederation and the Road to the Constitution*. Chicago: The University of Chicago Press.

Vaughan, A.T. (1995). *New England Frontier: Puritans and Indians, 1620–1675*. Norman: University of Oklahoma Press.

Vickers, D. (1990). Competency and competition: economic culture in early America. *William and Mary Quarterly* 47: 3–29.

Wade, H.T. (1948). *A Brief History of the Colonial Wars in America from 1607 to 1775*. New York: The Society of Colonial Wars.

Webb, S.S. (1979). *The Governors-General*. Chapel Hill N.C: University of North Carolina Press.

Webb, S.S. (1987). *1676: The End of American Independence*. New York: Knopf.

Webb, W. (1976). *Coastguard: An Official History of HM Coastguard*. London: Her Majesty's Stationery Office.

Weber, D.J. (1992). *The Spanish Frontier in North America*. New Haven: Yale University Press.

Weigley, R.F. (1991). *The Age of Battles: The Quest for Decisive Warfare from Breitenfeld to Waterloo*. Bloomington: Indiana University Press.

West, J. (1991). *Gunpowder, Government, and War in the Mid-Eighteenth Century*. Rochester, NY: Boydell.

Whisker, J.B. (1997). *The American Colonial Militia*. Lewiston: The Edwin Mellen Press.

White, E. (October 1989). The Marshall court and international law: the piracy cases. *American Journal of International Law* 83 (4): 727–735.

White, R. (October 1981). Outlaw gangs of the middle border: American social bandits. *The Western Historical Quarterly* 12 (4): 387–408.

White, R. (1991). *The Middle Ground: Indians, Empires, and Republics in the Great Lakes Region, 1650–1815*. Cambridge: Cambridge University Press.

Whitton, F.E. (1929). *Wolfe and North America*. Boston: Little, Brown and Company.

Wilkinson, C. (2004). *The British Navy and the State in the Eighteenth Century*. Rochester, NY: Boydell.

Williams, G. (1897). *History of the Liverpool Privateers and Letters of Marque, with an Account of the Liverpool Slave Trade*. London: William Heinemann.

Williams, J.B. (1972). *British Commercial Policy and Trade Expansion, 1750–1850*. Oxford: Oxford University Press.

Williams, N. (1961). *Contraband Cargoes: Seven Centuries of Smuggling*. Hamden, CT: Shoe String Press.

Jr. Williams, R.A. (1990). *The American Indian in Western Legal Thought: The Discourse of Conquest*. New York: Oxford University Press.

Wolf, S. (1993). *As Various as their Lands: The Everyday Lives of Eighteenth-Century Americans*. New York: HarperCollins.

Wood, G. (1969). *Creation of the American Republic*. Charlottesville: University of Virginia Press.

Wood, G. (1982). Conspiracy and the paranoid style: causality and deceit in the eighteenth century. *William and Mary Quarterly* 39: 401–441.

Wood, G. (April 1990). Classical republicanism and the American revolution. *Chicago-Kent Law Review* 66 (13): 13–38.

Wood, G. (1991). *The Radicalism of the American Revolution*. New York: Knopf.

Wood, Joseph, The New England village. Doctoral dissertation., Pennsylvani State University 1978.

Wood, P.H. (1996). *Black Majority: Negroes in Colonial South Carolina from 1670 Through the Stono Rebellion*. New York: Norton.

Wooster, R. (1988). *The Military and United States Indian Policy, 1865–1903*. New Haven: Yale University Press.

Worden, B. (2009). *The English Civil Wars: 1640–1660*. London: Weidenfeld & Nicolson.

Wright, C. and Fayle, C.E. (1928). *A History of Lloyd's from the Founding of Lloyd's Coffee House to the Present Day*. London: Macmillan.

Yirush, C. (2011). *Settlers, Liberty, and Empire: The Roots of Early American Political Theory, 1675–1775*. New York: Cambridge University Press.

Young, A.F. (1999). *The Shoemaker and the Tea Party: Memory and the American Revolution*. Boston: Beacon Press.

Zacek, N. (2010). *Settler Society in the English Leeward Islands, 1670–1776*. Cambridge: Cambridge University Press.

Zahedieh, N. (2010). *The Capital and the Colonies: London and the Atlantic Economy, 1660–1700*. New York: Cambridge University Press.

Zelner, K. (2010). *A Rabble in Arms Massachusetts Towns and Militiamen during King Philip's War*. New York: New York University Press.

Zemsky, R. (1971). *Merchants, Farmers, and River Gods: An Essay on Eighteenth-Century American Politics*. Boston: Gambit.

Zuckerman, M. (1978). *Peaceable Kingdoms: New England Towns in the Eighteenth Century*. New York: Norton.

Index

The Colonists' American Revolution: Preserving English Liberty, 1607–1783, First Edition. Guy Chet.
© 2020 John Wiley & Sons, Inc. Published 2020 by John Wiley & Sons, Inc.
Companion website: www.wiley.com/go/Chet/ColonistsAmericanRevolution